LOOTING GREECE

LOOTING GREECE
A New Financial Imperialism Emerges

by

Jack Rasmus

Clarity Press, Inc

© 2016 Jack Rasmus
ISBN: 978-0986085345
EBOOK ISBN: 978-0-9860853-5-2
In-house editor: Diana G. Collier
Cover: R. Jordan P. Santos

Clarity Press, Inc.
2625 Piedmont Rd. NE, Ste. 56
Atlanta, GA. 30324 , USA
http://www.claritypress.com

TABLE OF CONTENTS

To Brian, Ozzie, & Joe
on the anniversary of the great Oakland strike

And to those everywhere who stand and resist
regardless of the odds

Chapter One

THE MEANING OF THE GREEK DEBT CRISIS

The Greek Debt Crisis is over. The next Greek debt crisis has begun.

Some say the debt crisis in Greece was resolved last August 2015 with the latest restructuring of the debt. Greece now has sufficient refinancing to repay its debt and has begun to recover economically, enabling it to do so. Others conclude that the defeat of Syriza was so complete, and the Troika—the Eurozone's European Commission (EC), European Central Bank (ECB) and International Monetary Fund (IMF)—prevailed so thoroughly in negotiations that events of the past year 2015 proved resistance is futile. Therefore another rebellion by Syriza, or any other Greek government, is not likely in the foreseeable future. But the Greek debt crisis is not over. The conditions for yet another eruption have already begun to develop.

At the opposite end of the spectrum of analysis, other commentators on the 2015 events argue the Greek debt is so immense that, given Greece's small economy, it can never be repaid. Therefore, the ravages of austerity imposed on Greece will not only continue, but worsen. Resistance and rebellion is again inevitable. But the next time it will take place, the resistance will be more resolute and better organized. The yoke of debt will be severed, as Greece has no choice but to discard the Euro currency and 'Grexit' the Eurozone. If not, it will face perpetual economic depression and Troika-imposed austerity forever.[1]

As matters lie, one year after the Syriza government challenged the Troika, the former view seems more likely than the latter. However, appearances often prove deceptive, a weak shell encapsulating a more enduring reality that cannot be contained—a seeming defeat that will inevitably give way to a new and stronger resistance.

In January 2015, the Syriza party assumed control of the Greek government and immediately challenged the Troika—and clearly lost. As in previous challenges to Troika-imposed debt restructuring packages, in 2010 and 2012, the outcome of the latest Greek rebellion against Euro Neoliberal policies has concluded with the same result: yet more debt piled on existing debt and even more severe austerity measures imposed on the Greek populace as means to repay that debt.

Coming to power in January 2015 on a program promising to renegotiate the terms of Greece's massive government debt, and to roll back the 'austerity' program imposed on Greece by the Troika since 2010 associated with that debt, Syriza and its leadership collapsed just eight months later, in August 2015. In the process of attempting to negotiate and restructure that debt, it gave up virtually all its initial demands to reduce the magnitude of the debt burden and to end the worst elements of the austerity imposed to address it. In fact, the outcome was even worse than when negotiations began: the Syriza government agreed to continue austerity on even worse terms than before and accepted $98 billion more in new debt piled on the old. Now that additional debt would have to be paid for as well as the old, and even more onerous terms of austerity were imposed by the Troika to ensure that it would. In short, Syriza caved in, as had Greek governments in 2012 and 2010 in previous debt restructurings, and came out worse than when it went into negotiations.

The process and outcome was thus much like a labor strike, where workers and their unions demand improvements in their wages and working conditions, walk off the job, but then end up going back to work with less than they had when the strike began. The Greek Debt crisis of 2015 was thus a kind of a 'political strike'. As in labor negotiations, classes were clearly involved. But not all strikes are won—whether industrial or political--and especially when the relative forces are highly uneven at the outset, or when a walkout is threatened but never actually takes place. Syriza took a 'strike vote' by conducting a last minute plebiscite to let the Greek populace vote on the Troika's 'last offer'. That offer was rejected, but the leadership, even after having received its authorization to strike, failed to 'pull the plug' and allow the membership, the Greek people, to walk out. The consequences and results were predictable.

At one level, the 'meaning' of the Greek debt crisis reduces to which strategies and tactics of the respective parties—the Troika and Syriza—proved successful and which did not. How well did both sides play the hands dealt them by the conditions they confronted? How skilled were their negotiators? How well crafted were their proposals—i.e. to mobilize their base and put adversaries on the defensive—and how well timed were their moves? How well organized and solid were the class forces behind them? In short, how effectively did they play their cards?

Syriza's Poorly Bet Hand

The obvious question is how is it that the third Greek

economic insurrection, led by Syriza in 2015, imploded so quickly and so totally after the July plebiscite/de facto political strike vote? How could that have occurred under the leadership of a clearly left-oriented party and movement? In the preceding two debt restructurings in 2010 and 2012, the governments were conservative, pro-business or centrist. They either quickly agreed to the Troika's terms and self-imposed austerity with little opposition to the Troika demands. Or they provided a token resistance then quickly fell in line. But Syriza purported to be a coalition of left-oriented groups, which included significant elements of independent socialist and communist groupings. Unlike predecessor governments, Syriza's program and campaign promises were progressive, not conservative or centrist. The party and its movement clearly indicated their intention to fight it out with the Troika in 2015 on behalf of the segments of the Greek populace whose living standards had been devastated by the terms of debt servicing agreements previously imposed on Greece in 2012 and 2010. So how to explain why the resistance that started out in early 2015 led by Syriza— resistance which additionally proved to have clear majority support of the Greek people—subsequently dissolved and collapsed by mid-summer 2015 after less than six months of negotiations with the Troika?

Did the Syriza senior leadership, Alexis Tsipras and others, simply lose their nerve in the face of an ever-hardening opposition by the Troika over the course of the debt restructuring negotiations from late February to August 2015? Were Syriza leaders simply naïve about how far the Troika would go to ensure Syriza and Greece would not achieve any semblance of even partial victory in negotiations—including their willingness to accept Greek departure from the Eurozone? Was Syriza's strategy, and the tactics it employed, incorrect, thus contributing to their defeat?

Or was the problem deeper than leadership? Was Syriza, the party, composed of such conflicting elements that it was unable to ensure its leadership remained accountable to its demands and did not lose their nerve or otherwise cave in?

Or perhaps the source of the problem goes even deeper. Perhaps Syriza the social movement was just not dominant enough within Greek civil society to effectively rally the populace to undertake more than just negotiations and parliamentary action; that is, if necessary to directly confront the Troika where it was most potentially vulnerable—i.e. the Euro bond markets, the Euro banking system, and the Euro currency itself? And even if Syriza as social movement were strong enough, perhaps the remaining classes and elements in Greek society, apart from Syriza and its supporters, believed that remaining 'European', i.e. staying in the Eurozone and therefore continuing with the Euro currency, was more important than risking confrontation with the powerful financial forces of Euro Neoliberalism?

In other words, were Syriza leaders, party, and the movement psychologically and politically unprepared to undertake the kind of economic revolution that would be necessary to successfully confront the Troika? Was Greek society itself really desperate enough to take the fight with the Troika 'to the mat'?

As will be described in more depth in subsequent chapters, Syriza and its negotiators laid great emphasis on trying to convince their opponents that their proposals were financially sound and of benefit to all in the longer run—to the Troika, Euro bankers, the northern Europe neoliberal establishment, as well as to Greece. This view reflected, however, a strategic misunderstanding on Syriza's part as to the short term objectives and constraints of the Troika. Syriza's strategy was not only long-run focused but also attempted to appeal to the social virtues of Europe's once dominant Social Democratic heritage. What Syriza did not understand adequately, however, was that that heritage was now history, buried deep under a refuse pile of new Neoliberal values. Europe was no longer traditional social democratic; it was fundamentally now neoliberal. Appealing to the token remnants of European social democracy in France, Italy, and elsewhere in the Eurozone was therefore a 'DOA' (dead on arrival) strategy. No one anywhere in Europe was about to 'save' Greece, to side with it and defend what amounted to Syriza's avowed objective of resurrecting classical Social Democracy. Neither France nor Italy nor anyone else. Not when it came to taking on the banking and financial interests in their own economies and countries. Greece and Syriza thus stood alone from the very beginning, and remained so until the capitulation in August 2015. Syriza's strategy did not recognize this fact. Its strategy was burdened by the false assumption it could rely on allies it never really had; and that it could convince the Troika to make meaningful concessions to debt repayment and reducing austerity in the short run and did not have to play its 'ace card' of actually leaving the Eurozone monetary union and still remain in the customs union.

A customs union is about rules for exchanging goods and services between economies. The European Union is a customs union. A monetary union is where the countries share the same currency and rules are established for the flow of money and credit between the economies. The Eurozone is a monetary-currency union. A monetary-currency union means replacing one's currency (drachma) with the new union's currency (Euro), as well as turning over control of one's national central bank, and therefore private banking system in turn, to another higher-authority central banking institution (in this case the European Central Bank, ECB).

Which country, or group of countries, end up in de facto control of the higher authority central bank assume de facto control over the others' national banking system. Syriza's strategy grossly underestimated the ability of the Troika, which included the ECB, to economically pummel Syriza into submission over the course of 2015 negotiations by virtually shutting down Greece's banking system to force Syriza to submit to Troika demands and concessions.

So long as Greece continued within the Euro system, and did not 'Grexit', this leverage by the Troika proved determinative in Syriza's eventual capitulation to Troika demands. Syriza's two fundamental strategic errors therefore were to over-estimate potential allies and support from a Social Democracy in Europe that no longer existed as such, on the one hand, and on the other, an under-estimation of the power of the neoliberal Troika to bring Greece's banking system, and thus its economy, to its knees.[2]

But Syriza leaders' capitulation in August 2015 to Troika demands may not simply represent basic strategic errors, negotiating inexperience, or even perfidy on their part, as other left commentators argue or assume—as much as it may reflect divided forces and lack of solidarity within the party itself, as well as the broader Greek society's illusions as to what it means in the 21st century to be a periphery country member of the 'European' experiment.

The Troika's Stacked Deck

In fairness to Syriza, however, the events of 2015 cannot be laid solely at its door—whether leaders, party or movement. One cannot discount that the eventual collapse of resistance was due also to the superior cards that the Troika itself had to play in what it played as a 'winner take all' negotiation over austerity and the debt in 2015. The Troika enjoyed greater class solidarity among its elements; clearer objectives from which it never wavered; a superior strategy; allies both within Greece and globally without that it could, and did, call upon at critical junctures in the negotiations; and, not least, 'hard ball' tactics it was willing to employ, and lesser risks as the negotiations progressed and came to a head. In comparison, Greece and Syriza lacked all the above.

The Troika leaders proved the more competent negotiators, more devious in their maneuvers, and more skilled in debt restructuring negotiations. After all, they had far more practical experience in such matters, having concluded similar negotiations countless times before. Syriza was totally new to this game. The Troika skillfully played 'hard cop' and 'soft cop' with Syriza's negotiators. Members within the EC, for example, held out false hope to Syriza they might achieve some concessions from the Troika if only they, Syriza, gave up demands first or most. Syriza's negotiators responded, believing they were dealing with honorable men, when honor is an outmoded virtue where billions of Euros and wealth are concerned. Those false hopes were then dashed as ECB and Eurozone finance ministers, led by Germany's dominant coalition, repeatedly thwarted all attempts at compromise following Syriza's periodic concessions. Similar 'false hope' tactics were employed using Euro national leaders in France and Italy, who also held out the prospect to Syriza of their support in negotiations with the Troika, and when the US intervened via the backdoor to Syriza's negotiators, promising and threatening who knows what. But in fact Syriza had no allies—not even Russia or China, to which Syriza made overtures for support that produced nothing. The Troika, in contrast, had many allies, including within Greece itself, and as will be demonstrated in later chapters, they played one and then another against Syriza in a skillfully implemented 'poker hand' that steadily wore down Syriza negotiators' confidence and resolve.

Not only had the Troika more clever negotiating skills and allies, but their fundamental strategy and tactics also proved superior to Syriza's in the end.

So far as relative tactics are concerned, the Troika also held more cards in the negotiating game. For instance: it could shut down the Greek banking system at will through the bridge loans being provided by the ECB to the Greek central bank and private banking system in turn. And it consistently withheld interest on Greek bond earnings that were due for payment to Greece. In contrast, Syriza could have refused to repay any of the principal or interest coming due to the IMF or ECB during negotiations, to show its resolve and intention to exit if necessary. But it didn't. The Troika played tactical 'hard ball' with Syriza, while the latter conceded in the hope its show of 'reasonableness' and willingness to compromise would evoke some kind of similar response by the Troika. But it didn't.

But Syriza's implosion and capitulation cannot be attributed simply to Syriza leaders' inexperience, lack of bargaining skills, or loss of last minute negotiating nerve; nor can it be reduced simply to failures of Syriza's strategy, tactics, or its constantly shifting objectives; nor even to the lack of internal unity within the party and the movement. It must be at least in part explained by the relative strengths of its opposition, the Troika.

In the final analysis, the Troika was capable of imposing greater hurt on Greece and Syriza than the latter could on it and the Troika knew it, repeatedly making it clear to Syriza that it was prepared to do so. It never backed away from its original and primary objectives. Syriza and Greece continually backtracked from their initial demands over the course of negotiations. And once the backtracking began, the Troika pushed forward even more aggressively, with increasingly onerous proposals and demands.

Indeed, one may even ask whether, faced with such a great imbalance in the relationship of forces, Syriza and Greece could ever have prevailed, given that it, Syriza, and Greek society itself, was not psychologically, organizationally, or politically prepared to turn a rebellion into a bona fide economic revolution? And if it were prepared and somehow prevailed, could Syriza and Greece have survived thereafter, isolated and no doubt continually attacked by Euro Neoliberal forces economically and politically in the aftermath—from without and within Greece—as it surely would have been?

Therefore, the meaning of the third Greek debt crisis of 2015 at one level is that the Troika held a superior hand and additionally played that hand better than did Syriza, its leaders, and the Greeks.

But the Greek debt crisis has meaning and significance at an even more fundamental level, well beyond the events of the past year in Greece itself. This is true in at least three important ways.

Placed in context, the debt crisis at a deeper historical level reveals the limits and instability of the Euro form of Neoliberalism—i.e. what might be called a 'weak form' of Neoliberalism. Secondly, the Greek debt crisis shows that Euro Neoliberalism is fundamentally incompatible with classical European Social Democracy and economic policies and programs associated with social democracy. Proposing an incremental return to social democratic policies and programs as an immediate and coexisting solution to Neoliberal policies and programs is a contradiction in terms. The two cannot coexist. They represent a zero sum game. Third, the policies and processes evolved to address Greek debt, its deepening accumulation and its ostensible recuperation reflect the development of a new form of imperialism and colonialism that is taking root in Greece, which is a portent of things likely to come elsewhere wherever smaller states and economies choose to integrate themselves deeply in terms of trade and money capital flows with larger capitalist economies.

Greek Debt Crises and 'Weak Form' Euro-Neoliberalism

The Greek debt crisis is a reflection of the 'weak form' that Neoliberalism has assumed in the Eurozone. Before explaining how Euro-Neoliberalism represents a peculiar 'weak form', and how that differs from the stronger forms of Neoliberalism introduced by both the USA and UK, it's necessary to describe the major characteristics of Neoliberalism in general. From there, an explanation of how Euro Neoliberalism differs—i.e. is weaker—may be offered. And thereafter an explanation may follow describing how that weak form has resulted in the especially excessive debt accumulation and the repeated debt crises in the case of Greece.

Neoliberalism represents a fundamental restructuring of capitalist economic relations, implemented by leading capitalist economies in response to the general crisis of capital that emerged globally in the 1970s. At that time real investment and trade had begun to stagnate. The international monetary system based on the 1944 Bretton Woods agreement had collapsed. Productivity was stagnant and the growth period from 1946 to 1973 had passed. Both inflation and unemployment were rising. The working classes, their unions and parties were challenging capitalist ruling elites on various economic and political fronts. Non-capitalist states were making inroads on key resource markets and creating alliances in Asia, Africa, and Latin America. Nationalist movements in the 'Third World', as it was then called, were demanding and getting a greater relative share of returns from the global oil and commodities pie. Even the ideology of the system on various levels—including economic theory—was undergoing significant challenge and change. Neoliberalism emerged as a set of policies and programs designed to stabilize the global capitalist system and return it to growth. It succeeded in doing so in the 1980s and 1990s, although on a more fragile basis than in the 1948-73 boom period. In 2007 that fragile basis cracked and the Neoliberal model appeared to have run out of economic steam. Ever since 2009, global capitalist elites have been attempting to reconstruct and salvage it, with some apparent difficulty. Humpty-Dumpty hasn't quite yet been put back together again. Another major capitalist restructuring is now required—as had been achieved in the 1980s, before that in the immediate post 1944 period, and before that immediately before and after World War I.

Not all economies turned to Neoliberal solutions simultaneously in the 1980s or experienced a return to growth. Its leading, more aggressive proponents were the USA and the UK, during the regimes of Reagan and Thatcher. Others were late—in particular Europe and Japan which were more fully integrated into the US/UK dominated neoliberal global solution in the 1980s –1990s. China did not begin the transition to its own unique form of Neoliberalism until the late 1990s and after, following its internal reforms and its joining the World Trade Organization.

Although all Neoliberal regimes are different in particulars, the US and UK forms—or what might be called 'generic Neoliberalism'—shared in common certain similar industrial, fiscal, monetary, and financial policies. The differences lay in the particular 'mix' of policies and their relative weights. Neoliberalism of course also evolves over time as well as place, and the mix of policies emphasized also change.

Generic Neoliberalism

To briefly state the specific elements of generic Neoliberalism, it can be said to include:

- An industrial policy that focuses on containing wage incomes to help control corporate costs. The destruction of unions, limits on collective bargaining, and further restrictions on workers' right to strike and politically mobilize are the more obvious measures for nominal wage containment. Other measures include reducing and even reclaiming 'deferred' wages in the form of private pensions, and reducing 'social wages' in the form of national retirement benefits by means of legislation. Allowing minimum wages to atrophy in real terms is another. A more recent expression is the growing movement for what is called 'labor market restructuring', where wages are reduced by contingent and contract labor arrangements, the 'gig' or sharing economy, as well as other measures that reduce compensated hours of work per employee while expanding uncompensated hours and work.

- Neoliberal industrial policy also includes the privatization and sale of government public works, public services, and where still existent, government direct production. It means as well deregulation of industry.

- Neoliberalism includes a fiscal policy reducing government expenditures, typically for low-profit social programs, but also for government funded infrastructure projects. The tax side of fiscal policy favors tax reductions for corporations and investors, but tax hikes for sales and VAT, other forms of regressive taxation, and little or no tax reduction for middle income or below households. Neoliberal taxation policy also includes tax credits and incentives to move capital investment offshore, and thus reduce employment and wages in industries that relocate 'offshore'.

- Neoliberalism also places more relative emphasis on monetary and central bank solutions. Monetary policy is primary, and central bank injection of liquidity into the financial system is envisioned as the means by which to generate both economic growth and ensure stability.

Critics of Neoliberalism often emphasize the above more obvious elements, especially the first three, but they overlook its other important defining elements. That focus is in part a consequence of defining Neoliberalism based just on its initial Reagan-Thatcher forms. Critics thus overlook how removing barriers to international trade and money capital flows is central to Neoliberal regimes. Or how financial system restructuring since the 1980s has constituted a further important element of evolving Neoliberal industry policy.

A significant factor in US Neoliberal trade policy, for example, has been the emergence of what is called the 'Twin Deficits'. The twins are the US trade deficit (US imports more goods than it exports) and the budget deficit (US federal government spends more than it receives in tax revenues). Both began to accelerate during the Reagan period. Both are thus highly correlated. But more than that, it is the trade deficit that has enabled the escalating budget deficit in the US since Reagan.

Prior to Reagan, US trade policy tried to maximize exports over imports. That was necessary to maintain a balance of payments given that US policy has always been since 1945 to encourage US corporations' investment offshore. But that created a negative money capital outflow that had to be somehow 'offset' by a positive export-import inflow to the US in order to maintain a balance of payments. The US failure to continue that postwar formula by the late 1960s led to the collapse of the US dollar by the early 1970s and the end of the Bretton Woods system which Nixon declared 'dead' in 1971. The US fumbled throughout the 1970s to try to re-establish a new balance of money capital inflows-outflows. The Twin Deficits was the new solution.

Now, under Reagan, US trade policy reversed: the US decided to run a trade deficit, allowing imports to exceed exports. US dollars consequently began to flood global markets even more than before. Arrangements with trading partner countries were negotiated in which the latter agreed to recycle their accumulating dollars back to the US in the form primarily of purchases of US Treasury bonds. The bond purchases in turn allowed the US government to run huge budget deficits, mostly to enable massive cuts in taxes for corporations and investors, offsetting the loss of revenue by the recycled dollars the government now borrowed to fill the 'deficit' gap.

The key here is the dual idea of trade deficits tolerated, so long as trading countries benefited from the increased US purchase of their goods, and recycled their dollars. US multinational corporations were allowed to increase their offshore foreign direct investment. Money flows, unions and workers' wages were reduced by the offshoring so US corporate profits were subsidized both by lower wages in the US and lower wages abroad. Cheap imports offset the lack of wage increases to some extent, and recycled dollars allowed the reduction in US taxes, allowing the US to fund wars abroad for the first time in its history without raising taxes, and generally allowed the US to run continual and rising domestic budget deficits. Twin Deficits policy was thus foundational in various ways to US Neoliberalism. But the Eurozone, as will be explained below, would not prove as successful in establishing a 'twin deficits' arrangement to ensure the recycling of money capital flows from the periphery to its core.

Twin deficits and the recycling of money capital flows required the elimination of limits and controls on money capital flows between states. Thus a second major element integral to US Neoliberalism was the elimination of controls on international money capital flows. If Twin Deficits required allowing US multinational corporations, including banks, to move money capital in greater volume and rates offshore into emerging and other markets, restrictions and limits on those flows would have to be reduced or, better yet, eliminated. The ending of controls was necessary not only for recycling dollars back to the US by foreign central banks, private banks, and investors purchasing US Treasury bonds and other government securities, but also for uninhibited recycling of money capital as direct investment by foreign corporations back to US financial and other investment markets.

The US lead in eliminating global money capital controls was quickly adopted by Europe and Japan in a series of key negotiations in the mid-1980s held in the US and Europe, sometimes called the 'Plaza Accords' and the 'Louvre Agreement' between the US and Europe which quickly followed the 'Accords'. European banks and investors were prompt in agreeing to lift controls. Finance capital benefited in those regions as well as in the US. It was not a question of US pressuring them to do so. Had they not, and insisted on retaining controls into and out of Europe, it would have meant an even more uncompetitive position for Euro economies vis-à-vis US and UK than they already faced.

In addition to eliminating controls on international capital flows and establishing a 'twin deficit' capital recycling system, a third element of generic, US-UK Neoliberalism that also emerged in the 1980s, which accelerated rapidly in the 1990s and after the restructuring and deregulation of the global financial sector. This included the rise of non-traditional bank 'capital markets', shadow banking, and the associated revolution in financial derivatives and financial securities proliferation. Here again the US, and to an extent the UK, were leading initiators.

As with establishing a twin deficit arrangement, Europe also lagged in this particular Neoliberal element of financial restructuring, and remains still to this day in 'catch-up' mode, compared to the US-UK. For example, capital markets (i.e. non-traditional bank sources of credit) are generally acknowledged as undeveloped in the Eurozone. Shadow banks are barely established there, with US and UK 'shadow banking' mostly setting up the 'shadow banking' shop in the Eurozone. Homegrown Euro shadow banking remains undeveloped. And only recently has the Eurozone begun to develop and regulate derivatives markets.

Twin deficits, unrestricted money capital flows, and the rise of the capital markets-shadow banks-securities revolution were all elements of generic Neoliberalism. They all represent elements which the Eurozone has lagged at introducing into its particular form of Neoliberal regime. For all three elements to function in a Neoliberal regime, they require a global currency (or regional currency in the case of Europe), a true banking union to breakup logjams in money flows, and a fiscal union of sorts to smooth out imbalances in the accumulation of debt that periodically occur.

The Eurozone's introduction of the Euro and a single currency union after 1999 helped establish a 'twin deficits' system, but the lack of a true banking union and fiscal union created a caricature of a 'twin deficits' Neoliberal regime. The Eurozone consequently has proved unable to ensure the full recycling of money capital between Eurozone 'core' and 'periphery', resulting in the buildup of excess debt in its periphery—most severely in the case of Greece.

Eurozone Neoliberalism

There are five distinct elements of Euro-Neoliberalism which render it a 'weak form':

- Weak capital markets and undeveloped shadow bank institutions have resulted in over-dependence for economic recovery on the traditional banking sector in the Eurozone. Since 2009, however, that private banking sector has been mired in at least one and a half trillion dollars in non-performing bank loans (NPLs). Bank lending has never fully recovered since 2009, and Euro banks remain loaded with debt, highly fragile and susceptible to instability, which appears again to be on the rise. Because of their own debt-burdened balance sheets, core Eurozone banks have been unable to acquire, consolidate and thus 'bail out' periphery Eurozone private banks. Excessive bank debt remains endemic in the Eurozone. Without bank lending, growth and inflation solutions to bank and sovereign debt levels do not occur.

- Facing the problem of the lack of bank lending, the European Central Bank (ECB) has had to engage in massive liquidity injections to prevent financial market collapse and to try to generate economic growth. But Eurozone central banking is an undeveloped form of central banking. The ECB is not a true central bank and the Eurozone lacks a true banking union. ECB liquidity injections have consistently lagged events, and have resulted in the money capital flowing out to other financial markets in the US and elsewhere. The ECB-to-private bank lending conduit has thus broken down (as it has to some degree in all advanced economies). ECB growth policy has therefore attempted to use liquidity injections to reduce the Euro exchange rate to stimulate Euro exports and therefore growth. But in a slowing global economy and global trade, that too is proving to have minimal effect. At the same time, the ECB has been basically prohibited from directly bailing out periphery government debt. ECB inability to either grow out or bail out periphery bank and government debt has left the process of debt bailouts for both in the hands of special pan-Eurozone bodies like the European Commission and, more distantly, the IMF. That approach has politicized the bailout process and made it even more difficult. In short, no debt reduction occurs, and when the real economy, already weak from lack of investment and growth, periodically stagnates or slips into recession, more credit and therefore debt must be provided to both banks and governments in the periphery to enable them to continue paying interest on the previously incurred debt.

• With private banking and central bank policies neutralized, fiscal policy would be a logical alternative. However, Eurozone Neoliberalism has no fiscal union. It is therefore unable to use fiscal policy, whether directed to Greece or other periphery economies, in emergencies to help generate recovery and pay for debt by means of economic growth. To hold the lid on rising debt that monetary and banking policies have failed to effectively address, Eurozone Neoliberalism subsequently has resorted to 'negative fiscal stimulus', or what is referred to as 'austerity' policies, to try to keep a lid on debt increase. However, that has not only failed to keep a lid on debt, but has led to its further growth.

- In the absence of fiscal stimulus, and given the failure of ECB monetary stimulus and traditional bank lending to generate real economic growth, the Eurozone has resorted to 'labor market restructuring' in a desperate attempt to drive growth through exports. Labor market restructuring aims at reducing wage growth in what is called an 'internal devaluation' in order to lower export prices and gain global export share. This has boosted a narrow list of export industries while reducing household demand across a broader segment of the economy. The net effect is negative.

- While the foregoing illustrates how weak form Euro-Neoliberalism is unable to reduce the accumulation of debt since 2010, the origin of that debt problem is rooted in the 1999 creation of the Euro and the caricature of the 'twin deficits' arrangement that was introduced in the Eurozone in the mid-2000s. In the Eurozone, Germany has attempted to fulfill a role similar to that of the US. The essence of the US Neoliberal twin deficits arrangement is for money capital in-flow from an exports surplus to be recycled back to keep the circular flow of money capital going and to prevent destabilizing debt imbalances from arising. But the Eurozone 'twin deficits' is a caricature of the US-global twin deficits. As will be described in more detail in Chapter two as a result of the creation of the Euro, money capital flowed from Germany and the core northern Euro banks of the Eurozone to the periphery after 1999. Germany's exports were cheaper and the periphery economies purchased German exports in large volumes, thus recycling the money back to Germany and northern core banks. In the process debt in the periphery rose. The rising debt could be successfully serviced, but only so long as periphery growth and inflation continued to rise, which it did ... until 2008. Growth and inflation then quickly reversed. With internal Eurozone growth stagnant or declining, by 2010 Germany shifted its exports-driven growth strategy from the slowing Euro periphery, now stagnant or in recession and reducing purchases of German imports, to the now rapidly growing economies in China, emerging markets, and even the US, where growth was slowly recovering. Northern core banks shifted as well, reducing lending to the periphery banks and governments. The servicing of debt incurred prior to the 2008-09 crash became thereby increasingly difficult for periphery economies, especially Greece. Core bank lending to the periphery to purchase German and northern Euro imports was replaced by lending just to ensure continued payments on prior debt and, when that proved insufficient to repay previous debt, the Eurozone special pan-European institutions (EC, ECB, IMF) had to step in to take up the slack.

How does this translate into the Greek debt crisis? As in the other periphery economies, the Euro enabled the rise in lending by northern core Euro banks to Greece. Euro banks purchased and invested in Greek banks. And Greek companies. They set up subsidiaries of their own banks in Greece. Money capital flowed into Greece, was borrowed and debt correspondingly was incurred. The Greek government also borrowed heavily to expand infrastructure and provide income growth for public sector businesses and public workers. Government borrowing allowed taxes to be reduced, with the borrowed money used for government projects and normal operational expenditures.

With the onset of the 2008 crisis, however, the money inflow slowed dramatically. Simultaneously the ability to pay the previously incurred debt collapsed as the Greek economy fell into recession (then depression). Private businesses could not repay previous loans either to Greek banks or Euro banks in Greece. Collapsing Greek government tax revenues meant they could not repay their debt either. With normal money flows into Greece from the private banks and businesses of the northern Euro core disrupted, normal recycling back to Germany in the form of goods purchases or debt repayments also slowed or ceased. But the requirements of debt servicing from prior borrowing and debt did not cease, even as the economic growth that enabled servicing that debt was now gone. To restore the broken cyclical money flow, pan-European government institutions (ECB, EC, IMF) were required to step in and restructure the Greek debt—by lending more and raising debt further simply in order to allow Greek banks and government to repay the old debt. The Troika in effect loaned Greece to money to repay itself, the Troika. Often the new lending never even went through Greece; the Troika loaned to itself and sent the debt 'bill' to Greece. Money capital was thus provided to Greece, replacing the now defunct natural private money recycling, but it was new money and debt provided to repay old debt. And it was not money to grow the Greek economy to repay existing debt. It was the Troika repaying itself, and private core banks, on behalf of Greece.

So the nature of Euro Neoliberalism—specifically its weak banking union, its non-existent fiscal union, its frozen traditional bank lending, its lack of alternative capital markets to fill the bank lending void, and the disruption of its 'twin deficits' money capital recycling arrangement between the Euro 'core' and the periphery due to German and northern Eurozone businesses shifting to emerging markets—combined to create a condition in which stop-gap Euro institutional lending was provided in lieu of private money capital flows just in order to continue the repayment of prior Greek debt.

But providing debt to repay debt is no long-term or permanent solution. It's just a stop-gap interim arrangement— one that leads to worse debt repayment requirements over the longer run.

The Euro Neoliberal 'twin deficits' arrangement, made possible ultimately by the creation of the Euro currency union after 1999, was the engine of the buildup of debt in Greece and elsewhere in the periphery. That engine collapsed in 2008-09. The remaining peculiar characteristics of Euro Neoliberalism—i.e. its ineffective monetary and undeveloped banking system, its lack of fiscal union, and the central importance and role of Germany, etc.—all these peculiar Euro Neoliberal characteristics prevented a normal resolution of the Greek debt buildup once the twin deficits money capital recycling arrangement collapsed in 2008-09. The makeshift pan-European alternative of the Troika, and its stop-gap solution to the debt (adding more debt to repay debt) has not resolve the Greek debt crisis but has actually made it worse. It's not simply a matter of Eurozone austerity measures making it worse. Austerity is the symptom. The various 'weak form' characteristics of Euro Neoliberalism are what lies behind the appearance of the austerity measures. Austerity is the Eurozone's desperate and failed gamble to address its form of Neoliberalism's failures.

That deeper institutional failure of Neoliberalism is why the Troika's 2010 debt restructuring led to yet another restructuring required in 2012 when the Eurozone underwent a double-dip recession, and then led in 2015 to yet another Greek debt crisis and another debt restructuring. The bigger meaning is that Greek debt restructuring by the Troika will continue, and it will continue to result in subsequent Greek debt crises as well—the next appearing as soon as Greece and the Eurozone experience their next triple-dip recession.

The Greek Debt Crisis and Euro Social Democracy

Understanding the Greek debt crisis is important as well for understanding why Euro-Neoliberalism today has displaced what was classic Euro social democracy and why there is no returning to the latter so long as the former is dominant. Neoliberalism and social democracy are fundamentally incompatible and contradictory. They cannot co-exist. One must inevitably displace the other. That fact too is bound up in the events of the Greek debt crisis.

The Greek debt crisis of 2015 not only reveals the peculiar, weak character of Neoliberalism in its Euro form. It also reveals that classic Euro social democracy cannot co-exist with neoliberal policies and regimes. They are fundamentally contradictory. That is why Syriza and its leaders' delusions about the restoration of social democracy in Europe were so self-defeating and misleading to its followers and supporters.

Neoliberalism is entrenched in the Eurozone today. Appeals and references to the superior qualities of Euro social democracy are an ideological illusion. They are designed to keep Europeans believing they are 'exceptional' in their progressive and caring nature, compared to other advanced capitalist societies and economies. It is not unlike the myth of US exceptionalism fed to US society, where much of the populace believes the USA is exceptional in its degree of liberty and freedom where anyone can be a millionaire. The real conditions belie that ideological claim in both..

Social Democracy in Europe has been incrementally repealed since the 1980s, both economically and politically. The institutional evidence politically is the rise of the pan-European political institutions, such as the European Commission and European Parliament, created to unify Europe under the banner of its wealthy capitalist elite and their interests. Political centralization prevents component states from exercising better programs and policies in their own interests. That's why the same elite is so concerned, and adamant about preventing, the breakaway of existing nation states in Europe— the UK, Spain, Italy, and Others.

Economic social democracy is actually the antithesis of economic Euro-neoliberalism. The northern Eurozone economic elites weren't about to allow Greece to restore any semblance of economic social democracy. This would have opened a Pandora's Box of similar pressures and movements elsewhere in the Eurozone. Allowing Greece to retain more liberal pensions, even as the Eurozone was attempting to reduce pensions elsewhere, was simply untenable to the Troika as was allowing more collective bargaining and strike freedom to Greek unions while it was further restricting the same elsewhere. To let Greece 'off the hook' for implementing labor market restructuring when elites were struggling to pass it in France and Italy, would be tantamount to giving up on those efforts in those key economies. A good part of average German lack of support to Syriza and Greek efforts to retain restored social democratic benefits like pensions and union and worker rights during the 2015 debt negotiations derived from the fact that German workers had been forced to give up the same or similar benefits back in 2004-5. An oft-heard backward response by German workers in 2015 was "why should the Greeks be allowed to have better pensions, when we had to give up ours?" German unions and political parties, like the Social Democrats, were brought under the Neoliberal political umbrella, given a minor voice, so why should Syriza and the Greeks think they should be treated any differently?

The Emerging New Debt-based Imperialism

There is yet a third, historical meaning evolving out of the Greek Debt crisis—a new form of financial imperialism, and associated colonial-like wealth extraction, which has emerged with the Greek debt crisis.[3]

Imperialism implies the existence of empire. In the most obvious sense, an empire exists when one state exercises direct political control and dominance over the political affairs of another. The control is overt and if necessary ensured by military force in its extreme form. But political control may be exercised by non-military, or latent military, means. A political bureaucracy and government run by the imperial state—i.e. the colonizer—directly decides the affairs of the colonized state. But empire need not refer only to direct control—whether exercised by military force, bureaucratic rule, or the takeover or displacement of political institutions like legislatures, courts, etc.

Imperialism may also be exercised economically, in content and form, by one state over another, with minimal or even no direct control of political institutions. There may be no need for the imperial state to militarily occupy the colonized state or extend its bureaucratic apparatus extended to the colony and operate 'on site'. It may allow the elites of the colony to run their own political institutions—so long as those institutions do not interfere with the extraction of economic wealth and export of that wealth back to the imperial-colonizer state. In such cases of 'economic imperialism' the assurance of wealth transfer is not achieved by means of the imposition of an imperial government, bureaucracy or military on the colony. It is achieved through various institutions of economic control—such as control of the currency (including denial of the colony's own currency), control over sources of capital, relationships governing trade and capital flows, legal ownership or effective control over institutions of production, commerce, and sources of money creation, monopoly of resource extraction, and control by the colonizer of international economic institutions and their rules (such as IMF, World Bank, WTO, etc. today).

Domestic elites in the colony are brought in as partners to the imperial-colonizer, given a generous share of the wealth extracted, and allowed degrees of independence in running their own political institutions and bureaucracy. Imperial military force is kept 'outside' the colony, and works with the domestic military force to ensure the latter's ultimate loyalty to the domestic elite and the imperial state's military apparatus.

The former example is typical of 19th century European imperial strategy; the latter, more typical of US 20th century strategy. The latter, economic imperialism, is far more efficient and therefore a less costly and more profitable way to exercise imperial rule indirectly and extract even greater surplus and wealth from the colony. There is no cost of bureaucracy, or of political institutions of direct rule.

Should the domestic elite, now partners in economic imperialism, depart from the consensus with the imperial power, or lose control to domestic insurgents and revolutionaries not willing to continue the partnership, then the imperial state reorganizes the remnants of its domestic elite partners and its influence within the colony's military wing of the elite, and reasserts control by civil war and counter-revolution. Historical examples of the latter include US intervention in Iran in the 1950s, Brazil and Indonesia in the 1960s, Chile in 1973, Central America in the 1980s.

In rare, severe cases, when the domestic partners are in total disarray and the domestic military is unreliable, the imperial state may be forced to intervene directly and militarily itself. Vietnam represents such an attempt to reassert Imperialist rule, which was botched, however, due to the failure of achieve smooth transfer of that rule from one imperial state (France) to another (US).

The wars in the middle east since the 1990s might be viewed as a series of premature and ineffective pre-emptive interventions by an imperial state into what were prior colonies to re-establish more direct control—i.e. Iraq, Libya—as a result of ideological and naïve adventurists (US Neocons) capturing US imperial policy; or the unnecessary redirection of the US imperial policy by other regional client states—like Israel, Saudi Arabia, Turkey—as in the case of Syria today.

US 20th century economic imperialism may be more economically efficient at extracting surplus wealth from colonies, but that doesn't mean economic imperialism doesn't break down, to be replaced with more over 19th-century-like political-military imperialism. Breakdowns are periodic and are appearing to become more frequent in the early 21st century.

Nineteenth century direct imperialism extracts

surplus and wealth by direct labor exploitation. The imperial state (e.g. Britain) establishes in-colony mining and production at low labor costs. It then, through its direct monopoly of commerce and transport in the colony, exports those low cost resources and goods back to its home market, from which it resells them at a higher price internally and/ or re-exports at a higher price to other country markets. Low costs are obtained by working the colony labor force longer hours, more intensely, and at low wages. This is the model of a single imperial state and a single client colony state.

Twentieth-century indirect economic imperialism differs in that it employs multiple ways of extracting surplus and wealth. Corporations invest in local client-colony production. They may relocate operations there via foreign direct investment, to maximize profits by lowering labor and other costs (taxes, etc.) both at home and in the colony simultaneously. This is a model of dual cost reduction. Goods and resources produced are not exported back to the home colonizer market necessarily, but may be directly exported to the rest of the world and the surplus retained in the colony. A greater share of the surplus is shared with the domestic elite. The colony economy and its internal market is expanded, producing a larger surplus than otherwise and allowing resale of goods at higher prices within the colony, as well as the home market and other global markets. Multi-directional trade becomes more important for surplus generation, compared to just colony-colonizer one-directional trade. Expansion of markets becomes as important as direct labor exploitation, commercial exploitation, and direct resource exploitation. It is still goods and services exploitation—procured at lower price than resale price. But market expansion is significantly greater, so that total surplus is higher—while the costs of maintaining this form of economic imperialism is relatively lower. This is a model of a single imperial state with a multiple of colony states integrated by expanded trade connections and a network of interconnected expanding internal markets.

Whereas the 19th century form was primarily low-cost, geared to reselling at a higher price to the home and other markets, 20th century economic imperialism is both that, as well as expanding the colonial market via reinvestment and expanding other markets by trade integration. Exploitation and price differential is key in the former; these are supplemented by internal-external trade and market expansion in the latter, expanding the surplus by growing the volume of resales as well as higher price of resale.

Twenty-first-century imperialism, and the new emerging form of colonial exploitation, however, is based on neither of the above. In fact, it is not at all about extracting surplus and wealth from the colony from low cost production or expanding production and markets for the goods and services involved. It is about extracting surplus and wealth from *debt*. It is not about price and volume of goods. It is about price and volume of credit extended to the colony. Price in this case representing the 'price of money'—i.e. the interest rate—at which credit was extended to the colony, and the interest rate at which it is eventually repaid by the colony. Volume in this case represents the volume or magnitude of debt incurred by the colony. As the volume of debt rises, the ability of the colony to repay it becomes more tentative. Therefore the price of the debt rises in real terms in the global market. Inability to repay the rising debt requires the imperial state to provide further volume of credit, i.e. to 'roll over' the old debt and enable the repayment of the old debt as well as the new debt. That again results in further inability to repay and the rise in the price (interest rate) of the debt, and so on. More debt is provided with which to repay the interest due. Total interest payments thereby continue to rise of the longer term, keeping the colony in perpetual debt. As more debt is provided to service the old, the terms imposed by the imperial state on the colony become increasingly severe. The colony must work harder and longer to pay sufficient taxes to the colony's client government, which the latter must remit to the imperial state in the form of interest payments due.

The idea of this model of 'financial imperialism' and 'interest rate' driven colonial wealth extraction as imposed by a single imperial state is perhaps also inaccurate. Regional blocs of states participate as the 'imperial-colonizer', although within the regional bloc a single hegemon state may exercise disproportionate influence. This is clearly the condition within the Eurozone, with German relative influence in an alliance with other northern European economies allowing that German-led alliance to dominate the Eurozone. The 'colony' in this case, in its most extreme form, is of course Greece. But degrees of this same kind of 'interest rate imperialism' and 'financial colonialism' prevail to lesser degrees in other Eurozone periphery economies from Cyprus to Portugal, in a somewhat different version in the case of Ireland, and eventually as well in other smaller east European states and economies.

A similar phenomenon may evolve as well, as the US comes to financially further dominate Latin American economies that have, or may, adopt the US dollar as their currency. Longer term, the same may be conjectured for the US-promoted Trans-Pacific Partnership, and still further in the future, China's efforts in Asia to accomplish the same. Free trade agreements are still very much part of the 20th century US economic imperialism model. But trade integration is the requisite for moving beyond trade and markets expansion as means to expand surplus and wealth extraction—to the 21st century model of financial imperialism based on credit-debt and interest rate financial wealth extraction from the colony.

With the creation of the European Union in the early 1990s, the trade integration step was achieved between the Eurozone and Greece. In 1999, with the creation of the Euro money currency union, which Greece joined in 2002, the second step was concluded. Exports and credit flows thereafter established the basic debt relationship in Greece. The Troika restructuring of the Greek debt in 2010, 2012, and most recently 2015 has escalated the volume and magnitude of that debt beyond sustainable levels, debt that will not go away. Thus the Greek debt crisis is destined to continue—and to arise repeatedly so long as the debt remains unsustainable and economic conditions periodically deteriorate in Europe, within Greece, or both.

Greece has had to, and will continue to have to, 'exploit itself' more severely, in order to generate a surplus with which to repay the interest due to northern Eurozone bankers and pan-region economic institutions (the Troika itself that 'owns' much of the Greek debt directly).

A new kind of imperialism is thus on the rise—a financial form of imperialism, where the surplus and wealth of a colony is extracted in a money capital form, as interest and other forms of financial payments, and that surplus from these forms of financial payment is, through various financial channels, exported back to the private and government institutions of the multi-state (Eurozone) imperial host.

This book will return to this theme and explanation in further detail in the concluding chapter. First, however, the next chapter must further explain in more detail the process by which after 1999 the Greek debt rose to such unsustainable levels, and the central role played by the structure of the Euro monetary system and the dominant role of Germany in the process. Subsequent chapters three through five will describe the conflict between the Troika and pre-Syriza Greek governments, led by the PASOK and New Democracy parties, up to and through what is known as the Greek debt crises of 2010 and 2012. Thereafter, in chapters six through nine, the third Greek debt crisis of 2015 is addressed, including the respective strategies and tactics of the Troika and Syriza government from January 2015 through the spring of 2016.

The book concludes with a review of critical views and assessments of the events of 2015-2016 in Greece by other commentators, within and outside Syriza and Greece, as well as this writer's perspective and analysis as to why Greek and Euro debt crises have occurred, are not yet over, and are destined to again re-emerge in Greece and Europe. A Postscript to the conclusion provides an economic explanation why Greek and other debt crises represent a new financial imperialism now emerging, of which Greece is but an early case example.

Endnotes

1   By 'austerity' is generally meant government fiscal policies designed to reduce budget deficits, in the form of either tax hikes and/or government spending cuts. The tax hikes are often regressive, impacting wage earners and small businesses disproportionately compared to larger corporations and financial institutions. Similarly the government spending cuts target layoffs and wage cuts for public workers, reduce social pensions and health benefits, and cut or eliminate social subsidies for transportation and other essentials for the poorest and working classes. Austerity also typically involves government sales of public works, government services, and nationalized industries and companies to private interests. But what many definitions of austerity miss is financial measures that are designed to extract savings and interest earnings from median income depositors to bail out and subsidize the banking system at the expense of wage earners and small businesses. In other words, 'austerity' is not just a fiscal policy. It includes financial-monetary measures as well.

2   A more thorough analysis of Syriza's strategic and tactical errors

during the 2015 debt negotiations—as well as a consideration and critique of other analysts' assessments of the events—is addressed in the final, concluding chapter 10 to this book.

3   The various forms assumed by financial imperialism are considered in more detail in the final 'postscript' to this book.

Chapter Two

THE GERMAN ORIGINS OF GREEK DEBT

The Greek debt crisis of 2010—and the subsequent second and third crises of 2012 and 2015 respectively—are all ultimately rooted in the 1999 creation of the European Monetary Union (EMU). That historic event established the Eurozone (EuZ) and its single currency, the Euro, as well as activated the European Central Bank (ECB) as the central bank for the region. It also introduced a set of related monetary and fiscal policies that, together with the single currency and central bank, have led directly over time to the excessive buildup of debt in Greece and that country's periodic debt crises since 2010.

The 1999 creation of the EMU set in motion a monetary policy-driven, export-centric economic strategy that has been the hallmark EuZ economic policy ever since. The newly created central bank, the ECB, was now able to inject increasing amounts of the new currency, the Euro, thereby increasing the money supply and in turn devaluing the new currency. Devaluation by means of central bank money injection meant lower costs for Euro exports—the aim of which was to enable EuZ business to gain a larger share of external global trade. At the same time, expanding the supply of the new currency also resulted in a significant increase of available credit for investment internally, within the EuZ region. That boosted internal exports-imports flow within and between the Eurozone states as well. Stimulating both 'external' and 'internal' EuZ exports was clearly one of the primary strategic objectives behind creating the EMU.

Complementing this central-bank, exports-driven economic strategy was an EuZ fiscal policy based on austerity. Austerity policy is designed to reduce government social benefits spending, cap or cut government jobs and wages, and to privatize and sell off public works. Fiscal austerity reduced government workers' wages and benefits, as well as compensation benefits costs (pensions, paid leave, etc.) to the private sector working class. It's often overlooked that this inclusion of what is referred to as 'labor market reform' measures targets the private sector workforce as well—also designed to reduce business wage and benefits costs. Lower unit labor costs translates into more competitive 'external' exports sales from the Eurozone to the rest of the world. Thus 'external devaluation' by means of central bank currency and monetary policy is complemented by 'internal devaluation' by means of labor market restructuring and wage compression.

The ability to deploy both forms of devaluation to boost exports were key objectives behind the creation of the EMU in 1999. External devaluation was to be achieved by the creation of the single currency and the new central bank; internal devaluation was to be achieved via what at the time was called the 'Lisbon Strategy'.

Whichever country successfully controlled the policies of the new central bank, the European Central Bank, would benefit most from the monetary policy and the single currency. And which country within the EuZ carried out labor market reform/labor cost compression first and most aggressively would also capture a lion's share of intra-EuZ trade at the expense of its EuZ country partners.

From its very inception, therefore, the creation of the Eurozone was a neoliberal class-based, incomes redistribution project designed to boost corporate profits through expanding exports, with complementary fiscal austerity and labor market reform policies designed to contain and compress wage and benefits incomes.

Further, both policies expanded income inequality. The ECB monetary policy did so by stimulating financial asset prices (stocks, bonds, etc.) consequently buttressing and expanding capital gains incomes, while Eurozone austerity fiscal policy did so by containing, and even lowering, working incomes by reducing government employment, cutting public sector wages and benefits, and reducing national pensions costs, subsidies, and other social benefit forms of compensation involving the general working populace.

The Lisbon Strategy and 'Internal Devaluation'

The labor market reform and labor cost compression elements behind the creation of the Eurozone in 1999 were initially presented in what was called the 'Lisbon Strategy', launched soon after.

Beyond the grandiose-sounding cover phrases about creating a 21st century European capitalism, in its essence the *Lisbon Strategy 2000* called for 'flexible labor markets'. Translating that into real terms: the new Eurozone economic elite would restructure their labor markets and reduce wage and benefits costs by hiring more contingent labor—i.e. part time, temp, and contract workers—in lieu of traditional full time labor which would be reduced by attrition and other means. The vast majority of new hires would be contingent and would grow increasingly by means of contingent labor.

That was not all. Greater 'flexibility' in labor markets, as it was called, also meant stretching out the workweek to raise productivity, which in turn meant rolling back the gains of the shorter workweek achieved in France and elsewhere. That required weakening the role of unions and bargaining— also a strategic goal of the Lisbon Strategy—and reducing state support for unemployment and other social benefits. Reversing the trend toward early pensions and retirement was another major element. So was eliminating the various legal restrictions on laying off or firing full time employed workers. The code for this was "labor mobility" and it was to be achieved by reducing job security. They said the goal was 'flexible' labor markets and they even coined the term *flexicurity,'* representing the reduction of job security.

In short, the Lisbon Strategy was a 10-year plan to transform the labor markets by reducing the rate of labor compensation gains and raising productivity in order to lower total labor costs, so that Eurozone exports would be more competitive in global markets. In essence, it was about making workers produce more at less cost in order to subsidize exports at their expense.

But while these policies might result in boosting Eurozone exports in relation to the rest of the world economy, so far as the distribution of exports within the Eurozone was concerned, the country that moved first and most aggressively to implement labor market reform (and reduce labor costs) would gain a relative advantage in intra-Eurozone exports and trade. 'Internal devaluation' not only could complement currency (euro) devaluation to boost external exports; it could also boost a given Eurozone country's share of intra-Eurozone exports and thus result in severe trade and money flow imbalances within and between Eurozone partner countries.

Now that there was one currency, the Euro, and one

central bank, the ECB, no member of the Eurozone could devalue their respective currencies independently against another Eurozone member in order to boost its exports and growth in order to remain competitive within the Eurozone. The 'external' devaluation route was now in the hands of the ECB only, and whoever controlled the ECB controlled that action.

Germany and its northern banker allies were at the apex of control of the central bank and monetary policy. Other Eurozone member countries, especially in the periphery (like Greece), could only compete with Germany and its northern friends by depressing the wages and intensifying the work of their labor forces. Labor market restructuring and labor cost reduction was their only open option. And whichever country and economy began that race first, ran the hardest, and thus resorted to internal devaluation by means of labor market reform the most aggressively, would be the country and economy that would garner the lion's share of intra-Eurozone exports and growth. And that country and economy would prove to be Germany. The Lisbon Strategy thus marked the commencement of an internal 'race to the bottom' with regard to wage incomes within the Eurozone.

Germany's Lisbon Strategy Implementation

A review of the Lisbon Strategy 2000 at mid-decade showed that indeed Germany had begun implementing restructuring and labor market reforms earlier and more aggressively than its EuZ counterparts. Between 2003 and 2005 Germany embarked on a major labor market restructuring, called the 'Hartz Reforms', after the director of personnel for Volkswagen, Peter Hartz, who was tasked with developing the formal proposals.

The German labor market reforms reduced German

workers' wages by converting many full time workers into part time, or what were called 'mini-jobs', and cutting hourly wages. Mini jobs were limited to 16 hours work a week. The reforms were successfully imposed because of the high unemployment afflicting German workers at the time, undermining their ability to resist. The Social Democratic Party, complicit in the implementation, was 'rewarded' with a junior seat in the new neoliberal government and regime.

German unemployment remained chronically high throughout the 1990s, in the 9%–10% range, rising to 10%–10.5% during the EMU transition years of 1999–2003. Germany was then often referred to as the 'sick man of Europe'. Through the 2003–2005 'Hartz' labor market reform phase, German unemployment rose still higher, average 11%–12% as late as 2005–2006, with a view to taming the German working class and getting it to accede to labor market reforms.

German labor costs did not rise at all in the first half of the decade as labor reforms were implemented. And once they were fully implemented, labor costs began to decline from 2005 on. Essentially they were flat for the entire period from 2000 to 2008, as a consequence. That kept German export costs low and even declining. Now stuck with the Euro, the rest of the Eurozone economies could not compete by lowering their own currency exchange rates, as they could have done pre–1999. They could only cut wages or raise productivity by reducing employment. But by 2005–2006 they were well behind the German curve. By leading the race, Germany was able to sweep up intra-Euro exports share at the expense of many of its Eurozone partners, especially in the southern periphery economies of the Eurozone which included Greece, for whom Germany was the single largest source of imports.

The successful internal devaluation effects of

Germany's labor cost reductions at mid-decade were evident in the shift in Germany's intra-Eurozone exports to other Eurozone countries after its labor market restructuring.

In the 1990s, two thirds of German trade was with other European Union countries. Germany ran trade deficits most of that decade, importing more than it exported. But after 2003, German exports accelerated. Exports as a share of its overall GDP rose from 37% at the start of 2005 to 50% by 2008, as exports surged from 731 billion euros at the beginning of 2005 to 984 billion euros by 2008—a 34% gain.

Even more impressively, Germany's trade surplus rose from 731 billion euros in 2003 to 984 billion in 2008, or more than 250 billion more annually. Its cumulative trade surplus over same five year period totaled 853 billion Euros—or more than $1 trillion in equivalent dollars. More than half of that surplus 853 billion came at the expense of its other EuZ and EU partner countries. And much of that was no doubt due to the wage compression/labor cost reduction advantages Germany achieved as a result of its early and aggressive Lisbon Strategy implementation. So German exporters gained a massive $853 billion Euro trade surplus, but German workers initially paid for it.

However, labor cost reduction via internal devaluation wasn't the only means by which Germany obtained a greater relative share of both external and internal exports sales. Germany's domination of the early ECB and the ECB's monetary policy also helped Germany attain that massive 853 billion trade surplus.

Germany's Bundesbank Dominates the ECB

The ECB is a federation of national central banks. Factions have existed within it from the very beginning. The

German central bank, the Bundesbank, with allies in other Euz members, has succeeded in dominating the decisions of the ECB in most cases. That was especially true during the beginning period of 2000–2003 and up to 2008, although that influence has been recently weakening.

The single currency, the Euro, facilitated the expansion of credit within the EuZ. The Bundesbank's influence insured that the ECB would especially enable a sufficient supply of credit to German and other northern 'core' banks, which it did, along with credit as well to other national central banks within the Euro currency union. Much of that credit to northern 'core' economies before 2009 was redirected to investment into the periphery economies. That credit was eventually recycled back via purchase of German and northern core economies' exports by the periphery. The ECB made loans to German-core banks, which in turn loaned to private banks in the periphery or invested directly themselves in the periphery. Credit also flowed to periphery economy central banks via ECB loans; national central banks in turn re-loaned to private banks in their economies, who in turn made loans to local businesses, consumers, and even local governments. These are conduits by which the Euro money capital flowed from the ECB into the periphery economies like Greece.

Residential and commercial real estate was a particular beneficiary of money flows to the periphery, and the excess lending to the sector led to housing bubbles in a number of periphery economies. Non-bank German and core business also provided the periphery with 'foreign direct investment' (FDI). Core northern EuZ companies expanded into the periphery by acquisitions, by buying majority stakes in companies there, providing capital for partnerships with periphery businesses, or by establishing wholly-owned subsidiaries, especially after 2005.

Through the various channels, massive money capital flowed into the periphery economies, including Greece, from the German-core north, made possible by the ECB's new Euro currency creation. As much of that headed south into the Euro periphery economies, real estate construction, housing, and relocated manufacturing boomed. And much would eventually again flow back again to the German-core north—either in the form of interest payments on private loans and debt, repatriation of profits by subsidiaries and operations of northern businesses that relocated to the periphery, and, not least, in the form of rising purchases of German-core exports by businesses, households, and governments in the periphery economies that experienced significant economic growth and income gains in the period leading up to the 2008 global crash.

Money capital was being recycled, as the EMU 1999 project intended. However, while that recycling was producing rising profits and income in the German-core north it was leaving a massive residue and overhang of debt in its wake in the periphery economies.

So long as new money capital was provided by the ECB to German-core banks and businesses, and so long as the latter continued to extend credit and expand in the periphery, the recycling would continue to work. But the cycle broke down with the banking-financial crash of 2008–09. Credit to the periphery reduced from a flow to a trickle. And with money capital and credit inflows to the periphery evaporating, periphery purchases of German-core exports plummeted in turn.

Without a continuing flow of credit from northern core to the periphery, the 'twin deficits' mechanism of credit provided to the periphery in order to purchase northern EuZ exports would break down. Which it did.

Levels of ECB credit flows to the periphery were

reduced by Germany and its allied financial elites' domination of ECB policy. The de facto 'German rule' was that the ECB could not provide credit to governments or private businesses, only to EuZ member national central banks. EuZ private banks were not lending, due to the 2008–09 crash. And EuZ periphery central banks were not bailing out their private banks after 2008 very well either—unlike the massive bank bailouts underway in the US and UK by their central banks—the Federal Reserve and the Bank of England—at the time. The Federal Reserve was also assisting German and French central banks bail out their private banks in the wake of 2008 by swapping a trillion US dollars for their currencies. Northern core Eurozone central banks, like the German Bundesbank, were addressing their own private banks' solvency and liquidity needs. Periphery private banks were not yet the focus of serious immediate concern. But they soon would be.

When EuZ periphery business and household demand for German-northern core exports declined sharply in 2008–09, Germany and the northern core exporters made another strategic error. Instead of ensuring money capital kept cycling to the periphery, Germany shifted its exports strategy. It relatively de-emphasized intra-EuZ exports and focused more on external exports sales outside Europe—especially to China and emerging markets whose economies began booming around 2010 and after.

The EuZ periphery economies were left to figure out for themselves how to restart their economies after 2008–09, without sufficient credit, with slowing German-northern core FDI, and with their own domestic banking system having collapsed. What they were left with was a residue of massive debt overhang from the pre-2009 period. No economy in the EuZ periphery was more exposed to this post-2008 dilemma than was Greece.

Greek Debt as Private Bank-Investor Debt

Greek government debt over the 2005 though 2008 period rose only modestly. Most of the pre-2008 debt buildup was on the private side, not public, during this period. Private Greek banks, as well as northern core banks doing business directly in Greece, may have been accumulating private debt. But, according to Eurostat statistics, Greek government debt rose only 13% from 2005 through 2008.

In contrast, Greek imports of German goods over the period rose by 70%. Germany was Greece's biggest trading partner. Greece's cumulative trade deficit with Germany alone rose between 2005 and 2008 by 201 billion Euros. That 70% and 201 billion required money capital from somewhere— either from Greek banks, who borrowed from the Greek central bank who in turn obtained the Euros from the ECB; or from private Greek borrowing from other EuZ banks who ultimately got their money from the ECB; or else by credit extended by German-Core businesses directly to Greek households and businesses. *The Greek private banking system had become bloated with debt, not the Greek government.* At least not yet. With an only 13% rise in government debt over the period, 2005 to 2008, a sovereign or government debt crisis was not a problem as late as 2008. It was private debt that was accumulating. Government debt would begin assuming central import with the first Greek bailout of 2010.

That private debt was owed primarily to German-northern core banks. According to a Bank of International Settlements report in early 2010, Greek debt owed to foreign banks was $303 billion. Of that, $43 billion was owed to German banks and $75 billion to French banks, as of third quarter 2009. And that did not count credit default swap debt held by the eight large German 'Landesbanks', the total of which was not reported.[1]

The first Greek debt bailout that occurred in May 2010 was therefore not really about bailing out Greece's government. It was about ensuring that German banks would not have to be bailed out if Greek banks and the Greek government failed to make required payments on their debt held by German and other northern core banks. It was about bailing out the banks.

As a former finance minister for Greece, Yanis Varoufakis, summed up the 2010 Troika-imposed debt deal: "more than 91 percent went to make whole the French and German bankers, by buying back from them at 100% euros bonds whose market value had declined to less than 20 euros".[2]

The Myth of Greek Wages as Cause of Debt

German-core apologists and economists—both then and today—like to argue that escalating Greek purchases of German-core exports was the consequence of rapidly escalating Greek wages, excessively generous increases in Greek pensions, excessive public employment hiring, rising Greek public workers' wage, and overly-generous Greek government subsidies spending which freed up real wages, allowing Greeks to purchase the exports. It was true that Greek workers' wages were 25% higher than German workers by 2008. But the differential was caused by German workers' real wage compression relative to the Greeks', more than it was by excessive Greek workers' nominal wage hikes.

To illustrate, average annual wages in Greece rose, but only moderately, in the first half of the decade. Annual wages were stagnant from 2005 through 2008. The average annual wage for a Greek worker was at around 22k euros per year in 2005. Wages thereafter rose by only 238 euros from 2005 to 2008. That's about 1%. After 2010 wages then declined sharply, due to the global crisis of 2008–09, falling annually to 21.8k euros annually in 2010. Wages would plummet after 2010, as austerity policies and a long economic depression became the norm in Greece.

What the record does show is that, while Greek purchases of German exports amounted to 289 billion euros in the four years from 2005 through 2008, Greek wages were already stagnating and then declining. Greek purchases of German-core exports could therefore not have been caused by rising Greek wages; it could only have been enabled by escalating credit and debt, a good part of which was eventually recycled back to Germany and others in the form of Greek household purchases of German exports.

Yet another way to deflate the myth that the Greek wages and consumer spending was the cause of the debt buildup is to consider household debt as a percent of GDP. According to Eurostat figures, in 2008 German household debt as a percent of German GDP was 55%. France was also 55% and Spain 80%. But Greek household debt as a percent of GDP was still lower—at 50%.

Private debt was only the beginning, however. The flow of credit from German-core north to Greece and the south, in order to buy exports from the German-Core north, was not the only cause of the total Greek debt build up. Sovereign or government debt would soon be added to total overall Greek debt.

From Private to Government Debt

Afflicting not only Greece but the entire global economy, the 2008–09 crash led to growing budget deficits in Greece as it did elsewhere globally. As in all deep economic contractions, Greek tax revenues fell sharply and government spending on essential 'safety net' programs rose. Private sector banks and businesses also required more government subsidies, more business tax cuts, and thereafter bailouts beginning in 2008. All that meant more government borrowing and thus rising government debt as well. So the deep contraction of the Greek economy in 2008–09 represents a second major cause of the rise of Greek total (private plus government) debt. Again, not by primary fault of either the Greek government or Greek consumers.

Greek sovereign debt as a percent of GDP rose by only 13%—to 113% of GDP—over the four years from 2005 to 2008. But, as the 2008–09 recession hit hard, Greek debt in 2009 alone accelerated 17%, to 130% of GDP. Clearly the harsh recession and rising deficits caused by falling tax revenues and rising social spending were largely responsible for the 17% jump in government debt.

But government debt rises not solely as a result of a slowing economy that creates deficits and a rising volume of borrowing. It can expand as well as a consequence of rising interest rates on that accumulating debt. As Greek sovereign debt grew in the course of the 2008–2010 crisis, global financial 'vulture' speculators—i.e. shadow bankers like hedge funds, asset managers, fund managers, investment banks, etc.—flocked in and drove up the cost of Greek government bonds. That increased Greece's debt financing costs, driving up sovereign debt levels even further.

Debt from shadow bankers' government bond speculation thus piled upon government debt incurred from deficits due to the economic crash of 2008–09, which piled upon debt from imbalances in exports and money (credit) flows to Greece. Debt is insidious. It develops multiple ways and begets itself.

While the ECB could provide more credit (debt) to the Greek central bank, to lend in turn to Greek banks and businesses requiring bailout, it could not directly lend to governments to refinance their government debt. German rules set up in 1999 and soon after prohibited this, and Germany and its majority faction on the ECB's governing board of represented Eurozone central banks enforced the restriction. So what EuZ institutions apart from the ECB could extend credit to the Greek government to make payments on its previous Greek government debt?

An appeal to the International Monetary Fund was one possibility. But the IMF's longstanding policy is not to provide funding alone. It required other institutions to participate in any government 'bailout' loan package. And the economy in question would have to 'put some skin in the game', before any IMF lending agreement. That is, Greece would have to cut spending, raise taxes, sell off public assets, or whatever in order to generate a surplus budget to ensure debt repayments. The ECB could not bail out Greek government debt. The IMF would not alone and only in part. Where would the rest of the lending come from, then? From the third member of what would come to be called the 'Troika': the pan-Eurozone's fiscal governing body, the European Commission.

When the Greek government's debt load continued to grow, Greece had to obtain further credit somewhere. Eurozone fiscal (German) rules also set up in 1999 did not allow a Eurozone member government to run budget deficits of more than 3% of annual GDP. Just as Eurozone member states could not exercise any independent monetary policy to boost exports, they could not engage either in fiscal deficit spending beyond a very narrow range, up to 3% of GDP.

Government debt rose as a consequence of Troika debt restructuring. In exchange for a new, restructured debt and loan, a member government had to make a clear commitment as to how it would repay the new (plus old) loans and debt. And in an environment of slow or no growth, with a 3% deficit cap, that meant debt repayment at the expense of government spending reductions and tax hikes and public works and public asset sales—i.e. debt would be repaid by fiscal austerity. Yet fiscal austerity leads to still further slowing of growth and the need for still more debt to service prior debt.

This was still not the entire picture with regard to causes of government debt escalation. As the Greek debt crisis 'matured' from late 2009 on, and concern over government debt and potential default spread to Spain, Portugal, Italy and other periphery economies, the value of the Euro currency declined. This meant, for Greece, that it would have to borrow more—i.e. increase Greece's government debt—because the Euro would now buy less given its decline. Greece would have to issue more Greek government bonds—i.e. raise debt even further—to obtain the same amount of money from bond sales.

And there was yet another related debt issue. With the Eurozone and global economy not recovering much from the 2008–09 global crash, Greece was earning far less from exports sales than before. That meant it had less income with which to make its payments on interest and principal on prior debt. Debt crises are the result of not only excess debt but also of insufficient available liquid income necessary to 'service' (i.e. pay principal and interest) that debt, and of the terms and conditions under which debt servicing is arranged.

Greece's government debt crisis, which erupted in late 2009–early 2010, did so due not only to the rising debt levels caused by the recession of 2008–09 and the intensification of speculation on Greek government bonds, but also due to the fall in the euro's value and the lack of Greek export income and flow of funds into Greece from northern banks and investors that occurred with the banking crash of 2008.

In short, in addition to private debt, there were multiple causes behind rising government debt after 2008. In addition to private debt from money capital inflows there was government debt increase due to:

- the 2008–09 global economic and banking crash and lack of normal economic recovery in the aftermath;
- global financial speculators driving up the cost of Greek bonds in 2009–10;
- fiscal austerity measures imposed on Greece by Eurozone 'Troika' members as part of the debt restructuring of spring 2010; and
- the decline in the euro currency itself at the time.

The German Origins of the Greek Debt

Greek private debt escalation is tightly correlated with the arrangements described above, by which massive credit from German and northern core banks (enabled by the ECB) flowed into Greece to finance German export purchases by Greece. German origins of Greek government debt was more opaque. It originates in German insistence in early 2010 that Greece solve its own debt problems, which was an invitation for global speculators to drive up Greek bond rates and thereby Greek debt. It also originates in German and allied core bankers' dictation of the severe austerity terms imposed on Greece in the eventual May 2010 first debt deal.

Data shows that the escalation of Greek private sector debt occurs only after 2004. Private debt to purchase German-northern core exports escalates beginning 2005. Greece's trade deficit with Germany and Greek private sector debt is thus highly correlated with the structural reforms implemented by Germany circa 2005. Greek government, or sovereign, debt only begins to escalate in 2008–09, correlating with the global economic crash and the government bond speculators that followed.

Between 2005 and 2008 German exports to Greece almost doubled, from roughly 54 billion to 92 billion and amounted to more than $250 billion by the time of the first Greek debt crisis in 2010. During the same period, Greek yearly exports to Germany rose from only $17 billion to $20 billion, for a total of $112 billion. Greeks were buying far more German goods and boosting German GDP than vice-versa. Greece therefore had to 'borrow' $138 billion from somewhere to pay for the difference. That borrowing, and thus debt, flowed directly from German and northern Europe banks, from Greek banks ultimately owned or provided capital from German and other northern Banks, or from Greek banks that borrowed from northern banks. Germany and the 'core' got export-driven growth; Greece got German imports and an ever-rising pile of debt.

Stuck with the Euro single currency, Greece could not compete with the German-northern core export juggernaut after 2005, by lowering their own currency exchange rates to devalue their own currency. The euro was now the currency and Germany controlled its fate through its faction on the ECB. Greece had only one vote in 17 in the ECB. Greece was further hamstrung with regard to fiscal policy by additional rules that required a Eurozone member country to run deficits of no more than 3% of GDP. Nor did Greece, or the other periphery economies, launch their own 'internal devaluation' via labor market reforms to compress wages and the cost of their own exports. That would be embedded later, in the austerity packages of debt restructuring imposed upon them.

In short, Greece—like the other periphery economy members—in effect gave up any sovereignty with regard to monetary policy, and for all but a narrow scope of action concerning fiscal policy, with its initial acceptance of the Euro as its single currency, the ECB as its central bank, and the 3% deficit rule. This left Germany and its northern allies not only with indirect control over decisions concerning those parameters—but also with the ability to impose penalties on those periphery states like Greece attempting to break ranks.

Both Greek economic growth and Greek government debt during the decade 1995 to 2005 was no more unstable or excessive than that of other Eurozone economies at the time. Greek GDP in 1995 was equivalent to 110 billion euros and had doubled to 200 billion euros by 2005 then rose by only $25 billion in the five year period 2005–2010. Greece's sovereign debt to GDP ratio in 1995 was 97%; by 2007 it had risen to only 107%. But by 2009—in the wake of the 2008–09 crash—government debt rose to 130% of GDP and in 2010 to 148%. The surge in government debt was thus clearly a consequence of the 2008–09 global banking crash and deep recession, the speculation on Greek government bonds by 'vulture' shadow bankers and investors, and the debt terms imposed on Greece by the Troika itself.

What happened around 2005 on the private side, and then after 2008 on the public side and immediately thereafter thus provides the true explanation for Greece's debt acceleration and the debt crises that began to erupt in 2010. German and 'core' banks plowed credit and money capital into Greek banks and businesses. In addition to bank provided money capital, German private foreign direct investment (FDI) into Greece also rose from 1.4 billion euros in 2005 to more than 10 billion by 2008. As the money and capital to Greece was recycled back to Germany and the northern core economies in the form of exports, Germany got business profits, economic growth and its money capital returned to it. In addition, as financial intermediaries in the recycling of money capital, both core and Greek banks got interest payments from the Greek loans and Greek bonds. Greeks got German and 'core' export goods for a few years, but loaded up on credit and debt in the process for what appears will remain an interminable period of debt repayments well into the future.

German-Core provided money capital, credit and its debt-fueled export binge after 2005 hobbled Greece's real economy, to put it lightly. The problems were covered up so long as credit flows from the northern core continued and economic growth in Greece up to 2008 continued. But once the credit flows, and income from economic growth, collapsed in Greece the growing mountain of private debt could not be 'serviced'—i.e. paid. Greek banks, and northern banks operating in Greece, then experienced massive losses requiring bailout. The first casualty of the excess private debt run-up were the banks. The 2010 debt restructuring would be all about bailing out those banks and northern core Eurozone investors, institutional and individual, as well as non-Eurozone global speculators.

By bailing out the banks and investors, the Greek government in effect 'transferred' their private debt into Greek government debt. The Greek debt crisis thus may have originated ultimately in the German-northern core, but it would be dumped on the Greek banking system at first, to be eventually dumped thereafter onto Greek taxpayers and especially Greek workers who would be required to 'pay the bill' through various fiscal austerity and de facto labor market reform measures imposed on Greece by the Troika. German-northern core gain thus became Greece and Greek workers' pain.

Endnotes

1   The same BIS report indicated that, in addition to the $43 billion Greek

debt held by German banks, which held an additional $240.3 billion of Spanish government debt, $47.3 billion of Portugal's and $209 billion of Italy's.

2   Yanis Varoufakis, *And the Weak Suffer What They Must*, Nation Books, 2016, p. 157.

Chapter Three

PASOK AND THE DEBT CRISIS OF 2010

2009: PASOK's Strategic Error

After 2008, with Greek wage incomes collapsing—and money credit inflows from the ECB and northern Eurozone banks and businesses into Greece drying up—private sector debt was no longer the primary contributor to total Greek debt. This was reflected in the sharp decline in Greek purchases of German exports, indicating a decline in the flow of money capital into Greece with which to purchase those exports. German exports to Greece collapsed by roughly 70% from 2009 to 2015.

But just the opposite was happening with regard to Greek government debt. Greek sovereign debt rose by only 13% from 2005 to 2008. However, it escalated rapidly after 2008, from 113% of GDP to 197% of GDP at the end of 2015, according to Eurostat statistics. In 2009 alone it accelerated 17%. At the same the Greek economy contracted in 2009 for the first time in a decade. Greece's unemployment rate rose to 12.7%.

In October 2009, parliamentary elections replaced the ruling party, the conservative New Democracy party, with the social democratic party, PASOK. Shortly after the October 4, 2009 parliamentary elections, PASOK revealed that its predecessor New Democracy government had been covering up its budget deficit by offloading from its books some of its spending by means of 'derivatives swaps'.[1]

The new government's motives for revealing the coverup may have been several: in order not to be held responsible for their predecessor government's coverup of Greece's economic condition; to possibly maximize the loans sought from Eurozone institutions' new bailout funds just being created; or the prepare the public ground for the necessity of deep austerity. This was a relatively common practice at the time throughout Europe, not just by Greece.

In revealing the depth of the problem, however, the PASOK leadership made an historic strategic error immediately upon assuming the reins of government. That error would eventually prove its undoing and lead Greece into depression and years of rising debt and austerity to come. The Eurozone media made a big deal of it. When PASOK re-adjusted the budget deficit, it revealed publicly that it really had a budget deficit of 12.7%, not the 6% reported previously by the New Democracy government. That 12.7% was well above the Eurozone's '3% budget deficit as percent of GDP' rule and threshold limit for an allowable budget deficit. Yet nearly every other Eurozone government's deficit was also above 3%, including most of the northern core economies. Some by more than 10%. For example, the UK's budget deficit at the time was in excess of 11% of GDP. That apparently did not constitute a budget crisis. But Greece's 12.7% did, according to the Eurozone press, which immediately trumpeted the new figures. The 12.7% vs. 3% was used to make it appear Greece's government finances were way out of whack with the rest of the Eurozone. The revelation was quickly exploited by bankers and speculators.

PASOK's Voluntary Austerity Program

A new budget with fiscal spending cuts amounting to about 12 billion euros was passed by the Greek parliament in December 2009. On January 15, 2010, PASOK's leadership announced it would introduce fiscal austerity measures to reduce the budget deficit by 4% by the end of 2010 by means of spending cuts and tax hikes. In the interim, Greek bond speculators drove up the cost of Greek bonds, adding to the Greek government debt totals. Greece's stock market fell from 2700 to 2100 by early 2010. The euro currency also plummeted, as did Greek export earnings necessary to finance the existing debt.

In a press conference in mid-January 2010, PASOK pledged to reduce Greece's budget deficit from its 2009 deficit of 13.6%—to a new target of 2.8% by the end of fiscal year 2012. A reduction from 12.7% to 8.7% was the target for 2010. PASOK's party head, George Papandreou, declared that Greece could solve its own deficit and debt problem, and didn't need help from other Eurozone countries, the ECB or the IMF. He provided public details of a fiscal program that would include major reductions in public spending, in pensions, and imposing a wage freeze on public workers, raising sales taxes, etc. Papandreou and PASOK were clearly trying to impress the bond markets, Eurozone bankers, and Eurozone finance ministers that they could successfully impose austerity themselves. The austerity announcement did little, however, to tame the bond speculators who continued to drive up Greek bond costs in early 2010, as Greece's economic conditions worsened.

Eurozone finance ministers did not believe Papandreou's January austerity proposals could achieve the intended goals. In response to Papandreou's January press conference, Wolfgang Schauble, Germany's finance minister, reiterated the Eurozone finance ministers' message that Greece must find its own way out of the crisis. Greece should seek assistance from the IMF, not from the central bank, the ECB, or the European Commission (EC), through which the finance ministers influenced policy. The head of Germany's own national bank, Axel Weber, publicly came out in opposition to any form of ECB-EC Greek bailout.

Schauble's explicit message was the Eurozone's 'rules' prohibited the ECB from making loans to governments. Pooling bilateral government to government loans through the EC was not the way to resolve Greece's debt crisis. His veiled message was that Greece should do what Germany did in 2005: introduce a Lisbon-like plan and cut government spending. Greece had too many unprofitable public companies. It should sell them. And introduce labor market reforms. In other words, Greece should impose even more fiscal austerity on itself than Papandreou had initially offered. Still more austerity measures were necessary. There was too much reliance on tax increases in the January 2010 Greek austerity proposals, according to Schauble, on behalf of the finance ministers. More pension reforms were needed. Periodic reports on Greece's actual progress in cutting spending were now also necessary.

Within days, Papandreou publicly responded by adding further details of the austerity measures. On February 2, PASOK unilaterally introduced further austerity measures, including freezing wages and raising excise sales taxes. Subsequent visits by the EC to Greece in late February-early March were followed by a third round of austerity measures by the Greek government. This time the VAT general sales tax was raised, wage allowances reduced and holiday bonuses for public workers ended. The Troika spoke, and PASOK delivered. It was not even what might be called a 'negotiation' in any real sense.

On March 9 the EC concluded that PASOK austerity to date was likely sufficient for Greece to meet its budget goals for 2010. It was not. Throughout March the Greek economy continued to deteriorate, GDP slowed further, tax collections lagged, and the cost of borrowing by the Greek government in private markets began to accelerate significantly. Initial Troika estimates earlier in the year that Greece would need a 25 billion euro bailout had now risen to 60 billion.

Growing more desperate as the economy continued to slide, Papandreou met directly in early March with Deutsche bank's CEO and German chancellor, Angela Merkel, and offered another 6.6 billion in budget cuts, the details in terms of austerity to pay for it to be determined. The EC responded by demanding more sales tax hikes by Greece, more public worker wage cuts, and other measures. Greece was also issuing more government bonds to raise funds in private markets, but was having to do so at ever-rising interest rates due to the bond speculation.

Meanwhile, Greek workers were responding by early March. The selective public worker strikes earlier in the year were now spreading and on March 11–12, a short general strike took place. Papandreou indicated Greece could not continue to borrow at an ever increasing rate. By late March, even the ability to sell bonds was hitting a wall and bond buyers were disappearing. Greek banks were downgraded by the rating agencies once again.

The IMF and Schauble continued to praise Greece for its voluntary efforts to impose austerity and its continued efforts to sell bonds despite the escalating cost and greater debt incurred. They were squeezing every last ounce of voluntary concessions from Greece before they would announce any details of their own bailout support. But the costs of the bailout continued to escalate as the Troika still delayed. The contagion was still spreading to other Eurozone periphery economies, and the threats to Greek, and in turn to northern core banks still shaky from the 2008-09 crisis, were growing as well. Similar debt crises in Portugal, Spain, Ireland and elsewhere were consuming Troika attention. Meanwhile, Greece's situation continued to deteriorate. On April 23, PASOK officially abandoned its position that it could introduce austerity on its own and raise additional loans privately. It requested the Troika for a multi-year bailout package.

Since Eurozone governments individually could not provide loans directly to other member governments, nor could the ECB provide loans to governments per the Eurozone treaty,[2] that left only the European Commission, i.e. the EC, and the IMF.

PASOK turned to the IMF and requested privately that it lead in providing loans to Greece. But IMF policies required Greece, or any other country seeking its assistance, to lay out in detail and begin implementing its austerity plan first. Only then might the IMF consider providing loans. The IMF did not 'lead' in these kind of deals, Greece was informed. Greece would need to line up other private lenders first, or issue and sell more Greek government bonds in private markets to raise money, or else obtain loans from the EC, before the IMF would consider providing funds in a packaged deal. The EC thus became the focal point in the 2010 bailout deal by pooling bilateral loans from various Eurozone governments. The separate governments would provide the loans, but the EC would manage and disburse them.

This arrangement revealed the weakness of the Troika and the Eurozone's fiscal system. There were as yet none of the major Troika bailout funds that would soon follow—the European Financial Stability Fund, the Emergency Stability Mechanism, and so on. They were in development but not yet the primary sources for funding government or bank bailouts. For early 2010, it was the EC managing on behalf of bilateral government loans.

Bond Vigilantes Escalate the Debt

Given the continuing delays in bailout funding, global speculators continued driving up the rates on Greek sovereign bonds throughout March and April, thus adding to total Greek sovereign debt costs. The run-up in bond rates also stimulated the derivatives market, as investors buying Greek bonds also purchased derivative insurance contracts called Credit Default Swaps (CDSs), as a hedge to a possible Greek bond default. Global credit rating agencies' downgrading of creditworthiness of Greek bonds were also exacerbating the situation. With every downgrade, the interest rate for the bonds rose further. Bond speculators exploited the downgrade announcements to bid up Greek bond rates and costs still further.

By February 2010 another major problem was arising. Simultaneously, the growing instability in Greece began to have a contagion effect, spreading to government bonds for Spain, Portugal, and even Italy. Now the threat to German and northern core banks was not only a possible default by Greece, but a chain reaction of potential defaults throughout the Eurozone southern periphery.

This probably explains in part some of the delays in finalizing the 2010 debt agreement between Greece and the Troika. Were the EC, ECB and IMF to offer bail out loans to Greece, it would certainly lead to similar, and even larger, demands for the same from other periphery governments and central banks at the time experiencing their own debt crises. The EC and ECB were initially therefore hesitant, for fear of precipitating more requests for bailout loans. Which country should get how much bailout and for what in return was just being worked out. So the EC and ECB played hardball and forced Greece to go into private markets and raise funds from private investors for months in early 2010, despite the escalating interest rates in private markets that piled on more debt in the process, while also pushing PASOK to introduce new and further measures of austerity unilaterally before an agreement was reached.

This 'one way' negotiation was significant. In what would prove a frequently employed tactic in this and future subsequent debt negotiations, the Troika typically provided statements of encouragement to Greece to self-impose austerity on itself, while not saying anything specific about what loans and bailout funds they, the Troika, might provide in exchange for ever more austerity. The Troika strategy was to elicit more details about austerity proposals and implementation, the Greek economy, and Greek revenues and budgets while signaling still more austerity was needed. Papandreou and PASOK were more than willing to follow this one-sided negotiating farce.

With major debt repayments due May 10, 2010 Papandreou and PASOK finally 'threw in the towel' and on April 23 asked the EC and IMF for a $60 billion, multi-year loan package, promising in exchange to accelerate labor market reforms to reduce public worker employment and wage costs, reduce pensions and health benefits, and impose austerity cuts totaling 30 billion euros, or about 11% of Greece's GDP at the time. The austerity cuts unilaterally offered by PASOK included 5.3% in spending cuts, 4% in tax hikes, and another 1.8% of further GDP budget cuts derived from what were called 'structural reforms' to the Greek economy. This 1.8% was also in addition to a previous 5% of structural measures agreed to by Greece in the preceding months. The total impact of the bailout package was therefore approximately equal to 16% of annual GDP, according to independent estimates at the time.[3]

The 2010 Debt Agreement

Representatives of the Troika's EC, ECB, and IMF visited Greece on April 21, Papandreou requested his multi-year bailout on the 23rd, and a package of bailout loans, with required fiscal and austerity measures, was agreed on May 2, 2010 between Greece and the Troika. The Greek parliament approved the measures on May 6. The EC and IMF announced a loan package of 80 billion euros of bilateral loans from the EC plus 30 billion euros from the IMF approved on May 9.

38 billion of the 110 euros would be disbursed in 2010 and another 40 billion in 2011, with the remainder of 24 billion in 2012 and 8 billion in 2013. But the 2010 package would never make it through 2012, when it collapsed and another, second debt deal replaced it that year. Of the 110 billion euros provided by the 2010 deal, 53 billion of the EC's 80 were actually disbursed and 20 billion of the IMF's 30 billion. The remaining amounts were rolled over into the 2012 agreement.

In exchange for the EC and IMF loans, Greece was required to impose a particularly severe total package of austerity measures. These included a wage reduction of 14% in 2010 alone, as holiday bonuses were abolished and wages otherwise frozen. Pensions were cut by 8%, and retirement ages raised. Social security was reformed and health care costs raised for workers. Labor market reforms were called for, including decentralizing collective bargaining, ease of firing introduced, more part time jobs allowed, and union regulation tightened.

The spending cuts totaled 7% of GDP and tax hikes another 4% of GDP, or about 25 billion euros in what was a 'front-loaded' austerity plan in the first year, 2010. On the banking side of the deal, the ECB provided more lending to the Greek central bank by extending what was called

'Emergency Lending Assistance', or ELAs, in short term loans when requested. The ECB also introduced allowing Greece's central bank to issue bonds, which it, the Greek central bank, could use as collateral for borrowing from the ECB as well. A special Financial Stability Fund for Greek banks was also set up, with 10 billion euros initial funding.

The 2010 debt agreement was predicated, however, on a long list of overly optimistic assumptions that would eventually mean its collapse in 2012 as the entire Eurozone entered a double dip recession and dragged Greece's economy—already reeling from austerity driven economic collapse—down with it. The deal assumed Greece's economy would contract by only 4% in 2010 and 2.5% in 2011 and then grow in 2012–13. It collapsed 25%. It assumed unemployment at a level of 15%. It exceeded 27%. It underestimated Greek government bond rates, a continued problem in the banking sector, and made overly optimistic assumptions of the implementation of the austerity measures by the Greek government as Greek governments and people undertook a form of 'rear-guard' defensive measures to protect their interests from the massive austerity brought on by the agreement.

Who Was Really Bailed Out?

Who received the 110 billion, or 73 billion actual, euros from the 2010 debt agreement? Not Greece.

Former Greek finance minister, Yanis Varoufakis' estimated in his 2016 book that 91% of the 2010 Troika package went to bailing out the banks, Greek as well as German and other northern core. As he notes "Mr. Papandreou was pushed into accepting the largest loan in history of which the bulk, more than 99.1 percent, went to make whole the French and German bankers, by buying back from them at 100 euros bonds whose market value had declined to less than 20 euros."[4]

An even more definitive recent study has concluded that more than 95% of the payments by Greece went to pay interest and principal on the debt to banks and for bank recapitalization purposes.[5] Government bilateral loans, originally arranged through the EC, were funds raised from banks and investors by the Euro governments involved, and Greek repayments to the EC and governments were in turn paid back to the banks and investors. So the Greek debt payments amounted to 95% payment to Eurozone bankers, paid for by the austerity. Or, more directly, redistributed from Greek workers' wages, pensions, consumption subsidies for the poor, earnings from Greek nationalized utilities, ports, and transport companies, sales tax hikes, and other tax measures. The bankers were bailed out from what amounts to ultimate income transfers from these sources. At the same time, Greece's debt continued to rise absolutely and in terms of a percent of GDP. Thus, Greece was not bailed out if its debt continued to rise and austerity extractions continued to grow. The banks that ultimately provided the money, through the conduit of the Troika, were in fact bailed out.

A key characteristic of the 2010 Troika deal was that the Greek private sector debt that had accumulated over the years leading up to 2010 was paid for—due to the way the Euro and the ECB were structured in the 1999 EMU agreement—by the 2010 bailout. The Troika took over this private debt, converting it to public debt, and then charged this assumed debt to the Greek government. While it is also true that a portion of the Greek debt was the consequence of the global economic crash of 2008–09 itself, with its collapsing government revenues and rising social costs, the private was perhaps the greater element of total Greek debt in 2010.

According to the independent research estimate at the time by the Center for Economic and Policy Research, "The only thing the rescue package really achieves is a major change in the ownership of debt. With Greek sovereign debt being transferred from the balance sheets of banks to the balance sheet of European governments (the EC), the real purpose of the entire operation is to save European banks by relieving them from holding debt titles upon which a potential default could be looming."[6]

The Troika no doubt thought the additional 110 billion euros loaned to Greece would prove sufficient to enable it to pay interest and principal on Greece's prior debt as well as the 110 billion new debt. But that would prove incorrect. Greece's debt burden would grow even worse after 2010, leading to a second debt crisis in 2012.

Endnotes

1 This was a widespread practice by governments both before and immediately after the crash of 2008-09. A derivative swap allowed a government to reduce its official debt load by exchanging debt for a derivative sold to it by a bank or shadow bank. The swaps were defined as non-debt forms of securities. Investment banks, like Goldman Sachs, were heavily involved on a global scale.

2 The ECB by its rules could only provide loans to its affiliated national central banks. The ECB controlled the currency, so national central banks had to obtain loans from the ECB, for which they paid interest and eventually paid back principal as well.

3 Ronald Johnson, '*Greece and the IMF: Who Exactly Is Being Saved?*', Center for Economic and Policy Research, Washington D.C., July 2010.

4 Yanis Varoufakis, *And the Weak Suffer What They Must?*, Nation Books, New York, 2016, p.

5 Jorg Rocholl and Axel Stahmer, '*Where Did the Greek Bailout Money Go?*', European School of Management and Technology, White Paper 16-02. More on this report in chapter two, since the conclusions combine the debt payments from the 2010 and 2012 agreements. The authors conclude that only 9.7 billion of 247.8 billion of the Troika

loans went to the Greek budget. The rest to banks, directly or indirectly.

6   Ronald Johnson, '*Greece and the IMF: Who Exactly Is Being Saved?*', Center for Economic and Policy Research, Washington D.C., July 2010, p. 1.

Chapter Four

THE SECOND GREEK DEBT CRISIS OF 2012

A Brief Recapitulation

An important theme of this book has been that Greece's debt crisis is primarily non-Greek in origin, and largely the consequence of the creation of the Euro and its monetary system.

Earlier chapters showed that Greece's debt from 1995–2005 was no greater than in other Eurozone economies, and in some cases less. The rise in Greek debt therefore began from 2005–2008, driven during those years by the imbalances in trade and money flows between Germany and northern core Eurozone economies and Greece (and other southern periphery economies). Money and capital flowed from the Germany and the core Eurozone north to Greece, mostly to finance Greek purchases of German and core exports. The money capital flowed from German and core private banks into Greece's private banks, and/or in more direct form, via foreign direct investment by German and core businesses into Greek businesses or their own Greek subsidiary companies. The debt escalation was thus largely private business debt at this point. There was some central bank (ECB) to central bank (Greek) money flows and some lending to the Greek government to finance infrastructure expansion as the Greek economy before 2008 grew, but it was not significant. Greek government debt as a percent of GDP rose from only 97% in 1995 to 100% in 2005 and 107% by 2008. Government debt was not yet an issue. But it would eventually become so, once the private debt accumulated was transferred into public debt after the crash of 2008–09 and the series of Troika debt restructuring deals that followed.

The outcome of the imbalances in private sector trade and money flows up to mid-2008—from the German-Core to Greece—was that Greek banks and businesses became over-extended with the massive cheap euro inflows. When the 2008–09 crash occurred, the money flows to Greece plummeted but the private debt remained. The continuation of private debt payments by Greek banks and businesses became difficult and defaults loomed. New money flows from the north to Greece were now required for Greek banks and businesses to continue debt payments—i.e. to pay debt on previous purchases, not to finance business investment or Greek export purchases. The new post-2008 money flows would cycle through Greece's central bank and Greece's national government via bailouts of a growing number of insolvent Greek banks and non-bank businesses facing default or collapse. Greek private debt became Greek government debt.

The conversion of private Greek bank and non-bank business debt to government debt occurred roughly as follows: Greece's government issued new Greek government bonds for its central bank to sell at subsidized rates to Greek private banks. The government bonds would then be used as collateral for the private banks to borrow from the European Central Bank (ECB), which provided new funds to Greece's central bank to lend to Greek private banks, using the new

Greek bonds as collateral. As others have pointed out, it was not unlike a 'ponzi' scheme.[1]

In addition to the conversion of Greek private debt of 2005-07 to Greek government debt, starting in 2008 Greek government debt would rise sharply as well as a result of the global financial crash and great recession of 2008-09. Greek tax revenues crashed and government spending rose—as occurred in virtually all other economies at the time. Deficits increased, as they did elsewhere, as did Greek government debt in turn.

By 2010, both the Greek private sector—banks and non-banks—and the Greek government required bailout. However, the Euro system created in 1999 had no provisions for central Eurozone fiscal assistance to peripheral economies like Greece. This awkward arrangement existed due to the built-in failure of the 1999 monetary union structure. Under that structure, the ECB, by its rules, could not lend to Eurozone governments, but only to Eurozone member national central banks. Conversely, the EC loaned only to governments, not to central banks.

Greece's private banking system became increasingly indebted to central banks—Greek and ECB—as well as to other Euro private banks, while the Greek government became further indebted as a consequence of issuing collaterable bonds to its banking system and as a result of borrowing from the European Commission and IMF.

The Greek government's debt thus rose rapidly from 2008 to 2010 due to (1) Greek government issuing bonds to its central bank to bail out Greek banks that had become over-extended during the boom of 2005–08; (2) Greek banks borrowing from other Euro banks using the new Greek bonds as collateral; (3) general Greek government deficits created by the deep recession of 2008-09; and (4) Greek government borrowing from the European Commission and IMF in 2010 as a result of (1), (2) and (3).

From 107% of GDP by end of 2007, Greek debt then accelerated rapidly to 170% of GDP by 2011 after the May 2010 first debt restructuring deal. Clearly Greek debt up to this point was due to German-created trade imbalances during 2005–07 before the crash, the deep crash of 2008, the first Greek bank bailout, and then the debt added by the Troika's 2010 debt restructuring as debt was piled on to repay previous debt.

Some Defining Characteristics of the 2012 Debt Crisis

The process of adding debt to pay for debt would be repeated in the second debt crisis and restructuring of March 2012. This time, however, the challenge for the Troika was even greater than in 2010. New negative variables were now part of the debt equation. One was the concurrent double-dip recession occurring throughout the entire Eurozone from late 2011 to early 2013. It was exacerbating debt conditions not only in Greece but throughout much of the Eurozone, hitting the Euro banks as well as governments. The emerging parallel debt crises in Spain, Portugal, Ireland and Italy in 2012 were another new factor. Now the debt crisis concerned not only Greece but the entire southern Eurozone periphery (and Ireland).

Troika government bailout funds were insufficient to resolve the spreading crisis. It was now a matter not just of a couple of hundred billion euros, but of well over a trillion. ECB liquidity injections targeting direct bank bailouts were also insufficient. Under its new chairman, Mario Draghi, the ECB provided a half trillion euros to banks during the first few months of 2012. With government debt defaults now looming across the periphery, the EC and Eurozone governments created a new, larger bailout fund of 1.2 trillion euros, the European Financial Stability Fund, or EFSF, in order to bail out not only Greece but Spain, Portugal, Ireland and Italy. In the midst of the deepening Euro wide recession, spreading banking system fragility region wide, and more governments experiencing sovereign debt deterioration, Greece experienced its second debt crisis. Greece's crisis accelerated contagion effects throughout the Eurozone periphery, while itself being impacted both politically and economically by the broader debt crises elsewhere.

The new developments of double dip Eurozone recession, spreading sovereign and banking contagion, and the new EFSF bailout stamped the 2012 Greek debt crisis as even more serious than in 2010. Even more debt would be piled upon preceding debt levels before it was over.

If one were to identify a single driving factor behind the 2012 crisis, it would be the Troika's intent to bail out the private banking system first and foremost, and in the process to lay the financial burden of that bailout onto Greece's government, which then would require Greek society to pay that cost by means of even more austerity than imposed in the 2010 debt restructuring.

That the primary Troika goal was to bail out the banking system while laying the bill on the Greek people was revealed in detail in a 2016 study done on the combined 2010 and 2012 debt restructuring deals by the European School of Management and Technology. After an exhaustive investigation of where the bailout funds during the two crises actually ended up, the ESMT study's authors concluded that:

> Only 9.7 billion (euros) or less than 5% of the total amount of 215.9 billion (actually disbursed to Greece) being distributed in the 1st and 2nd programme were not used for debt-related payments and bank recapitalizations and thus directly

contributed to the Greek fiscal budget. In contrast, 139.2 billion or more than 64% were used to repay the existing debt and serve interest payments. Furthermore, 37.3 billion or 17% were used to recapitalize Greek banks, while the remaining 29.7 billion or 14% provided incentives for investors to engage in the Private Sector Involvement (PSI) in March 2012.[2]

In other words more than 95% went to the banks, either directly or eventually, and mostly of that 95% to banks outside of Greece—the lion's share going to German and French banks.

2011: Interim Preceding the Second Debt Crisis

Despite the 110 billion euros cost of the first debt restructuring of 2010, the first Greek debt deal did not stabilize the Greek banks.[3] Greek lending within Greece continued to weaken after May 2010, and fell by 3.8% in 2011. Banks' non-performing business loans surged, doubling to 16% of all loans in 2011. Declining bank lending meant little investment by business and therefore a fall in bank revenues, which translated into banks' growing difficulty servicing prior Greek bank debt. Despite the Greek central bank repeatedly providing emergency loans to private Greek banks—from funds provided to it from the ECB—Greek banks were still insolvent by the summer of 2011, a year after the introduction of the 2010 debt deal that was supposed to bail them out.

The austerity terms associated with the 2010 debt deal slowed the Greek economy even further, raising Greek government deficits and debt in the process. Government spending was cut by $6 billion in 2011, but tax revenues also declined, increasing the need for more government borrowing and thus debt.

Greek businesses and households fared no better. 105,000 of Greece's 800,000 businesses failed in 2011, a rise from 68,000 a year earlier in 2010. Business investment fell by 17% in 2011, to approximately half that of 2007. Business net exports fell by half in 2011 compared to 2010. Businesses and wealthier households that still had bank savings continued to withdraw their deposits from Greek banks throughout the year and re-deposit them in other Euro banks in Germany, France and Netherlands. Deposits flowed out unimpeded at an 18% annual rate, with no attempt by the government whatsoever to limit the capital flight with capital controls or other measures. From the period following the 2010 debt deal through 2011, no less than $75 billion was withdrawn from Greek banks, mostly sent to German and other northern core Eurozone banks.

On the labor side, 51,000 government job cuts were announced as the May 2010 austerity plan was implemented. Government workers' wages declined by 25% over the 2010–2011 period. Total Greek employment fell by 6% bringing unemployment to 20% and youth unemployment to 48%. As a result of a reduction in the minimum wage and reducing wages in union agreements called for by the 2010 austerity plan, wage levels in the private sector also fell across the board by 5% from the third quarter of 2010 through third quarter of 2011. Deferred wages in the form of pension benefits were reduced by 12% as well. As part of the same 2010 austerity plan, income and property taxes were also raised while global oil prices rose in 2011—both of which further cut into real wages. All these combined job, wage, and pension cuts and inflation reduced consumer spending sharply. Adjusted for inflation, Greek consumption fell in 2011 by an unprecedented 9% annual rate.

Given these negative trends in business investment, household consumption, government spending and net exports, it is not surprising that Greece's real GDP fell by 9% in 2011. With the prior deep contractions from 2008 to 2010, Greece's total GDP decline by 2011 clearly meant that Greece was now in a bona fide economic depression, not just a recession. In just three years Greece's economy had contracted by more than 20% and the contraction was accelerating. As the Eurozone-wide recession began in the fourth quarter of 2011, Greece's economy contracted in the course of three months alone by 7%. That abysmal economic record of 2011 was the economic legacy of the May 2010 first Troika debt restructuring deal.

In the summer of 2011 the Greek PASOK party government tried to relieve the debt pressure on the banks by attempting to open negotiations on the debt with Eurozone private banks, hedge funds, insurance companies, foreign pension funds, and other 'shadow' banks still holding Greek debt. About 40 billion euros of Greek debt at the time was held by other Eurozone banks and another 70 billion by hedge funds and other shadow banks. The ECB held 55 billion. Greek banks and pension funds held another 80 billion.

The call to renegotiate was rejected unequivocally by the foreign bankers, hedge funds, and shadow banks. Leading players included Gramercy, Marathon, Greylock and Vega hedge funds and the global private equity firm, Carlyle Group. The hedge funds threatened to sue Greece in international courts for full payment. They had previously bought Greek debt at 40 cents on the dollar, and now wanted full value payment *to realize a 60% return.* Greece wanted to pay them 50 cents. On the market the bonds were now almost worthless, at 15 cents.

The Greek PASOK government tried as well that summer to relieve pressure on the government debt by raising income and property taxes. But that only depressed total government revenue receipts further, and accelerated the bank deposit withdrawals and money capital outflow from Greece.

The 2012 Debt Crisis and the Three-Way Negotiating Farce

As the Eurozone economy slipped into a double dip recession in fourth quarter 2011, Greece's second debt crisis erupted. Greece announced it might not be able to make its next 14 billion euros ($18.7 billion) debt payment scheduled for March 2012. The Troika announced it was withholding its next tranche of loans to Greece called for by the May 2010 agreement. In response, PASOK threw in the towel and resigned leadership of the government in November 2011, calling for a new election for February 2012. With a Greek government no longer at the helm, the Troika maneuvered successfully to install its technocrat to run the interim government, a former ECB official and Goldman Sachs Investment Bank vice-president, Lucas Papademos. A similar Troika move was made to place another Troika-friendly technocrat in charge of Italy, Mario Monti, who was also a former banker, as that country's debt crisis intensified as well.

By early 2012 private investors and hedge fund-shadow bankers, who made up what was called the PSI Group, still owned 70 billion euros of Greece's debt and northern Eurozone commercial banks another 40 billion. So long as the hedge funds and shadow bankers remained obstinate about restructuring Greek debt, the IMF by its rules had to refuse to participate in a second bailout. The 14.5 billion euros tranche payment by the Troika, scheduled for March 2012, could not be released without IMF approval and the IMF would not approve until settlement was reached with the PSI Group of shadow bankers and private investors.

The Papademos caretaker government met with the Troika in mid-January 2012 to explore a joint effort to get the Private Sector Investors (PSI) to accept a reduction in PSI bond debt payments, i.e. a 'haircut' of 50%, which amounted to roughly reducing by half what Greece owed them.[4] It should be noted, however, that 'haircut' refers to a price less than investors' original purchase price. The 'haircut' price is always greater than the prevailing market price, so the restructuring still provides the private investor a higher price than he could have obtained otherwise in the market at the time.

The Troika publicly threatened to withhold the March tranche payment if the PSI did not agree to a 'haircut'. Withholding the tranche meant a default by Greece. A default could mean no further payments to the PSI at all. But the threat of default was in reality no threat at all to the PSI. The private bondholders were OK with a default, since they had covered their investment in Greek bonds with extensive credit default swaps (CDSs), which were insurance contracts should Greece default. They might even have expected to realize an even greater payout if Greece did default.

The three way negotiation—Troika, PSI, and Greek government—represents a pattern in Greek debt restructuring strategy. The centerpiece of the government's strategy was to try to play one group of creditors off against the other (PSI-Troika) in the hope of achieving some sort of negotiating advantage. In early 2012 Greece thus attempted to elicit the help of the Troika against the PSI. However, neither the IMF nor ECB would get involved or take sides in the Greece vs. PSI negotiations. And the third Troika member, the European Commission (EC), was restrained from taking action by the German bankers-finance ministers coalition in its ranks. So the Greek government negotiators' strategy in 2012 was doomed from the start. Greece would try again in 2015 to leverage liberal elements in the EC against the

German banker coalition, as well as in the spring of 2016 by appealing to the IMF against the German coalition. It would fail in both those subsequent cases as well.

In their initial January 2012 opposition to the Greek-EC proposal to take a 'haircut', the PSI bondholders raised three issues as their justification: First, how could Greece and the Troika ensure that all private bondholders would voluntarily participate in the haircut? Some of the same hedge funds had gone through the Argentina debt crisis a decade earlier, refused to accept the debt restructuring Argentina deal and continued to fight for full repayment, which they eventually received.[5]

Secondly, they raised the warning of contagion of other southern periphery economies if they weren't paid in full. They forewarned that if they, the PSI, were forced to activate their CDS claims if the Troika allowed a default, the bond rates and CDSs on other government debt in the Eurozone would accelerate. If Greece was allowed to default and CDS payouts were made, the CDS contagion might easily spread to CDSs on Italian, Portuguese and Spanish government debt. If CDS payouts were made, the bondholders who purchased the CDSs would get full compensation, but other financial institutions which wrote the CDSs would experience a payout cost. So making the Greek government bear the cost in the form of bailout and more debt was preferable from a Troika perspective.

Third, the PSI asked what guarantees were there if they took the 50% haircut proposed by Greece and the Troika, that Greek debt was sustainable longer term on the remaining 50%? The Eurozone EFSF bailout fund by the EC had not yet been created to ensure Greece debt payments would be fully 'backstopped' by the EC. It was still a work in progress. Why then should they take a haircut when the rest was not firmly guaranteed to be paid later?

Negotiations between the Papademos rump government and the PSI group broke down in January 2012. The IMF and ECB refused to directly participate in any new debt restructuring unless the EC and Eurozone finance ministers and their governments significantly increased the commitment to provide more funds for Greece. The 'Greek Lending Facility' (GLF) set up by the EC in 2010 was generally viewed as woefully underfunded. A new, much larger bailout fund (the EFSF) would be required. It would have to provide not only for Greece's new bailout but for similar debt restructuring needed for Italy, Spain, Portugal and other periphery economies at the time (early 2012) which were now experiencing their own escalating debt crisis. This new fund was eventually called the European Financial Stability Fund (EFSF), and would become the primary lending facility in the second Greek debt restructuring of March 2012.

Following the breakdown of Greek government discussions with the PSI group in January, Germany publicly warned Greece it would need an additional 145 billion euros plus even more billions to cover the PSI debt in a new second debt restructuring that 'rolled over' old debt and added new to pay for the old. Germany went further and recommended that, as part of a new deal, Greece should turn over to the Troika the administration of Greece's tax system and submit all spending to Troika approval. Greece rejected that proposal, but the idea would come up again in 2015 and become part of that later deal.

The 'German Hypothesis'

The German position, which has remained unwavering from the first debt deal of May 2010 through the most recent third deal of 2015 and up to the very present, is sometimes referred to as the 'German Hypothesis'. That view is that austerity will actually lead to economic recovery and growth. It is a decidedly pre-Keynesian economic idea that sees business investment as determined by business confidence as the key to recovery.

The hypothesis maintains that, in the short run, budget cuts (i.e. austerity) lead to what is strangely called '*expansionary fiscal contraction*', or EFC for short. This obvious contradiction in terms is more economic ideology than theory based on historical observation. Austerity is supposed to lead to an increase in business confidence (for which there is no evidence), and in turn to more business investment. More investment leads to production and exports, which means more jobs, income and ultimately consumption in the final analysis. The German Hypothesis and EFC also requires expansionist monetary policy in the form of massive liquidity injections by central banks to offset the fiscal contraction. This is obviously a policy regime that bankers find attractive. It is a bankers' ideology. It has its ultimate roots in failed 19th century 'neoclassical' economic thinking, which argued at the time that whatever reduced business costs—i.e. wage cuts, interest rate reductions, tax cuts, deregulation, or whatever—would yield additional business savings. And that business would automatically reinvest that savings in new real investment in equipment, structures, inventories, and so on.

The theory fails, however, because reducing business costs does not automatically result in business re-investing the savings in job- and household income-producing real investment. The historical record shows clearly that, to the contrary, the savings from wage, interest rate, tax and other cost reductions is in the present era increasingly re-invested in financial asset securities—i.e. stocks, bonds, derivatives, etc.—which produce few if any jobs or income that leads to consumption. It doesn't necessarily get committed to real investment. If not diverted to financial investment in Europe or wherever, the savings may be shuffled to offshore investment, both real and financial. Or it may be distributed by the trillions of dollars back to investors in the form of stock buybacks and dividend payouts. Or it may simply remain on bank and business balance sheets undistributed and uninvested. These alternatives are exactly what has increasingly happened in recent decades, in the advanced economies in particular, and especially since the 2008 crash.

The Second Debt Restructuring Deal of 2012

On February 12, 2012 the EC and IMF informally called on Greece to voluntarily introduce further austerity measures. They recommended reducing the minimum wage and that the Greek government legally declare the expiration of private sector union collective bargaining agreements, requiring them to be renegotiated from scratch. In addition, they demanded that 25,000 government workers previously identified but not yet laid off be discharged over the next eight months.

The Greek government, in a show of willingness to impose further austerity, voluntarily cut pensions by $300 million, cut state spending on pharmaceutical drugs by more than $1 billion and reduced other government spending programs by an additional hundreds of billions of dollars. Protests and demonstrations erupted in Athens and throughout Greece in response to the cuts and in anticipation of the coming, even more severe, austerity measures soon to be demanded formally by the Troika.

As for the bailout of the banks, the Troika further indicated it was prepared to provide Greece 30 billion euros, for incentive payment to the PSI creditors—banks, shadow banks and private investors— to entice them to participate in a swap of their old bonds for new issues. Roughly 206 billion euros in old bonds were owed to private investors (PSI Group) and were thus eligible for swap and exchange for new bonds. The Troika indicated an interest rate of 3.5% could be paid out to the creditors on the new swapped bonds. Greece immediately thereafter formally announced a bond debt swap program.

The PSI held out for 4% interest rate payment on the new bonds, demanded the payment of past accrued interest on the old bonds, and complained that the old Greek bonds were subject to Greek law and thus Greece could decide on imposing another haircut anytime it wanted in the future. Therefore the new bonds should be subject to what was called 'English law', which meant the host government, Greece, could not unilaterally impose any further haircut in the future. Greece was already threatening publicly to impose a haircut on its own, since the majority of the bonds were under Greek law, which allowed that. The PSI Group's collective trade group, the International Swaps & Derivatives Association, warned that if Greek did so it would declare a 'credit event' and activate the trigger for CDS payouts on the 70 billion euros CDS contracts on the Greek debt the PSI group then held. That might have then precipitated unknown financial instability and contagion effects throughout the Eurozone.

The 'two way' negotiations thus continued—Greece and the Troika negotiating with the PSI private creditors, on the one hand, and on the other, the Troika negotiating with Greece on how much new debt would be offered in exchange for how much additional austerity imposed in return. Greece would prove the loser in both negotiations.

Greece's total debt as of February 2012 was approximately 350 billion euros ($467 billion given the euro exchange rate at the time). Roughly 90 billion were loans by the ECB, IMF, and Eurozone bailout funds. 260 billion euros were bonds, 55 billion euros of which was held by the ECB and other national central banks.

The remaining roughly 205 billion was private debt held by EU commercial banks (40 billion); by various shadow banks (i.e. insurance companies, hedge funds, private equity firms, sovereign wealth funds, pension funds, etc.) which held approximately 85 billion; Greek private banks (50 billion); and the Greek social security system (30 billion).

This latter 205 billion euros of private debt was the primary 'target' for refinancing and roll-over. And of the 205, the main beneficiaries would eventually be the EU commercial banks and shadow bankers combined debt of $125 billion. Satisfying this group, paying them off, reducing the private component of Greece's total debt in the course of restructuring, and doing so without precipitating CDS derivative payouts that would spread contagion throughout the Eurozone periphery was a major objective of the Troika during the course of the second Greek debt restructuring.

On February 23, 2012 the caretaker Greek Parliament approved the final debt restructuring deal offered by the Troika, by a vote of 202–80. In terms of austerity measures, the final terms of the Troika's debt agreement went even beyond the initial provisions suggested by the Troika earlier in the month.[6]

If paying off the private creditors was a major objective of the second debt deal, then making Greek workers pay for it all in austerity targeting their wages and benefits was the 'other side' of the deal.

The EC's summary report of the terms of the second restructuring immediately indicated the goal was "an ambitious internal devaluation". 'Internal devaluation' simply means reducing labor costs in order to make Greek exports more competitive. Selling more exports would result in higher GDP and national income with which to pay the rising debt load imposed on Greece. This focus on stimulating exports as the primary growth strategy reflected the German, and post-1999, Eurozone fetish with exports-driven growth strategy. Exports had enriched Germany under the Euro regime (at the expense of the rest of the Euro periphery, of course). Why shouldn't it stimulate Greece's economy, was no doubt the neoliberal logic. The focus showed the extent to which the Eurozone was under the ideological thrall of the German-core banker alliance and private investor group.

But Greece's exports had been rising under the effects of 'internal devaluation' since 2008—and had had no effect on Greece's steady decline into depression. For example, as Greece's average annual wage levels fell from 23,500 euros in 2009 to 19,500 by 2012, Greece's exports were rising—from 20.4 billion euros to 35.4 billion, according to OECD data. But that had little overall positive effect on Greece's growth, since the latter was collapsing far more due to other aspects of the crisis. No matter. The EC's report focused in terms of austerity on driving down Greek wages to pay back the Troika's ever rising debt loads on Greece.

'Internal devaluation' is synonymous in policy terms with what is called in Europe 'labor market restructuring' or labor market reforms. As noted in previous chapters, this was built into the Eurozone in its initial creation as fundamentally as the single currency, a weak central bank (ECB), focus on monetary policies that benefited banks and investors first, and austerity fiscal policies. The labor market reforms and restructuring derived from the initial 'Lisbon Agreement' addendum to the 1999 Euro treaty. The Troika's second debt deal for Greece thus emphasized strongly the deepening of 'labor market reforms'—aka wage and benefit reductions for Greek workers and small businesses in order to generate the government annual surplus necessary to pay the principal and interest on the rising debt.

The new agreement ludicrously projected that annual surplus to rise to 4.5% by 2014, even as the 'surplus' for 2011 was actually a deficit of -1.0%. In other words, Greece had to increase its annual GDP by 5.5% over the course of the new three year deal, and keep generating 4.5% growth rates thereafter—a rate which no economy in Europe, including Germany, was even close to attaining—since the total debt was projected for payoff only by 2060.

With the EC projecting Greek GDP to decline by another -4.7% in 2012, no growth in 2013, and only 2.5% growth in 2014, how was this 10% government surplus to be achieved? By massive further austerity cost cutting by Greece, as the following measures required by the second debt deal clearly reveal.

The new 'labor cost' reduction—aka labor market reforms, restructuring, internal devaluation, etc.—measures in the second debt agreement included:

- The national minimum wage was reduced by 22% and for youth by 32%, the latter defined as any worker under 25 years old. According to the EC summary report, that in turn would create a complementary reducing of wages above the minimum, by creating "additional room for downward wage adjustment to be decided by employers".[7]
- All scheduled wage increases, union or non-union, were frozen until unemployment, now at more than 20%, was reduced to less than 10%.
- Private sector wages were lowered further by reforming union collective bargaining. Reforms here called for all current union contracts to expire and be renegotiated within one year. If their current contracts expired before one year, unions had three months to sign a new contract. If they didn't, workers' wages would revert to the national 'basic wage'.

- The introduction of 'workers associations'—i.e. independent unions often dominated and controlled by management—further weakened unions. These now could also negotiate with employers, thereby lowering the floor of union wage demands. This would, according to the EC summary report, "allow wages and hours to adjust (downward) faster and in line with the needs of firms".
- Arbitration by independent third parties of year-end bonuses typically paid in Greece was no longer permitted. All arbitration of bonus issues was now strictly 'voluntary' for companies. Public workers' bonuses would be reduced further by 12%.
- The general wage level nationally must be reduced by an additional 15% over 2011 levels.
- Tenure for teachers and regulations for licensing of professionals was ended, thus increasing management freedom to fire and layoff teachers and professionals, in order to cut labor costs that way. Overtime pay for doctors was cut by 50 million euros.
- Pension benefits were to be reduced further over prior levels by September 2012. State owned enterprises (utilities, ports, etc.) pensions had to conform to private employer level pensions. If SOE pensions were higher, they would be 'brought in line' and reduced. The supplementary pension fund was cut by 300 million euros.
- The National Labor Agreement was to be overhauled by July 2012.
- Business contributions to the national social security program were reduced by 5%.
- The Greek government was to commit to reducing 150,000 government jobs by year end 2014—i.e. 50,000 a year.

- 50 billion euros of privatizations had to be completed by the end of the 3 year debt agreement by 2015.[8]

In addition to all this, the EC summary of the austerity measures declared, "we (EC) will review and are prepared to take additional corrective measures ... in order to ensure wage-flexibility. If by the end of 2012 efforts on labor market reform remain elusive, we will consider more direct interventions".[9]

All these extreme austerity measures were designed primarily to restructure and pay off the 206 billion euros owed to private banks, shadow banks and investors, and to 'roll over' and refinance the 73 billion euros disbursed to Greece to date under the 2010 debt plan.

Independent analyses show that the Troika provided Greece an additional 130 billion euros ($174 billion) in new loans as part of the second debt deal. Of the PSI group private creditors, 96% of them signed up to refinance 199 billion euros worth of the previous 206 billion euros private debt. The PSI Group came off well in the final deal. In addition to the 29.7 billion euro 'sweetener' incentive to participate in the swap deal, they were given, without charge, another roughly 30 billion in EFSF notes that could be cashed in within two years, plus another 63 billion in the new bonds. In addition 4.9 billion euros were paid the PSI for accrued interest on the old bonds. The new bonds, moreover, were now issued under 'English law', meaning Greece could not impose a future haircut on them. Given that the old Greek bonds at the time were likely worth no more than 40% at market value at the time, and therefore about 80 billion euros (40% of the $206 billion), that meant the PSI group 'realized' about 50 billion more than the prevailing market value by agreeing to the debt swap..

If the objective of the second debt deal was to reduce

Greece's debt by the end of the 3 year term, it completely failed. With a debt to GDP ratio of 170% in 2011, Greece's debt–GDP continued to rise to 177% of GDP by the end of 2014. In absolute terms, total Greek debt was about 300 billion euros at the start of 2010 and the first restructuring. It rose to 340 billion by the close of 2014, at the end of the second restructuring.

All this strongly suggests the purpose of the second debt deal was primarily to refinance, pay off and reduce the Greek debt held by the private investors. This is what the debt swap at the heart of the deal was all about. The debt of the private creditors was assumed by the Troika, which then transferred that cost in turn to Greece's government and central bank and through austerity, to the Greek people themselves.

With the announcement of the official terms of the new debt deal, workers' and public protests and demonstrations intensified in March. With new national elections set for May, it was not a done deal that the second restructuring agreement would be accepted by a new government. It was only an interim, caretaker government that had approved it in the first place. Given the growing uncertainty, interest rates on the new Greek bonds rose to 16.9% by the end of March. Non-performing bank loans were growing, and capital flight from the country was rising as well. On one day alone, 900 million euros were withdrawn from the Greek banks, what some might otherwise call a 'bank run'. The debt swap wiped out the balance sheets of private Greek banks, already insolvent and now in desperate need of the projected 45 billion euros they would receive from the ECB in the event of the debt deal being closed. The Greek economy was on track for another -5% GDP decline for 2012.

Elsewhere across the Eurozone, the second recession was deepening. Interest rates on Spanish, Portuguese, and especially Italian bonds were accelerating. The cost of CDS insurance contracts was rising. The Euro was falling in exchange value and stock markets Eurozone-wide were in retreat.

The outcome of the May national elections in Greece was inconclusive. No party, not PASOK, nor the pro-business and pro-Euro conservative New Democracy party, nor the new Syriza party rapidly growing in popularity, achieved a decisive majority or was able to form a new government. New elections were set for June 17.

Talk of the possibility of a 'Grexit' (Greek exit from the Eurozone) was rising—on both sides. The German central bank, the Bundesbank, let it be known that if Greece failed to sign the debt deal it should exit. Grexit would be manageable, if not for the Eurozone at least for Germany, according to the Bundesbank. Eurozone finance ministers were reportedly developing contingencies for a Grexit.

Between the May and June elections, Syriza's popularity was rising, according to polls, at 22%. Its program was to cut defense spending. Raise taxes on the wealthy. Halt the projected 150,000 layoffs, repeal the various proposals for wage cuts, reverse the labor market reforms and the reduction in minimum wages, and nationalize Greece's private banks. Syriza's young leader, Alex Tsipras, proposed that Greece should reject the Troika deal but still stay with the Euro—a contradictory option that would never be accepted by the Troika. But it did have popular appeal. Greeks did not want to leave Europe, which they viewed as synonymous with exiting the Euro currency regime. On the other hand, they didn't see any benefit from the austerity or Troika deal(s) that were destroying their standard of living and condemning them to perpetual economic depression. They wanted both. This public view would keep them trapped in their current condition, an economic 'doom loop'.

As even the Europe business press recognized at the

time, "the European bailout of 130 billion euros ($164.4 in May) that was supposed to buy time for Greece is mainly servicing only interest on this country's debt ... almost none of the money is going to the Greek government to pay for vital public services. Instead, it is flowing directly back into the Troika's pockets".[10]

On the eve of the second general elections in June, Syriza's leader, Tsipras, provided what he and Syriza considered the new hope and new way out of the debt-austerity trap that Greece was falling into ever more deeply. Greece required the opportunity to grow out of the debt, according to Tsipras. Electing Syriza would mean changes and stability. "We will set Greece on a new path to growth ... and replace that failed old Memorandum of Understand ing (i.e. March second debt deal) with a national plan for reconstruction and growth ... overturning the Memorandum is the only viable solution, for Greece and for Europe". If elected, Syriza would stabilize Greek government spending at 44% of GDP.[11] It would tax the wealthy and corporations, not middle and low income households. It would recapitalize and stabilize Greece's banks in the public interest. And it would do all this without leaving the euro.

But it was not yet Syriza's turn. The conservative center-right New Democracy party prevailed in the June elections. It received 30% of the vote and 129 of the 300 seats in the Greek parliament. Syriza received 27% of the vote and 71 seats. The now discredited PASOK party received only 12% and 33. New Democracy was able to form a government as several smaller parties joined it in a coalition.

But as did PASOK before it, New Democracy would also fail to deliver a way out of the debt-austerity Troika trap. At the end of the term of the second debt restructuring deal set for early 2015, New Democracy would give way to its main competitor Syriza. Neither PASOK nor New Democracy could pierce the financial armor of the Troika. Whether Syriza could succeed where they did not was the story of the third debt restructuring deal of 2015.

Endnotes

1   Yanis Varoufakis, *And the Weak Suffer What They Must*, Nation Books, New York, 2016, p. 160-163.

2   J. Rocholl and A. Stahmer, '*Where Did the Greek Bailout Money Go?*', ESMT White Paper No. WP-16-02, European School of Management and Technology, 2016.. The PSI was the group of private banks and shadow banks outside Greece that were holding approximately 105 billion euros of Greek debt at the time of the second debt crisis of 2012.

3   The actual amount that was eventually disbursed under the 2010 deal was 73 billion of the 110 billion euros allocated under the 2010 deal.

4   Greece's total debt at the time was estimated at about $450 billion.

5   They eventually prevailed in 2016 in Argentina when the government there was taken over by pro-business elements. One of the first actions of the new, Argentina prime minister, 'Macri', government was to immediately repay in full the hedge fund and shadow banker investors who refused to participate in the partial payment arranged by the IMF.

6   The following terms and conditions are summarized in the European Commission, '*The Second Economic Adjustment Program for Greece*', Occasional Paper No. 94, March 2012.

7   It might be noted that other Eurozone economies with higher minimum wages included Netherlands, Belgium, Luxembourg, France, and even Ireland. Other Europe economies, like the UK, were also much higher.

8   See page 118 of the European Commission, '*The Second Economic Adjustment Program for Greece*', Occasional Paper No. 94, March 2012.

9   European Commission, '*The Second Economic Adjustment Program for Greece*', Occasional Paper No. 94, March 2012, pp. 110-111.

10 Liz Alderman and Jack Ewing, *Financial Times*, May 30, 2012, p. B1.

11 Which was approximately same as that of Germany's and much less that other European economies.

Chapter Five

COLLAPSE OF NEW DEMOCRACY & RISE OF SYRIZA

The conservative New Democracy party prevailed in the June 2012 runoff elections mostly due to two factors. First, it pledged to renegotiate the $218 billion bailout with the Troika, if elected. Second, the Syriza party at the time was still very much a coalition of parties and groups, with little structure or experience in contending for Parliamentary elections.

In contrast to New Democracy, Syriza's main electoral campaign message was that the agreement with the Troika had to be overturned, i.e. thrown out. While it clearly stated it was not in favor of leaving the Euro, Syriza's message was to restart negotiations from scratch, which appeared less pragmatic to centrist, conservative voters in Greece.

The Troika rejected New Democracy appeals after the election to renegotiate certain details of the debt deal. It insisted the Greek government would have to begin implementing the austerity measures associated with the deal first, before it would even consider its request. This pattern would prove similar in all the debt negotiations: the Greek government would pursue some kind of adjustment and debt relief changes to the original deal that were affordable as its economy fell further and it was unable to achieve the target budget surplus with which to repay the accumulating debt. The Troika would subsequently respond by demanding first more austerity to offset the surplus gap and Greece's inability to repay. The Greek government would then reluctantly implement the further austerity, as the Troika dribbled out the promised loans in stages, but only after requiring proof by the Greek government of its austerity implementation. If the implementation was only partial or behind schedule in the opinion of the Troika, the Troika would withhold the loans called for in the original deal. The ECB would threaten to withhold bridge loans and emergency credit to the Greek banks. In the meantime the Greek economy continued to worsen as the process went on—Greece implementing austerity and the Troika releasing loans only sparingly and after significant delays.

In other words, there was a double standard: the implementation of austerity had to be timely and complete, but the disbursement of loans from the Troika were neither.

New Democracy Pleads to Renegotiate

Upon assuming office, the dilemma the New Democracy government faced was that the entire Eurozone economy had fallen into deep recession by mid-2012. Moreover, the debt crises in Italy, Spain, Portugal and elsewhere were worsening and were perceived by the Troika as far more serious than Greece's. As the Troika negotiated bailout loans to these larger economies, it held an intransigent line in the Greek negotiations, out of concern it might send signals that were too concessionary to the other countries seeking bailouts.

Immediately after the June 17 election, New Democracy asked for a two year extension, from 2014 to

2016, to repay the $218 new debt. That would lower its debt payments. Germany and the EC finance ministers at the end of June refused extension, or any consideration, including adjusting the 2012 agreement requirement that Greece produce a 4.5% of GDP surplus by 2014. The Troika demanded, moreover, that Greece first implement all the required 11 billion euro ($14.5) austerity measures before it would release any funds. It complained that the privatizations and tax code changes weren't happening fast enough and that the layoffs of public workers called for under the agreement were not yet occurring, despite Greece having already laid off 100,000 in the previous two years.

The Troika then went further. It noted that the economy was declining faster than before during April-June and so another 2 billion euros in spending cuts, beyond the 11 billion, were also now needed. Greece's previous 2012 GDP forecast of -4.7% made in March was now estimated at -7% for the year. The Troika withheld a 2.4 billion euro disbursement called for by the 2012 debt deal in the meantime. Another 4.1 billion was scheduled for August, when the Greek government was predicted to run out of cash, but would not be released until austerity measures were implemented.

After Troika representatives visited Greece in early July 2012, the New Democracy government dropped its request for a two year debt payment extension and pledged to accelerate austerity measures, especially the privatizations. The European Commission's president, Barroso, raised the bar further almost immediately after, saying Greece would need an additional 20 billion euros loan in 2013-14, which would require even more austerity measures.

In Germany, where the original debt deal loans to Greece had yet to be approved, opposition to the Greek deal was rising. A common topic of German public debate at the time was that Greece's deepening depression was due to its failure to implement structural reforms in labor and product markets, and not due to the austerity measures. Talk about letting Greece exit the euro (Grexit) gained ground.

In August, the European Central Bank (ECB) increased pressure on Greece, refusing to provide any more bridge loans until the Troika released its report in September on Greece's progress toward implementing the terms of austerity. It was estimated at the time that 20% of all Greek bank loans to Greek businesses (48 billion euros) were 'non-performing'—i.e. interest or principal was not being paid.

Given the ECB's refusal to release funds, Greece's central bank was forced to issue four billion euros in new Greek government bonds to private investors at exorbitant interest rates, just in order to make its August payment on previous debt. In short, Greece was making payments and implementing austerity per Troika demands, but the Troika was not releasing loans it had agreed to provide six months previous, in March 2012, under terms of the original 2012 debt deal. And that itself was deepening Greek debt.

The Troika in late August then upped the pressure, declaring Greece must cut spending and implement $3.7 billion more in austerity measures in 2012, plus another $14.2 billion in 2013-14, as a condition for releasing the first tranche of loans to Greece.

Greece's president, Antonis Samaras, traveled to Berlin in late August to plead for reconsideration, meeting with Merkel and others. Merkel rejected Samaras' proposals for any kind of debt extension or relief. Samaras asked for an extension of 20 billion euros in IMF loans due 2014 to 2020. The IMF and other Troika members immediately rejected the proposal. German finance minister Wolfgang Schauble declared any kind of debt relief was 'illegal'.

At the end of October the Troika had still not

released any loans to Greece, insisting more implementation of austerity was required before the first tranche of 31 billion euros ($40 billion) was distributed. Conceding once again to the Troika, in early November the Greek parliament approved an additional $23 billion in austerity measures, including pension cuts, wage cuts, tax hikes and services reductions. President Samaras publicly declared "Greece has done what was asked of it and this has been admitted by all ... the money from the aide tranche, the billions that we will be paid, will come in time".[1] The Troika replied it would meet November 20 to decide whether to finally release the funds.

About this time a difference within the Troika publicly emerged. The European Commission's Jean Claude Juncker, a 'liberal' member of the Troika, publicly noted that the Troika would consider reducing Greece's interest rates on its debt and possibly extend the IMF share of the debt payments to 2020. IMF director Christine Lagarde immediately rejected the idea. There was now a public split within the Troika ranks between the EC and the IMF. For the IMF, a simple extension would violate its rules. The Juncker-Lagarde differences would eventually be resolved in coming weeks by what would be called the 'buyback boondoggle'.

The Bond Buyback Boondoggle of December 2012

The extended delays in releasing the Troika funds, now nine months after the agreement, and the eruption of the IMF-EC differences concerning debt relief, likely reflect developments behind the scenes designed to benefit private speculators and investors who had bought Greek bonds on the cheap during the spring crisis period. New Democracy wanted some kind of formal debt relief, the IMF wanted its rules respected, and the EC wanted to help New Democracy get through the transition to a new technocrat-led government that would continue to adhere to the Troika's program. (Samaras had announced his departure from the Greek government and New Democracy anointed a new candidate to replace him, Stavros Dimas, a former technocrat who had worked for the EC.) The Troika wanted to ensure 'their man' remained at the helm of the Greek government. The key to the arrangement that was to satisfy all the above interests was the 'bond buyback boondoggle'.

Revealed in late November, the deal called for Greece to buy up the debt of private bondholders and speculators who had acquired Greek bonds during the 2012 spring crisis and renegotiation and who were not part of the original 'old for new' debt swap in the original March debt restructuring. The new 'buyback boondoggle' had the Troika lending Greece an additional 11 billion euros in the form of Troika short term notes, that Greece would use to buy back the private bonds. Under terms of the buyback, Greece would pay 35 cents on the dollar value of the bonds to hedge funds and other bondholder speculators who had bought the bonds at 11 to 17 cents on the dollar during the spring crisis. The buyback would result in a 100-200% profit for the speculators. The original face value of all the bonds was approximately 31 billion euros. So the 11 billion euro buyback would eliminate a net 20 billion in overall Greek debt. That is, Greece would add 11 billion in debt from the Troika, with which the privately held bonds were bought. Greece's net debt would decline by 20 billion euros. The hedge funds and speculators would realize the 100% to 200% profit, depending on whether they purchased the bonds at 11 or 17 cents.

Reducing Greece's net debt by 20 billion also satisfied the IMF's Lagarde, ending her differences with the

EC's Jean-Claude Juncker over whether to extend IMF loans beyond 2014. Greece was granted an IMF loan payment extension to 2020, while the rest of the 2012 debt deal would expire in early 2015 as part of a three year deal. The insuperable IMF rules could now, apparently, be ignored.

As a consequence, in December 2012, the Troika loaned Greece 44 billion euros, instead of the scheduled 34 billion first tranche: 11.6 trillion euros for the boondoggle and the rest as the first tranche disbursement to Greece of the original March loan deal.[2]

What the whole buyback boondoggle affair reveals is how debt restructuring deals in general (and indeed, IMF rules) are ultimately about redirecting loans in various ways to pay off private investors and bankers. The boondoggle and similar financial arrangements represent how the more than 300 billion euros loans by the Troika to Greece eventually ended up in the pockets of private banks—as documented in the European School of Management and Technology's study referenced in the previous chapter.[3]

Who Benefits?

How could Greece and its economy have benefited? The truth of the matter is revealed in Greece's debt to GDP ratio. If Greece had benefited, its Debt-GDP ratio should have declined. After all, hundreds of billions of euros in additional debt was piled on Greece as a result of the 2010 and 2012 debt deals.

Despite the 110 billion euro in loans to Greece under the 2010 deal—and the additional roughly 200 billion euros in loans provided Greece under the March 2012 agreement— Greece's debt to GDP ratio continued to rise throughout the Troika debt restructuring period, 2010-2015, as the table that follows shows.

Table 5.1
Greek Debt as Percent of GDP

Debt % GDP	Period
107%	2007
113%	2008
130%	2009
148%	2010
157%	2012
177%	2013
197%	2015

It is important to note that Greece's continually deteriorating debt to GDP ratio was not due to Greek government spending and budget deficits. Government spending declined from 118 billion euros in 2010 to 99 billion in 2012, and declined further 86 billion by 2014. Greek budget deficits contracted even more, from 25 billion euros in 2010 to 12.4 billion in 2012 to 7 billion in 2014. So it wasn't runaway spending or escalating budget deficits that was responsible for Greek debt rising as a percent of GDP.

Greece's continuing depression accounted for some of the debt-GDP ratio decline, as GDP continued to contract. But not all can be explained by GDP decline. Greece's GDP fell from 240 billion euros in 2009 to 200 billion by 2012 and thereafter to 180 billion by 2014. That's 40 to 60 billion.

But Troika loans to Greece during the period of 2010-12 and 2012-14 rose to approximately 320 billion euros.

Where then did the huge difference of $260 billion in loans to Greece go? It went to bail out banks and investors—and not just Greece's own banks but banks in Germany, the rest of the Eurozone, and international speculators, as the aforementioned 2016 ESMT study documents.

If banks and investors were the prime beneficiaries of the bailouts and debt restructuring, other indicators show who clearly did not benefit from the 320 billion euro additional debt piled on Greece between 2010 and 2012 by the Troika.

It certainly wasn't Greek workers, public or private sector. Greece's total employment beginning 2008 was 4.6 million; by year end 2012 it was 3.7 million. The unemployment rate rose from 12.7% to 24.4%. (A similar decline in the US economy today would equal 38 million unemployed). Average annual wages in Greece during the period fared no better. Average annual wages were 23,581 euros in early 2009. They fell to 19,469 euros by the end of 2012, and continued falling further through 2014. (In the US, assuming a median annual wage of $50,000, it would be an equivalent wage cut of $8700 a year for those that still had jobs.) Add to these wage figures cuts of 30-40% in pensions, health care services and benefits, and other elements of national 'social safety net' benefits, and the result is a massive reduction in living standards for Greece's 11 million population.

Whether estimated at 260 or 320 billion euros, at least 95% of the total represents an extraction and transfer of income and wealth to bankers, speculators, bondholders, and Troika governments—paid for by Greek workers, taxpayers, and the general populace.

It was a wealth seizure on a scale never quite seen in the advanced economies.

Muddling Through: 2013-2014

For the next 18 months, from 2013 through mid-2014, Greece's depression moderated. The economy continued to contract but not at the depression level GDP rates as during previous years—at a 2%-4% annual rate instead of the previous 8%-9% of 2011-2012. The Eurozone economy's double-dip recession that began late 2011 had also ended by mid-2013. Greek government bond interest rates declined from 2012 record highs or more than 30% to settle around 10%. The Greek stock market more than doubled by mid-2014. Government levels of debt held steady around 320 billion euros. Unemployment rates peaked at 28% and then backed off slightly to 25% by 2014. Wages continued to decline, however, as did consumer prices which slipped into deflation by 2014.

The picture in 2013-2014 was therefore one of an economy settling into a chronic low level stagnation, remaining in depression conditions but neither getting worse nor getting much better.

The lack of sustained economic growth meant Greece could not achieve the 3.5% surplus needed to enable it to continue to pay interest and principal on its more than 300 billion euro debt. Consequently, by early 2014 it was once again becoming clear that Greece would need still more Troika loans if it were going to be able to repay its old loans. Either that, or more austerity. Or pay exorbitant interest rates selling government bonds to private investors. In June 2014 Greece was forced to do just that in order to raise another 6 billion euros from new government bond sales. But that only enabled it to make the latest interest and principal repayment to the Troika on prior debt and bought a couple of months' time. A more fundamental solution was again required.

The Greek government therefore tried once again to reopen negotiations with the Troika in mid-2014 as it had tried to do in mid-2012. The outcome would prove no more successful. It offered the Troika evidence that it had fully complied with the debt repayment program and had implemented all the demanded austerity measures. The Troika rejected Greece's study, however, claiming its own data showed otherwise and that Greece was actually 2.5 billion euros short of compliance. Greece would have to add more austerity. It was déjà vu once again.

Syriza Comes of Age

As the New Democracy government continued dutifully to implement the Troika's austerity measures, while simultaneously pleading yet again for consideration on debt relief, the formerly loose coalition of groups and parties that composed Syriza was beginning to transform itself into a parliamentary party preparing to contend to lead government.

Syriza held its first founding convention in July 2013. Thereafter, in May 2014 it stood for elections to the European Union parliament, to which it successfully elected six Syriza members, the most among the Greek parties. On September 13, 2014 Syriza then developed its own full list of proposals it would implement were it in government, called the Thessaloniki Program.

Briefly, the Thessaloniki Program—which Syriza declared was 'non-negotiable'—called for ending the severe austerity measures imposed on Greece up to that time. It called for:

- debt reduction based on the model of the London Agreement of 1953, where German debt was significantly reduced
- a National Reconstruction Program to restore social spending; a more aggressive system of progressive taxation and ending of tax evasion by the wealthy
- a New Deal-like public investment program financed by the European Investment Bank
- the introduction of new forms of direct democracy.
- a restoration of prior wage and pension cuts; and
- a restoration of 300,000 jobs and social subsidies that were eliminated or reduced, among other measures.

It was a classic social democratic program. But would a classic social democratic party like Syriza and a Thessaloniki Program from a bygone era ever be tolerated by the Troika in a Europe now firmly grounded in neoliberal policies and programs?

The Eurozone Stagnates Once Again

The Eurozone's recovery from its 2011-2013 double dip recession began to weaken significantly once again by late 2014. As in all 'epic' recessions, recoveries were proving short and shallow, punctuated by repeated brief and moderate contractions and stagnation.[4]

In the second half of 2014 the Eurozone economy at large began showing signs of rapidly slowing growth and a drift toward stagnation once again. GDP was essentially flat, at a mere 0.2% growth rate, as even Germany failed to grow and Italy entered another recession. Unemployment remained stuck at 11.5%, bank lending continued to slow, and the economy drifted toward deflation. Calls rose for the European Central Bank to introduce a quantitative easing

(QE) policy of buying back bonds, much like the US and UK had done previously, and Japan most recently. At the same time US Treasury Secretary, Jack Lew, publicly warned Europe that it was risking a 'lost decade' and would fall into a deeper slump if it didn't take measures to stimulate the Eurozone economy fiscally in addition to QE.

In this environment, with Greece slowing as well, New Democracy's Antonis Samaras planned to strengthen Greece's negotiating position with the Troika by announcing he supported the former Eurocommission technocrat, Stavros Dimas, to head the government in 2015. According to Greek constitutional rules, Dimas would have to be approved by 180 of the Greek Parliament's 300 members. In the initial vote within Parliament on December 17, 2014, Dimas received only 160 votes. A second vote taken polled on the 23rd not much better, and a third vote on December 29, 2014 resulted in only 168 votes. Under the same Greek rules a 'snap' general parliamentary election was therefore required. It was set for January 25, 2015.

The Troika intervened to encourage the Greek public to vote for New Democracy—just as it had successfully in the June 2012 elections. Although the current 2012 debt agreement was scheduled to expire at the end of December, in an effort to assist the Samaras government, the Troika extended the deadline for another two months, until the end of February.

Sensing the historic opportunity, Syriza's leader, Alexis Tsipras, on December 20 laid out the Syriza program. It was Thessaloniki, but now with further clarification regarding Syriza's approach to debt negotiations. Tsipras proposed Syriza would call for a European-wide Debt Conference, based on the model of the London 1953 Conference which provided extensive debt relief—ironically—to Germany. The proposed new Debt Conference would address not only

Greece but the entire southern periphery of the Eurozone. Tsipras further proposed that future Greek debt payments to the Troika must come out of economic growth, not budget cuts. In other words, not austerity. A moratorium on debt payments would be further necessary to give Greece a chance to grow economically. Tsipras then called for a 'European New Deal' of public investment financed by the European Investment Bank and an immediate 4 billion euro investment in Greece. He also advocated in favor of a QE policy by the ECB, which was then being debated and considered throughout the Eurozone, and a change in ECB rules that would allow it to directly purchase sovereign bonds. Other key elements of the Thessaloniki program were also highlighted, such as restoring salaries and pensions, introducing progressive taxation and stopping tax fraud, and incentives to small and medium businesses. It all amounted to what Tsipras called a 'National Reconstruction Plan' for Greece.

As the Greek parliament voted to reject the Troika-Samaras hand-picked successor, Stavros Dimas, a third time on December 29, Tsipras declared in a speech "Austerity will soon be over. The Samaras Government, which looted society and decided to take further austerity measures, is finished."[5]

The intervening weeks, up to the election date of January 25, 2015, would witness an intensely competitive race between Syriza and New Democracy. During the pre-election period, the Troika and pro-Troika press, both inside and outside Greece, mounted an aggressive campaign to discredit Syriza. Reports were issued and rumors started that, if Syriza won, Berlin was prepared to have Greece leave the Eurozone.

But Tsipras and Syriza had made it abundantly clear the party's intent was not to exit the Eurozone or the euro regime. In that they were in agreement with the majority of the Greek people who consistently indicated in polls they did not want to leave the Eurozone either. They, like Syriza, wanted to end the austerity, but stay in Europe and keep the Euro. Neither thus understood that the root of the austerity lay in the neoliberal euro regime they wanted to keep.

Tsipras and the Greek electorate wanted to return to a social democratic Europe that was already history, buried by a neoliberal transformation throughout Europe in preceding decades, and especially since 1999, that was fundamentally incompatible with social democracy programs and policies. As neoliberal forces, led by financial elites throughout the region, were rolling back social democracy and social democratic parties everywhere, Syriza was proposing a resurrection and unification of social democratic institutions—economic and political—and a return to social democratic programs. Greek workers, small businesses, and farmers were yearning for a return to a better social democratic reality. Greek bankers, investors and wealthier households, who were doing well, avoiding taxes, speculating in their government's own bonds, and sending their incomes to banks and shadow banks outside Greece since 2009, were not.

Neither the electorate nor Syriza-Tsipras fully comprehended at the time that they stood virtually alone against the rising neoliberal tide throughout the region. They would call for a social democratic counter-offensive, but no one would rise yet to join them. What was left of social democratic parties in Europe had already capitulated to neoliberal forces or, in some cases such as in Germany, had allied themselves directly with the bankers and investors running the Eurozone-wide pan European institutions like the EC and ECB. Syriza wanted a European version of the US 1930s New Deal. But this was 70 years later and history was not about to repeat itself. European Social Democracy was a mere shadow of its former self. And Syriza and Tsipras now stood alone.

Their grand strategy to reignite European social democracy by their example—in the process aligning sufficient elements in Europe to support their cause to lift austerity and generate growth through fiscal policy activism—would ultimately crash against the neoliberal wall erected by the Troika and its finance capital elite in governments and without. Neither so-called socialist governments, like Francois Hollande's in France, or falsely presumed 'liberal' elements in the European Commission, would in the end support them.

Syriza-Tsipras wanted to remain within the Euro regime but without the extreme austerity it demanded of them and Greece. But Euro-based neoliberalism required the arrangement of goods and internal money flows that had indebted Greece (and other periphery economies) and ensured some form of perpetual austerity. That is how the system was designed to work. The Euro and austerity went hand in hand for the periphery economies. It was not an aberration. It was the very essence of the neoliberal system itself—which was structured and designed to enable, through new pan-European institutions, core northern European finance capital elites to extract wealth from the periphery by means of trade flows and money flows.

In the run-up to the third Greek debt restructuring deal of 2015, Syriza and Tsipras would discover *there was no option* to return to social democracy and social democratic policies, without austerity. The choice was either to leave the Euro and the neoliberal regime, or remain caretakers for that regime on the system's periphery, condemned to some degree of perpetual indebtedness, austerity, and long run negative economic growth.

Over the course of the third debt restructuring negotiations in 2015, Syriza would at first deny and resist this reality, then concede in steps as it retreated from its positions and its Thessaloniki program. In August 2015, it capitulated. Like its political predecessors, New Democracy in 2012 and PASOK in 2010, Syriza would also eventually settle into the 'caretaker' role for the neoliberal Troika.

Endnotes

1   *Wall St. Journal*, November 12, 2012, p. 13.
2   For a detailed analysis, J. Zettlemeyer, C. Trebesch, M. Gulati, *'The Greek Debt Restructuring: An Autopsy'*, Duke University, 2013.
3   That study found more than 95% of payments from the 2010 and 2012 deals accrued to private banks. See ESMT, *'Where Did the Greek Bailout Money Go?'*, WP-16-02, 2016.
4   For this author's explanation of the phenomenon of 'epic recessions', and how they differ from normal recessions and depressions, see Jack Rasmus, *Epic Recession: Prelude to Global Depression*, Pluto Press, 2010.
5   Sara Sjolin, *Marketwatch*, December 29, 2014.

Chapter Six

SYRIZA
TAKES THE
OFFENSIVE

The weeks following the dissolving of the Greek Parliament at the close of December 2014, leading up to the new elections on January 25, 2015 saw intense political competition between the New Democracy party—aided by its allies among wealthy Greek oligarchs, their media, and the Troika—and Syriza and its sympathizers in emerging left groups and parties in Spain (Podemos), Ireland (Sinn Fein), Germany (Die Linke) and elsewhere. The weight of money and institutional power was heavily imbalanced in favor of Syriza's opponents, however, both within and outside Greece.

Remarks by Michael Fuchs, parliamentary leader of Angela Merkel's party in Germany, were typical of the attacks by German politicians and media on Syriza. Fuchs declared at the start of the campaign in early January that "Greece does not have systemic meaning for the euro" and if Tsipras backs off from austerity reforms "then the Troika will also have to pull back on credits for Greece". His view was widely echoed by northern Eurozone finance ministers, like Wolfgang Schauble, by leaders within the European Commission, like Jean-Claude Juncker, and even by leaders of social democratic parties throughout the region. The best support Syriza received was statements of neutrality from Hollande, president of France and leader of the French socialists, who took the position that the Greeks should be allowed to vote as they wished.

At the start of 2015 more than 85%, or about 270 billion euros, of Greece's 317 billion euro public debt was now held by Troika institutions, central banks and EU governments—the largest part of which, 142 billion, was held by the EC's EFSF fund. What was once predominantly private investor-held debt had been largely converted by now to public debt after the debt restructuring of 2012. Investors were largely paid off in 2012-2013 from the new EC bailout funds, the bill for which was thereafter added by the Troika to Greece's total debt. With most private investors now out of the picture, the EC and its Eurozone country finance ministers, led by the German-northern faction of ministers and national central bankers, were calling the Troika's shots by January 2015. And they had amassed a multi-trillion dollar bailout war chest with which to intimidate Syriza if necessary, should it win the January 25 election. And they didn't waste time communicating that fact.

The Troika's $2.8 Trillion Grexit Firewall

In addition to the 780 billion euro European Financial Stability Facility (EFSF) established in 2010 for purposes of government bailouts, and under the control of the EC, the Eurozone's bankers and political elites now also had a Long Term Refinancing Opportunity (LTRO) fund, created in 2012 and controlled by the ECB. The LTRO provided an additional 500 billion euros, available specifically to bail out banks. By 2015 the two bailout funds—EFSF and LTRO—had been integrated into a new European Stability

Mechanism (ESM) fund, as it was called, with a combined total of more than $1.5 trillion. In addition, at the start of 2015 there was pending another trillion euro source, called quantitative easing, QE, created by the ECB. While consisting of ECB money injections into Euro central banks and private banks, there was also the potential for its use to bail out governments as well by indirect means.[1]

The ECB's new QE program, announced on January 22, 2015, called for the central bank to inject about $69 billion a month into the Eurozone banking system, or roughly $1.3 trillion, over the next eighteen months. QE was primarily designed (like all QE programs everywhere) to stimulate stock and bond prices. The ECB loaned to private banks and the latter in turn loaned to financial market investors, or directly invested themselves in financial securities. That prop to stock and bond prices anticipated for early 2015 was to offset potential negative effects on stocks and bonds from a new Greek debt crisis and a Grexit, should it occur.

Insofar as it transmitted a negative message about the health of the Eurozone economy, QE also served to lower the euro currency's exchange rate, in order to make Euro exports—especially German goods exports—more competitive globally. More exports meant more production and supported economic growth, especially Germany's, which was heavily focused on exports to emerging markets, China, and elsewhere outside the Eurozone. QE's currency devaluation effect added little to Greek exports, however, which were mostly focused intra-Europe.[2] Potential disruption to the Eurozone economy from a Grexit might thereby also be offset by the $69 billion a month QE, according to Troika and friends.

With more than $2.5 trillion in hand in the form of the three funds—EFSF, LTRO and QE—the Troika, the German faction and their allies in particular, were taunting Syriza—'go on, exit the Eurozone, we dare you'.

Troika Strategy to Defeat Syriza at the Polls

The general strategy of the Troika and German financial elite to block Syriza was to resurrect their previously successful campaign of June 2015 that enabled the New Democracy party to prevail over Syriza. The central theme of that strategy was to paint Syriza and its leaders as incorrigible radicals that were incompetent, insofar as understanding financial realities and negotiating complex financial deals was concerned. As in 2012, the Troika general message was a Syriza victory would mean bankruptcy and the economic collapse of Greece.

The Troika also flooded the public media with the declaration that Syriza would never be able to deliver on its promise to force the Troika through negotiations to concede on debt relief or austerity reduction. What Syriza was promising to do was futile, Troika interests claimed—with some veracity, since Syriza promises hinged on the Troika's willingness to accommodate them. Syriza in 2015 had far less leverage compared to 2012 or 2010. Troika representatives and the media argued that Europe was now in a much better condition and prepared if necessary to weather another Greek debt crisis—even to absorb a possible Grexit. Financial 'firewalls' had been erected in the form of the new funds now available to the EC and ECB since the prior debt crisis and restructuring in 2012. The risk of contagion effects from a new Greek debt crisis on Spain, Italy, Portugal and Ireland was now much reduced. Eurozone banks were also now in much better condition. And while the Eurozone real economy showed signs of weakening in late 2014, the Eurozone was not in recession, as in 2012 and 2010. Moreover, it argued, the ECB's forthcoming QE program starting in March would soon boost real economic recovery.

In addition to suggesting the Troika would not back down, and that it was financially and economically far better prepared in 2015 to resist Syriza demands for an end to austerity or more debt relief, the Troika strategy was to portray Syriza's leader, Alexis Tsipras, as a hard-line radical, de facto Marxist, who would engage in high risk and dangerous initiatives once in office.

The Troika's joint public relations campaign with New Democracy declared that Grexit was Syriza and Tsipras's real objective—and Grexit would result in a suspension of ECB emergency loans to Greece's central bank, a subsequent collapse of Greece's banking system, and in turn a massive wiping out of Greek households' and small business's deposits in Greek banks.

But Syriza's Thessaloniki program of late 2014 was anything but Marxist. And Grexit was never part of its program. Thessaloniki was a social democratic national restoration program, much more in the tradition of 1930s Roosevelt 'New Deal' reforms designed to redirect income from oligarchs and tax evading wealthy investors—who at the time were sending their money capital out of Greece at an accelerating rate—and to redirect income through fiscal and monetary means to Greek small businesses, professionals, and working class households, with the goal of stimulating aggregate demand and economic growth.

When Syriza raised the demand for debt relief, it meant reducing part of the 142 billion held by the EC's ESFS fund. It never sought to reduce the IMF's 24 billion euro debt, nor to ask for debt relief from the ECB. Nor for relief from the remaining 15% of the total 317 billion debt still held by private investors. As future finance minister, Yanis Varoufakis, during the election an advisor to Tsipras, made clear, "a Tsipras led government would not make a private sector haircut a priority."[3]

As the weeks went by in the January run-up to the election on the 25th, the Troika and New Democracy grew increasingly worried. Public opinion polls showed Syriza slowly but steadily pulling away from New Democracy. One reason was the revelation of secret emails from Samaras to the Troika leaked just weeks earlier. The emails revealed that New Democracy and its leader, Antonis Samaras, had already agreed to the Troika's request to implement more austerity once the current 2012-14 three year debt deal expired on December 31.[4] The revelation seriously undermined New Democracy's credibility. So too did persistent rumors that the Samaras government was planning to allow banks to sell homeowners' mortgages to investors, which might in turn lead to widespread foreclosures. New Democracy's credibility was also damaged by its pledges in 2012 to reduce Greek government debt and austerity by means of negotiations. But those negotiations had not occurred, and both the debt and austerity measures had actually risen.

All the above posed a serious problem for the Troika. Should Samaras and New Democracy lose on January 25, the understandings surreptitiously reached between them in 2014 would be 'off the table'. The Troika-compliant New Democracy party government might no longer be available to guarantee the Troika's plans for a post-February 2015 further restructuring of the Greek debt. Greece needed to repay 28 billion euros in debt in 2015, with 4.5 billion due on March 31, and another 6.5 billion August. To do so would require still more austerity in any new 2015 memorandum of agreement on debt restructuring. Negotiations with a Syriza government would be, at best, a lot messier and more uncertain.

The Greek stock market had already declined by 15% in December alone, and government borrowing costs, once at 3.5% in July 2014, rose to 12% by the start of 2015 and to nearly 15% on the eve of the election. By mid-January, non-performing business loans, for which payments had not been made for more than 90 days, amounted to no less than 77 billion euros. Such trends raised the likelihood of a 3rd Greek debt restructuring in 2015, leading to even more debt added to Greece, and in turn eventually more austerity to pay for it.

Syriza's Electoral Offensive

Syriza's January campaigning constantly reminded voters that New Democracy had failed to deliver on all its key 2012 pledges, that the secret deal making by New Democracy and the Troika signaled even worse austerity was in store for Greeks should New Democracy win, and that secret plans were even being developed to sell off their homes to speculators. Syriza promised not only to stop the anticipated foreclosures and sell offs, but also to repeal unpopular property tax measures introduced in 2014 by New Democracy affecting 80% of households. The measures were especially aggravating, since they valued properties at pre-2008 market values even after home prices had fallen by 40%-50% since that time.

Yet another election issue raised with success by Syriza was the 'Lagarde List'. New Democracy was cozy with Greece's oligarchs and ignored their widespread practices of tax avoidance and tax fraud. The 'Largarde List' that appeared at the time indicated there were more than 2000 very wealthy Greeks who had failed to pay more than $1 billion in taxes and instead were sending the money to Swiss bank accounts or to their offshore corporate subsidies from which they were paying themselves. Their profits from capital gains from property sales in Greece—often to investors outside Greece—were generally unreported. Tax evasion by the wealthy was rampant, Syriza pointed out, at a time when New Democracy and the Troika were raising sales taxes on the rest of Greece and cutting essential subsidies on food and utilities. Syriza pledged to put a stop to tax evasion by the oligarchs and ensure transparency in property sales.

Another Syriza pledge to take on the oligarchs had to do with their control over the media and their financial funding of center and right wing politicians in New Democracy, PASOK, and other parties. As a US embassy cable released by Wikileaks indicated, "Greece's private media outlets are owned by a small group of people ... related by blood, marriage or adultery to political and government officials and/or other media and business magnates." Media companies were given no charge licenses and virtual free loans from local Greek banks. In exchange favored politicians got free media time. New Democracy Prime Minister Antonis Samaras, for example, appeared frequently on the 'Star TV' network, owned by Greek oil and shipping oligarch, Vardis Vardinoyannis.

At the Syriza Party's Congress on January 3-4, Tsipras gave a keynote speech that revealed more of Syriza's electoral strategy, as well as its likely program should it win the elections.

The speech promised to "put an end ... to the absurdity of memoranda and austerity". But there was no reference whatsoever to a possible 'Grexit' or leaving the Eurozone as the means by which to end austerity. Grexit has never been an option to Syriza or Tsipras. Ending austerity would be accomplished "by way of sincere but resolute negotiations"... that would result in "a waiving of most of the debt." Reducing the debt—i.e. debt relief—would relieve the burden, imposed by the Troika, of an impossible fiscal surplus of 3.5% needed to pay interest and principal on the debt. That in turn would allow Greece to reverse the worst of austerity and employ the rest in fiscal stimulus to grow the economy once again. Growth would enable the payment of the remaining debt.

So the Syriza formula for ending austerity was via "resolute negotiations" that would convince the Troika to "waive most of the debt".[5] Neither would prove possible in the end, however. And there was no plan for Grexit.

Tsipras declared Samaras and New Democracy were fear-mongering when they declared that Syriza planned for a Grexit and thus bankruptcy. Rather, Syriza argued, it was Samaras and New Democracy that were responsible for half the Greek population, 6.3 million, now living in poverty; for one third the workforce unemployed, for the cuts in wages, pensions and rising sales taxes on medicine, food and utilities; and for plans in the works after the election to sell off millions of mortgages and foreclose and evict homeowners.

In contrast, Syriza would, if elected, reduce unrealistic primary surpluses, re-allocate surpluses to public investment, protect citizens' bank deposits, and "delete most of the nominal value of the debt" just as the allied powers—the US, UK and others—at the London conference of 1953 had deleted Germany's post-world war II debt. There would be a moratorium on debt payments, a 'European New Deal' to release public investment for growth, and support for the ECB to directly purchase government bonds via QE. All this would somehow be accomplished by negotiating "within the framework of the EU and European Institutions"—i.e. by negotiating with the Troika.

Providing more detail, Tsipras spoke of four 'pillars' of the Thessaloniki program, the 'National Reconstruction Plan': immediate relief of the 'humanitarian crisis' by initiatives for the poor, including raising pensions, providing shelter, food vouchers, free electricity and healthcare. A second pillar to restart the economy by providing support to small and medium businesses in the form of loans and tax relief. A third pillar to recover 3000,000 jobs cut since 2010, and restoring minimum wages, union rights, and collective bargaining. And a fourth pillar reforming government and the media. The program was envisioned as a spark that would resurrect social democracy throughout Europe. A Syriza victory would send a signal to Spain, Ireland and elsewhere, making "Greece a positive example of progressive development in Europe". Tsipras concluded with a call "for a mandate to negotiate."

Despite its call for reversing austerity, restoring cuts to jobs and incomes, and expunging the majority of the 142 billion euro debt held by the EC in its EFSF fund, it was clear Tsipras meant to achieve this by negotiating with the Troika—not by Grexit or more radical means. From the very beginning Syriza's assumption was that a negotiating strategy could succeed. That assumption grossly overestimated Syriza's leverage in negotiations with both the Troika and with potential Syriza allies. And it grossly underestimated the insistence of Troika hardliners, led by Schauble and Germany's allies, to continue austerity and their refusal to deploy the resources they had now demonstrated were at their command toward Greek debt relief. Negotiating debt and other restructuring deals was the turf of the bankers and financial-economic elites running the Troika. They were good at it. They knew all the financial tricks and accounting legerdemain. They had done this countless times. And they were more confident than ever in 2015.

The coming weeks and months would reveal the inexperience and disadvantages of Syriza and its negotiating team, as it retreated step by step from its non-negotiable Thessaloniki program. It was a classic example of elevating negotiations, a tactic, to a level of strategy itself. And once it became clear that Syriza had no true allies elsewhere in Europe, or even liberal sympathizers among certain elements of the Troika, as it had hoped, all it could do was either mobilize the Greek people toward a Grexit or fall back to a concessionary policy in negotiations that eventually accepted the Troika's demands.

This dilemma for Syriza was clarified in an interview with Tsipras the week before the January 25 election. The interviewer asked him: "Your opponents, on both the Right and Left, claim that your position on abolishing the Memoranda and austerity, and renegotiating the debt will result in one of two possible outcomes: you will either have to backtrack, recognizing that you can't achieve your goals or you will be forced out of the Eurozone ... What is your response to such claims?"

Tsipras' reply was he didn't believe Greece would be forced out of the Eurozone, since "it's not allowed under the European treaties". Furthermore, "a voluntary exit is extremely risky, with dangerous consequences for Greece and for Europe". So a Grexit, initiated either by the Troika or Syriza, was not going to happen. Grexit would destabilize Greece, Tsipras conceded, and Europe itself.

Grexit was avoidable if the EU accepted that Greece and other smaller European countries "are equal partners", Tsipras contended. But were they in fact equal? Did the creation of the Euro in 1999 institutionalize equality of its members—or were some created more equal than others? Did not the 1999 agreement, by creating the ECB, strip the smaller members of their right to exercise independent monetary policy? And did not 1999 also freeze any possibility of independent fiscal policy by requiring member states to not exceed a ceiling on fiscal budget deficits? In reality, Germany and friends dominated the ECB and the larger countries—like France and others—were allowed repeatedly to violate the budget deficit limits while the smaller states, like Greece, were held accountable to it. That was not equality. And there was no prospect of either the monetary or fiscal-budget arrangements changing soon—and certainly not to accommodate Syriza and Greece. Tsipras apparently believed that the powers in the Eurozone would come around to Syriza's view, recognizing that the European experiment was itself at stake. As he put in, "I'm personally optimistic about the developments we can expect".

Tsipras believed the Troika would eventually recognize the Greek debt was not a Greek problem, but a European problem and that the logic and sensibleness of Syriza's proposals would prevail as a consequence of negotiations. Elements within Europe, apart from the Troika hardliners, would come to Syriza's position and force Schauble and the Troika hardliners to reform the Eurozone itself. The only way to repay the Greek debt was to give Greece the opportunity to 'grow out of the debt' by stimulating its economy fiscally—not by fiscal austerity measures which had the opposite effect. Surely progressive elements in the Troika and Eurozone would see the logic and necessity of creating a 'European New Deal'. The issue of the debt has to be dealt with at the European level, he added. Negotiating with the Troika was the only option, but that option could only succeed if Europe beyond the hardliners came to Syriza's defense. As Tsipras put it, "we're not just fighting for change in Greece—ours is a struggle for political change across Europe". What Tsipras was in effect saying was 'restoring social democracy in Greece', in one country, would lead to its restoration and revival across Europe as well. Neoliberal interests of course were not in the slightest interested in allowing the resurrection of the old European social democratic order that they had successfully displaced.

But this vision of a social democratic Europe had already been pushed aside by the Euro Neoliberal revolution that had been deepening for the past quarter century. And that Euro Neoliberalism had passed a point of no return with the creation of the Euro system in 1999. If Greece's negotiating with the Troika were to prove successful—in turn proving that Grexit was not necessary—then forces favoring a social democratic return elsewhere in Europe would have to throw their weight in favor of Syriza and Greece in the negotiations. But the old forces that once were social democratic had capitulated to neoliberalism and become its junior members years ago—and the new would-be proponents of social democracy—like Syriza, Podemos in Spain, die Linke in Germany, etc.—were still too small and undeveloped to aid Syriza in more than just words.

This overestimation of the forces outside Greece that might come to its assistance in securing a new debt deal through negotiations was perhaps Syriza's and Tsipras' strategic weak link. Without that assistance, negotiations would fail. And if they failed, Grexit was the only alternative to an eventual collapse back into concessions and further austerity. That of course was the interviewer's original question—which Tsipras chose not to answer directly. Negotiations would succeed because Europe would rally around Syriza and Greece. Thus, Grexit would not be necessary.

On January 26, 2015 Tsipras was sworn in as the new prime minister. Syriza had won the election and 149 seats in the Parliament. It formed a majority of 162 out of 300 by establishing a coalition with the right wing party, Independent Greeks, which was also vehemently opposed to austerity. The Troika immediately warned the new government to abandon the idea of any kind of debt write-off. Debt relief had been promised by the Troika in 2012 if Greece produced a positive budget surplus, which it did in 2014. However, the Troika had ignored its prior promise of debt relief then, and had no intention of debt relief now. Debt relief for Greece might open a Pandora's box of similar demands elsewhere in the Eurozone. A successful Greek negotiation might also provide a political and electoral impetus to new left, and right-wing, formations rising in popularity and influence.

Within 24 hours, Troika spokespersons reminded Greece it had debt payments of 4.3 billion euros due to the IMF in March and another 6.7 billion owed to the ECB in July and it expected Greece to pay up. Until it did, the 7 billion euro latest disbursement of funds under the 2012 agreement would be withheld. Social democrat party leaders in Germany and France chimed in supporting the Troika, noting in public statements that Greece should forget about cancelling debt. The new Dutch finance minister and president of the Eurozone council of finance ministers, Jeroen Djisselbloem, immediately flew to Athens to initiate informal, back room discussions with Tsipras.

In response, the new Greek government within days of the election suspended privatization projects in progress, raised the minimum wage by 30%, restored some pensions, and promised to rehire thousands of public workers. Tsipras publicly declared "We are not going to continue the politics of subjugation", and further indicated Greece did not support European sanctions against Russia over the emerging conflicts in the Ukraine. Greece's newly appointed finance minister, Yanis Varoufakis, further suggested Greece would take an aggressive line in negotiations and further aggravated the Troika by calling the preceding Greek debt deals "a toxic mistake" and Troika-imposed austerity an example of "fiscal waterboarding." Greece did not want the Troika's 7 billion additional debt disbursement, he added. In a joint press conference with Djisselbloem, Varoufakis then called for a Euro-wide conference to consider Greece's debt, which Djisselbloem promptly rejected publicly in turn, declaring that the conference already exists as the Eurogroup of finance ministers.

The Troika hardliners came out swinging, as the vice president of the EC, Jyrki Katainen, a strong ally of German finance minister, Wolfgang Schauble, retorted "We expect them to fulfill everything that they have promised to fulfill," and that talk of debt relief was a non-starter. Schauble himself declared Germany would not be "blackmailed".

At the same time, rumors arose that the EC might consider lowering Greece's fiscal surplus target, now at 4.5% of its budget, and perhaps extending debt payments out additional years to lower payments. Splits were beginning to emerge within the Troika, which Syriza planned to exploit in the coming weeks.

By early February, the positions of both sides were becoming entrenched. Syriza's coalition with the anti-austerity Independent Greeks, appointment of the outspoken Varoufakis, disagreement on Russian sanctions, suspension of privatizations, and rollbacks of pension, wage and job cuts were playing into Schauble and the hardliners' hands. At the same time, the Greek government declared it was no longer going to cooperate with the EC's monitors in Greece, and indicated it was not interested in renewing the 2012 debt deal when it expired February 28. Instead, it would offer its own proposals.

To organize support in Europe, Tsipras and Varoufakis set out on visits to explore support from social democratic governments, visiting Paris, Rome and other destinations. Following the round of meetings, the new government planned to introduce its new proposals to the Greek government on February 7. Thereafter, Tsipras planned to travel to the EU leaders summit on February 12 to seek out likely responses by Euro heads of government, including Merkel and German allies in Brussels and elsewhere.

Then the real negotiations would really begin.

Endnotes

1   While the ECB could not directly bail out governments, there were ways around this rule. The nation could issue government bonds, sell them to its central bank, which could then use them as collateral to borrow loans from the ECB. The national central bank could then lend to local governments, relieving the central government from otherwise directly having to do so .

2   In fact, the prospect of more Greek instability and Grexit might even serve to reduce the euro currency's value, and therefore was considered not necessarily all bad—as least from the perspective of some northern Eurozone bankers and exporters.

3   Landon Thomas, 'Voices Join Greek Left's Call for a New Deal on Debt', *The New York Times*, January 9, 2015, p. B5.

4   Samaras' failure to get New Democracy's handpicked candidate approved by the Greek parliament in December 2014, despite three votes, held up the new agreements in principle. The Troika and Samaras therefore agreed to extend the then current 2012-14 debt agreement another sixty days, until after the elections, after which to work out the details of a subsequent 2015-2018 new debt restructuring deal.

5   By waiving or writing off debt, according to sources, Syriza apparently meant deploying approximately one-third of the $142 billion held by the EC in its EFSF fund.

Chapter Seven

THE TROIKA COUNTER-ATTACK

Within a couple days of the Greek election, Angela Merkel, leader of Germany, made it explicitly clear that the Tsipras-Varoufakis proposal for debt relief—i.e. a haircut or reduction of the existing Greek debt—was out of the question. In an interview to the influential German daily newspaper, *Die Welt*, she pointblank declared "I don't see a further debt haircut". She emphasized that the recent ECB decision to launch a QE monetary program did not change anything as far as Greece was concerned. The Germans and Troika were still awaiting an official response from Greece.

Nor could Greece expect any support from its presumed social democratic allies in France or elsewhere. In a meeting with France's finance minister, Sapin, on February 1, Varoufakis was told in no uncertain terms that France was sympathetic but it would not support proposals for debt relief. Varoufakis was also warned that after the current debt agreement expired February 28, Greece could expect no further lending from the Troika. That meant not only from the EC but likely also from the ECB, whose support was critical to keeping the Greek central bank and private banks afloat throughout the bargaining period ahead.

This absence of public support when it counted would be typical of social democratic parties and leaders throughout the remainder of negotiations. Germany may have been the 'hard cop', but the social democrats—in and out of government—would consistently play the role of 'soft cop' in the emerging negotiations.

An initial sign of concession by the Syriza government arose soon after February 1. Greece's initial disagreement with the EU extending sanctions on Russia was reversed; Greece now endorsed the EU's extension of sanctions for another six months. The EU's foreign policy chief, Federica Mogherini, called the Greek shift "extremely constructive". But if Syriza thought this concession would soften Troika resolve, it was mistaken. Repeated subsequent concessions would be accepted by the Troika with little, if anything, offered in return.

The ECB was a particularly potent weapon deployed by the Troika. The Eurozone central bank had several levers of power over Greece. First, it had the authority to issue loans to Greece's central bank, for disbursement to Greek private banks. Up to now, the ECB allowed the Greek central bank to issue bonds which were equivalent to 'junk bond' quality, and those bonds were used by the ECB as acceptable collateral for issuing ECB long term loans to the central bank.[1] Second, the ECB could also provide very short term loans to the Greek central bank, from the ECB's Emergency Loan Assistance (ELA) program. Third, it could disburse loans not yet distributed under the old 2012 agreement, which was still in effect until the 28th of February. Fourth, it held onto the interest earned on prior issued Greek government bonds that it was officially required, under the old agreement, to disburse but was withholding as well.

These last two measures, three and four, in effect represent violations of the old agreement. But withholding funds to Greece, even when legally required by the prior agreement, was too powerful a tactical weapon for the Troika to relinquish. Paying Greece what it was owed would likely have strengthened its bargaining hand and delayed further the eventual capitulation to Troika demands. And the Troika was turning every available screw to come to that conclusion with Greece.

Why the Syriza government did not make a greater issue of this Troika refusal to pay it what it, the Troika, had previously agreed is interesting. The Greek government of course did demand the loans and payment it was due. But it also asked for a bridge loan, suggesting it really didn't think it would receive the scheduled loans or be paid the interest on its bonds held by the ECB. The Troika was more likely to issue new loans—after an agreement was reached—than to provide the old loans and payments prior to an agreement. Like the old loan disbursement due and the interest on Greek bonds due, the Troika never conceded to a temporary bridge loan during negotiations either. The Troika strategy was to drain Greece of all money and funding for both Greece's banks and its government to function. To disburse old loans, pay Greece interest, or provide Greece a bridge loan would have directly contradicted and undermined that Troika strategy.

On February 4, the ECB met to decide on what, if anything (including what it owed!), to provide Greek banks in terms of additional liquidity. In the wake of the election, Greek banks were experiencing increasing financial difficulty. Greece was running out of cash. The value of Greek banks' stocks had fallen by 50%. Deposits were being withdrawn at record rates, mostly by corporations, and sent outside Greece. In December the withdrawals were nearly 5 billion euros. In January, 9 billion. And in early February, at an even faster rate. In public statements, the ECB suggested indirectly that it might not agree to accept new Greek central bank bonds as collateral for loans, and it might even stop providing short term emergency loans.

The US global corporate rating agency, Standard & Poor's, then downgraded Greek bonds to 'deep junk' status, adding more pressure. That meant it was virtually impossible for Greece to borrow from private markets. Greece was therefore totally dependent on ECB and Troika lending, and all indications from those sources was 'no loans' or loan rollovers unless Syriza agreed to extend the current debt agreement of 2012 beyond February 28, 2015. Troika representatives were indicating a six month extension.

The Troika and ECB initial goal was to force Greece to accept an extension of the current debt agreement on its terms. If it could achieve that, it would signal weakness in Greek government resolve. For its part, Tsipras and Varoufakis pushed for what they called a 'bridge loan' to cover Greek debt payments coming due in March, June and July while they negotiated an entirely new agreement 'from scratch'. Their vision was an agreement concluded at the national government levels in the Eurozone. They hoped to leverage allies, like France and Italy, who also wanted relief from Eurozone budget cap spending limits. But France and Italy had consistently received exemptions from their limits, unlike Greece, and so did not need to push for a Eurozone-wide new fiscal spending and infrastructure investing regime— which was strongly opposed by Germany and its allies who insisted on fiscal austerity and central bank monetary policies as the strategy. Syriza's grand strategy of eliciting a new pan-European resolution of their (and other countries') debt problems was thus a doomed strategy from the start.

The Debt-Swap Proposal and Euro Tour

Nonetheless, Tsipras and Varoufakis adhered to it

and pushed it in the early weeks of February. Both went on a 'tour' of European capitals to try to garner support for this strategy and support, which they hoped they could leverage and ride to get some relief from austerity to enable them to reverse the worse income effects from Greek austerity and invest and grow Greece's way out of its debt conundrum.

Varoufakis traveled to Paris, London, and then Berlin to explore with his finance minister counterparts if there was receptivity to Syriza's grand strategy: inter alia, swapping old Greek debt for new growth bonds. Growth bonds meant interest and payments would be indexed to Greek GDP growth. The more the growth, the more the repayment. This was a clever proposal, for growth meant the Troika would have to reduce its current '4.5% Greek surplus as a percent of GDP' rule. The surplus was necessary to repay the Troika the level of interest and principal due based on prior debt. But if the surplus was used to repay debt, it would not be available for Greece to stimulate and grow its economy. Reducing the surplus to 1.5%, as Greece proposed as part of the debt swap arrangement, meant Greece could use the 3% budget difference to fiscally stimulate its economy and to reverse some austerity measures, together which it hoped would further stimulate private consumption and Greek GDP growth.

The second element proposed by Varoufakis on his tour was to replace some of the old debt as well with what were called 'perpetual bonds'.[2] That meant replacing current bonds on which both interest and principal were due, with bonds that never matured and on which only interest payments had to be made. That would reduce Greece's total payment, leaving funds available for fiscal stimulus and austerity reduction. Varoufakis also proposed, as part of this package proposal, that Greece would accelerate tax collecting from the wealthy. And in the meantime, while negotiations were progressing, so he proposed, the ECB would grant Greece a four month emergency loan. In other words, at this point in negotiations Greece did not want an extension of the old agreement after February 28, 2015.

What was especially significant about this new position offered by Greece was that it dropped altogether any demands for debt relief in the form of writing off a portion of the old Troika debt, specifically the 142 billion held by the EC. Greece was more than willing to repay the debt coming due owed to the IMF and the ECB. Its strategy was thus, in part, also to placate the IMF and ECB in the hope of allying them to push the EC, the third member of the Troika and Greece's 'target' for debt negotiations, into accepting in principle the idea of a 'debt swap' as described above—along with a bridge loan in the interim plus a Troika agreement to abandon the old 2012 agreement as the structure on which to conduct new negotiations and rather begin a new deal 'from scratch', as Tsipras put it. This was an old negotiating trick, called setting and controlling the agenda, which provided its proposer a negotiating advantage. But the Troika were old hands at this kind of maneuver, and would have none of it, holding to the old agreement from which negotiations would commence. And that meant the old agreement had to be extended past February 28. Whoever blinked first on this matter would be forced to assume a defensive position in bargaining.

From Paris, Varoufakis went on to Frankfurt to meet with Mario Draghi, chair of the ECB, to seek agreement in principle and, more importantly, to secure some kind of agreement on the idea of a 'bridge loan'. The media and press at first reported their meeting as positive, with some support for debt swapping. Greek bank stocks and Greek stocks immediately surged, as Greek government bond rates eased. But it was a false indicator. Immediately after the Varoufakis meeting, the ECB decided to suspend its previous rule allowing Greece to issue near worthless bonds as collateral for ECB loans. But the ECB approach was 'part stick and part carrot', as the saying goes. The ECB did decide to give its OK for Greece's central bank to issue bonds to private sellers. The cost of such bonds to Greece, however, shot up to 20%. So the consequence was a further increase in Greece's total debt. Greece could raise money from the private lenders globally, but the latter would only buy Greek bonds if they paid a usurious 20%. The ECB thereafter noted that the emergency lending assistance, ELA, program might soon be limited as well if there were no extension past February 28. The ECB decision was thus the Troika's way to signal Greece that, in exchange for Greece dropping altogether its demand for debt relief, the ECB would assist it in incurring more debt in the private marketplace for its bonds. However, even this token 'concession' by the ECB was contingent on Greece agreeing to an extension of the old agreement. The Troika took one step forward, as Greece took three steps back, in other words.

If Varoufakis got nothing out of Paris but vague words of support, and then a questionable concession from Frankfurt and the ECB, he ran into a brick wall in Berlin. Wolfgang Schauble, Germany's finance minister, remained adamant that nothing was discussable unless the current agreement was extended and therefore the austerity measures under it were implemented. The German position remained: extend the current agreement, no relief in debt principal or interest. Greece must stick to its austerity measures. No bridge loans. And negotiations on a new agreement to commence from there, on the framework of the old agreement, at the level of the Troika, and not some new supra-government level 'from scratch'. Both did agree, however, that Greece would stay within the Euro. Schauble and Varoufakis held a press conference following their meeting, at which Schauble concluded, 'we agreed to disagree'. Varoufakis added, 'we didn't' even agree to disagree'—a kind of statement that qualified, according to some, as a diplomatic faux pas.

Varoufakis had embarrassed and alienated EC representative Djisselbloem when the latter had visited Greece immediately after the election; now he had done the same with Schauble. In reality, however, while the press made a big deal of these diplomatic discourtesies, it made no difference whatsoever in the respective parties' negotiating positions and outcomes. But it would provide the Troika with an excuse later in the summer, on the other hand, to demand Tsipras remove Varoufakis as finance minister, which he would do, consequently undermining Syriza's bargaining authority even more. The Troika knew how to play these games; Syriza was just learning— the hard way.

As Varoufakis toured the first week meeting with finance ministers, Tsipras met with his official government-state counterparts. His tour produced a similar lack of support. Social-democratic party and government counterparts in France, Italy, and Holland issued similar carefully worded but noncommittal statements of support. Merkel and Germany remained obstinate, calling on Greece to show its official proposals first before negotiations or new loans might be made available.

The end of the first week of February and the first 'grand tour' of Euro capitals might have been scored as 9 for Troika and (perhaps) two for Syriza: The ECB would provide no bridge loan, would not distribute Greece's interest earned on bonds or the 11.5 billion euro disbursement of loans under the old agreement; social democratic governments and parties were supporting no debt relief and agreeing Greece should extend the current agreement; there was no indication of a growing Euro-wide challenge to austerity in the works; and the EC did not embrace debt swap. Greece got in exchange a temporary, unwritten assurance to continue ELA and short term loans from the ECB that was subject to ECB cancellation at any time. Syriza gave up a prime demand of debt relief, backed off its initial position on Russian sanctions, committed to remaining within the Euro regime, and, as Varoufakis added, indicated it was willing to accept 70% of the previously imposed austerity measures of the old agreement.

The basic contradiction at the heart of Tsipras and Greece's proposals was evident in Tsipras' public remarks delivered after he met with EC officials in Brussels. As he put it, "Our goal is to respect the people's sovereignty in Greece ... and at the same time we respect the rules of the EU." But respecting EU rules meant not respecting Greece's sovereignty. It was really one or the other, not both. Syriza could not have it both ways, it would eventually discover. It would have either to decide on sovereignty or decide on the Troika's terms for debt renegotiating. There really was no middle ground. The Troika would never consider it.[3] If it did, that would signal the end of neoliberal policies administered out of northern Europe and imposed on the rest. And the Troika was now in a stronger bargaining position than in 2012: there was no European recession, other peripheral governments' bonds were not in freefall, the Euro banks were not as widely insolvent in 2015 as in 2012, and now the ECB had another big pot of money, QE, from which it could disburse trillions to governments or banks in trouble— except to Greece, of course. Somehow these ballasts to Troika intractability were lost on Syriza.

Tsipras returned after his tour to address his own Greek Parliamentary majority. His speech mentioned none of the rebuffs or adamant rejections of Greece's proposals offered to the Troika during his, and Varoufakis', tour of

Eurozone capitals. He reaffirmed his party's anti-austerity pledge and indicated Greece did not want the Troika's final loan under the old agreement. He also noted that continuing the old agreement past February 28 would be "a mistake and disaster". Greece wanted a bridge loan until June 1, and a reduction of the budget surplus to 1.5% to get some space for the government to invest in expansion and lift the worst elements of austerity. He reiterated the party's campaign pledge to raise the minimum wage, halt pension cuts, and restore jobs and year end wage bonuses. Exemptions for the property tax were raised from 5 thousand to twelve thousand euros and a crackdown was planned on wealthy tax evaders.

It was clear from the speech that Tsipras still had in mind the grand strategy of a general European-level solution. As he put it again, "The problem is not just Greece. It never was. The crisis is not just Greek; it's European." He also still held the position that negotiations therefore were best conducted at the higher inter-government level and not with the Troika. And if that was not aggressive enough, he threw in the fanciful vow to seek German World War II reparations of $71 billion. This all appealed to the party faithful in Parliament, though most of it had already failed, or was sure to, with EU or Troika counterparts. In a separate interview, Varoufakis echoed the hard line, publicly stating if Greece were to exit, the Euro regime would "collapse like a house of cards" and that the day of "the Troika is over".

Through all the bombast and rhetoric, it was clear that Greece had dropped the proposal for debt relief as well as the idea of ending all austerity—it was proposing to end just 30% of it. And after China, which was bidding to buy Greece's main port, Piraeus, complained about the halt to privatizations, Tsipras reversed that as well and pledged to meet the 2.8 billion euro goal of privatizations scheduled for 2015. As both Tsipras and Varoufakis repeatedly assured the Troika in the preceding week, dropping the euro, i.e. Grexit, was not on the table in any form. The core of Syriza proposals was now the debt swap, not debt relief; a reduction of the surplus target to 1.5%; a partial rollback of austerity; accelerated tax reform focused on wealthy evaders; and some kind of EU government level investment program. Greece had come a long way in terms of concessions and implied concessions in just one week. In contrast, the Troika had not budged: nothing was offered until Greece agreed to extend the current debt arrangements beyond February 28.

The February 20 Interim Agreement

Another round of meetings with finance ministers followed at mid-February. Now Greece was willing to accept disbursement of the last loan under the old deal, unlike before. And Tsipras agreed to meet and negotiate with the Troika. In response the Troika suggested it was willing to stretch out the current payment periods on the loans, lower the interest rates further, and release 7.2 billion euros. In exchange it insisted, however, that previous austerity measures had to continue, and this time under Troika direct supervision. Moreover, the 22 billion euros of privatizations had to occur, as well as labor reforms and restructuring (i.e. reversing the government's recent restoration of job, wage and pension cuts).

Given the economic deterioration resulting from the January election and events that followed, plus the prospect of a protracted negotiation period, it was estimated Greece would need another 38 billion euros in loans in addition to rolling over the old debt. Yet Greece still held firm to the idea of a totally new agreement, scrapping the old 2012 deal, which was a negotiations stopper for the Troika. As an un-named Greek government official put it, as Tsipras headed off to another meeting of EU summit heads of state on February 15, "The basic difficulty is whether the basis for discussion is the previous program … we're looking for a new program."

Meanwhile, deposits were being withdrawn from Greek banks at a rate of more than $2 billion a week—already 20 billion euros. At that rate Greece's remaining 145 billion deposits would evaporate in seven weeks, by April. Greek banks would be completely cashless.

The February 15 EU summit meeting produced no agreement. Discussions were abruptly halted after only four hours. The negotiations had clearly broken down. The sticking point was the Troika's demand for a six month extension of the old agreement. With no agreement on this key Troika demand of extension based on the old agreement, the Troika gave Greece an ultimatum: either agree on extension or ECB short term ELA loans that were keeping the Greek banks afloat might be halted—i.e. a 'nuclear option' as it was called. There was simply no alternative, echoed EC officials. The threat to withhold short term emergency lending was exactly the move made by the Troika that had forced Cyprus to capitulate during its debt negotiations in 2013.

The 'carrot' accompanying this stick was that the Troika would consider lifting some austerity terms—but at a later date and only if Greece did not reverse additional past austerity measures unilaterally while negotiations were underway. German finance minister Schauble reaffirmed Germany's hard line, publicly declaring after the session that he was "very skeptical" of any deal occurring and that Greece was behaving "irresponsibly" and "insulting those who have helped Greece in the past few years." These strong statements were answered in kind by Greek government spokespersons. Negotiations had not only collapsed but were now also growing more acrimonious and even personal.

Immediately following the February 15 summit, the ECB decided not to pull the plug on ELA loans to Greece yet, although it reportedly began planning for a possible Grexit that would definitely mean no more loans of any kind. Greece shortly after requested another meeting with EU finance ministers, scheduled for February 20, and indicated it planned to submit another proposal—this time specifically addressing the Troika demand for extension.

At the February 20 meeting Greece blinked and made significant concessions to the Troika. Most significant, it backtracked on its two most important prior positions: not to negotiate with the Troika directly and not to accept the old debt memorandum agreement as the basis from which to restart negotiations for another four months until June 30—thus adding to the government's previous major concession earlier in the month to drop its demands for direct debt relief. Greece henceforth also referred to its Troika bargaining opponents as 'the institutions' or the 'European Group', as a way to avoid its pledge never to negotiate with the despised Troika.

In exchange, the Troika would allow Greece to redefine the austerity measures under the old memorandum, instead of the Troika. Whether the total austerity spending cuts had to add up to the total of the old memorandum was left ambiguous. But at least Greece was left to define them. In other words, Greece could now choose how to cut its economic throat, and do the dirty work to itself. However, the ambiguity of how the totals might add up would soon arise as another critical bargaining issue.

As part of the deal, the Troika also implied it might later discuss reducing the percentage figure for the annual budget surplus. And that the ECB would continue providing short term ELA emergency loans to Greek banks, necessary to keep Greece's banking system afloat while negotiations were occurring. Both the Troika's representatives and the Greeks claimed the new interim arrangement as a 'victory'.

Ireland's finance minister, Michael Noonan, publicly stated, "This is a reversal of their election position. There is absolutely nothing on the table that could be considered a concession." And Germany's Wolfgang Schauebel added that the "Greeks certainly will have a difficult time to explain the deal to their voters". Varoufakis declared the deal was a victory because Greece could now co-author the austerity reform measures, not the Troika alone.

The Troika may have thought the Greeks, given this leeway, would choose between which austerity measures to implement. But to the Greek government, the authority to define austerity meant raising taxes on the wealthy, who had underpaid taxes since 2010 by an amount of 78 billion euros, and then using part of the additional taxes to restore wages and benefits to the poorest of Greece's households.

In the days that followed, rumors spread the Syriza government was planning to restore at least some minimum wages, rehire some of the 10,000 fired, and partially halt some of the privatizations. And that it planned to go after tax evaders aggressively and recover at least 10 billion euros of unpaid taxes. Also to restore subsidies to the poorest, including food, electricity, transport vouchers, and assistance to homeowners in foreclosure.

The February 20 interim deal was brokered primarily by the EC. The terms were reported by the EC as "sufficiently comprehensive to be a valid starting point." But the deal was not accepted by either the ECB or the IMF. IMF director, Christine Lagarde, complained it "failed to adhere to the current program as Athens had promised last week." ECB chairman Draghi also voiced strong reservations. The list of austerity measures would have to expand, and then actually be implemented as well, before the 7.2 billion euros final loan tranche called for under the old memorandum agreement—half of which was IMF money—might be distributed.

It is worth noting that at this point in late February the Troika had not disbursed any loans under the old agreement to Greece since August 2014. That included, as noted previously, the scheduled disbursements under the old agreement which it, the Troika, had agreed to extend until February 28. This treatment of Greece contrasts sharply with Troika treatment of France, Spain and Italy where failure to meet fiscal budget rules and limits resulted in repeated exemptions and extensions of the rules. Germany and other core countries in the Eurozone (and larger EU) liked to talk of adhering strictly to 'rules' as an excuse to take a hard line with Greece. But there was one set of rules for some and another set for others. Greece was unfortunately one of the 'others'.

Tsipras' concessions of February 20 resulted in a political firestorm among the various elements of Syriza and its government. Long time and highly respected party members resigned and stated their reasons publicly, declaring the agreement reneged on Syriza's party platform of principles and the January election promises it had made to Greek voters. Internal resistance was particularly strong with regard to backtracking on rehiring, raising the minimum wage, and unfreezing privatizations. The government's minister in charge of privatizations, previously frozen, independently declared there would be no privatizations on his watch. However, in a raucous 12-hour party meeting, the decision was to approve the deal—although unofficially.

On February 27, based on Schauble's assurance the deal was in effect a four month extension of the same old agreement, Germany voted to approve the new interim agreement. But despite a written agreement, the Troika did not follow up and disburse any of the 7.2 billion euros pending loan. Nor did the ECB follow through on allowing Greek banks access to its ELA emergency short term lending facility. The Troika demanded more details in Greece's proposal, since the IMF and ECB were still not accepting it. Greece thereafter drafted and submitted a second 11 page letter on March 6 outlining more details, which the Troika rejected again as still insufficiently detailed.

In response, Tsipras gave another angry speech to the Greek Parliament on March 11, a day before another round of negotiations were to begin with the Troika. Appealing to the growing discontent in the Parliament, and perhaps also as a concession to the more radical among his MPs, he raised the Greek demand once more that Germany owed Greece 160 billion in reparations from German occupation of Greece during World War II. The Troika, equally incensed and not to be outdone, demanded its monitoring team be allowed to return to Greece to inspect Greece's economic accounts. Schauble in turn assumed an even harder line, adding that nothing would change, and no funds would be disbursed, until Greece fully implemented the austerity measures required by the old agreement.

The Syriza government was clearly losing what little support it may initially had among other governments in the Eurozone and within the EC. This was not all due to Tsipras' and Varoufakis' defiant attitudes. Smaller state members of the Eurozone did not want Greece to succeed in any event, lest its success encouraged other internal political competitors to demand similar debt reconsiderations for their countries. These states, mostly allied with Germany, furthermore viewed more bailout money for Greece as paid for at their own expense. Germany itself believed that Syriza's election upset the progress that was being made in 2014—a progress enabled by the austerity measures the German coalition had demanded.

On the other hand, the Greek government's frustration with the Troika was also rising, as it had made major concession after concession in exchange for vague assurances, almost all of which were never delivered. Understanding it had the 'green light' to 'move the money around', so to speak, and facing the necessity of delivering something to Greek voters as it had promised, the Syriza Parliament passed what was called the 'Humanitarian Bill'. This was a series of measures designed to lighten the heavy austerity load afflicting the poorest sectors of Greek society. It included food assistance, electricity subsidies for 300,000 poorest Greeks, rent and transport voucher restoration, and similar measures. Upon hearing of the bill's passage, the Troika were angered. The law was passed without prior notification to the Troika and its approval. In its view, Greece should be identifying and implementing austerity, not reversing it—even for token relief targeting the poorest.

On March 19 yet another EU summit meeting was convened. Following the meeting, at a press conference German chancellor Merkel made it clear that none of the pending 7.2 billion euros loan to Greece required by the current, extended agreement would be released until Greece implemented austerity measures. Merkel then referred to the December 10, 2014 austerity reforms, indicating that Greece could replace them with their own new austerity measures but the net effect should be the same as provided in the December 10, 2012 measures defined by Greece's predecessor Samaras' government. Now it was finally clear what the Troika meant by its token concession in February allowing Greece to redefine 30% of the austerity measures: The form of austerity could change but not the final content or total value. As Merkel put it, "The Greek government has the opportunity to pick individual reforms that are still outstanding as of December 10 and replace them with other reforms if they ... have the same effect."

Merkel's move was a classic concession bargaining tactic: the weaker party is allowed to put the money wherever it wanted, so long as the total did not change. It could 'move the money around', as they say in bargaining, but the total value could not change. In classic union bargaining tactics, it means divide the total austerity as you may like but the total remains unchanged. In the case of Greek debt negotiations, the 'moving the money around' bargaining tactic meant total austerity required was the same as it was December 10. Greece could identify how to allocate the cuts, the tax hikes and adjust the budget surplus, but the total austerity required and implemented remained unchanged from December 10.

Merkel's 'hammer' to enforce this was the ECB, which now reneged on its assurance in February to provide short term ELA loans to Greece to keep its banks afloat while negotiations proceeded. The ECB now denied raising the cap on Greece's ELA allotment. That meant, in effect, no more ELA. That—plus no loans using Greek bonds as collateral, no release of any part of the 7.2 billion prior loan, ECB withholding of interest earned on Greek bonds since 2010, and Greece's inability to raise funds in public markets—meant Greece was about to run out of money to make an upcoming IMF payment, as well as funds needed to pay for its daily government expenses. In turn it meant Greek banks were about to exhaust all their available liquidity. There would almost certainly be a 'run' on the banks within weeks, even days.

In a private letter from Tsipras to Merkel at the time, revealed well after the March events, Tsipras asked Merkel for a short term loan until May; it again was rejected. The Troika demanded Greece allow Troika monitors to return to Greece and inspect its economic accounts henceforth without interference. Greece's finance ministry quickly complied. As of March 2015, Greece's GDP had collapsed by -26%. Its unemployment level had risen to 26%. Wages since 2010 had fallen by -33%. And Greece's combined spending cuts and tax increases amounted to 45% of its budget.[4]

Facing a desperate situation—with Germany, the Troika, and the ECB tightening the economic squeeze, Tsipras announced a planned trip to Russia on April 8. At the same time, the Syriza government announced it would submit a third set of new proposals to the Troika in exchange for short term financing.

The Lessons of Bargaining: February-March 2015

In a brief period of just a little more than five weeks, Syriza had retreated from its initial bargaining positions on a number of fronts. Several retreats were on major negotiating demands on which it had sworn to voters it would never surrender: First, the idea of some kind of debt relief was dropped. So too was the 'non-negotiable' demand never to directly bargain with the despised Troika. The government's finance ministry acceded publicly to keeping 70% of the austerity measures. And a number of previously implemented anti-austerity measures quickly introduced after the election were in part rolled back, including the freezing of privatizations.

The Troika had successfully launched concession bargaining. Initially it made negotiating all issues conditional upon Greece's acceptance of extending the old memorandum agreement of 2012 as the basis for negotiations. It succeeded breaking the Greek government's resolve on that matter, and thereby set the pattern for subsequent negotiations.

The Troika's concessions were vague, ambiguous and subject to reinterpretation as conditions required, in contrast to those imposed on the Greek government: the ECB promise to lift the cap on short term ELA loans was broken by mid-March. The meaning of allowing Greece to define austerity—hailed as a 'victory' by Varoufakis when agreed to—in reality meant Greece could 'move the December 10 austerity around' but the austerity total could not change.

To achieve its goals, the Troika was fully prepared to provoke a banking crisis and induce a run on the Greek banks. How might Greece economically harm the Troika similarly? The only option might be a Grexit, but that was unilaterally removed—by Greece—before negotiations ever began.

Contrary to Tsipras' expectations, the EC was not the real power within the Troika. That power lay with Schauble's coalition of finance ministers. At key junctures in negotiations that coalition would prove able to successfully check other forces within the EC that may have been sympathetic to Greece. Power also lay with the ECB, which had the most tactical leverage over Greece with its banking system; and the ECB mostly followed Schauble's finance minister majority faction. Deeper still, however, power ultimately lay with Merkel and Germany, with its majority of heads of state allies in northern and eastern Europe that regularly sided with Merkel and Germany on Greek debt issues. They ultimately had to agree to whatever the Troika was able to negotiate

The initial tour of European capitals by Tsipras and Varoufakis showed that social democratic forces elsewhere, in and out of government, were not prepared to support Greece beyond carefully phrased words of support. Tsipras' grand idea of Greece providing a 'spark' around which social democracy in Europe might rally—and together reverse neoliberalism and central bank monetary policy and replace it with a fiscal, investment spending renaissance in Europe that Greece could 'piggy back' off of in order to generate economic recovery—was simply wishful thinking. It was Syriza's core strategy for negotiations, but a strategy without foundations. Daily negotiations on a new agreement depended upon it. When it did not materialize, Greek negotiators were left without leverage in bargaining. With little they could do to potentially cause economic harm to the Troika, given that Grexit was not an option, Syriza negotiators were left with moral demands—and bankers, whether public or private, have no morality concerns where hundreds of billions of euros or dollars are at stake. The Greek government fell into the concession bargaining trap as a result.

That trap was consciously laid by the Troika. Its negotiators understood the importance of an early breaking of Syriza's resolve—hence its resistance on an immediate issue to hand: the question of extending the old agreement. Once the Greek government started the retreat, they knew it would continue and they promptly introduced 'all or nothing' replacement demands after the extension concession was achieved: let Troika inspectors back in, define austerity measures in acute detail first, and then implement the austerity measures before any funding is released. If and when Syriza leaders balked at the repeated bargaining roadblocks raised by the Troika, its ECB stood ready to squeeze Greece's banks and precipitate if necessary a collapse of its banking system and all the consequent political upheaval that necessarily follows such an event.

Greek negotiators were also at a disadvantage in that the Troika was a tripartite opponent. One of the three heads of the dragon could imply, or even agree to a Greek demand, to elicit concessions in exchange from Greece. One or both of the remaining heads then would refuse to join in the deal. So Greece's concessions would remain while the Troika's were pulled off the table. The Troika were old hands at this sort of thing—i.e. concession bargaining tactics, move the money around, soft cop-hard cop double and triple teaming. In contrast, the Syriza negotiators were newcomers, destined to learn the lessons the hard way as negotiations progressed.

This was class-based bargaining at a capitalist state level where the stakes were even higher than at a company or industry level and affected millions instead of hundreds or even thousands. The Troika had its 'strike weapon'— i.e. the ability to slow squeeze or even crash if necessary Greece's banking system which it wielded effectively. The Greek government had no similar strike weapon—apart from the threat of a Grexit which it disavowed from the very beginning and throughout negotiations. The Troika was determined to defeat and humiliate Syriza and the Greek government as an example to others. And in 2015 it had exceptional resources at its disposal with which to do so— unlike in prior debt negotiations in 2010 and 2012 when it was at a greater relative disadvantage.

Endnotes

1   'Junk bond' quality refers to high risk, high yield bonds that only the most risk-raking investors, mostly speculators, were willing to buy in the open market.

2   The 'perpetual bonds' idea was not new; both Portugal and the Netherlands had perpetual bonds in their government portfolios.

3   This basic contradiction, it should be noted, was not merely Tsipras' or Syriza's. It had its roots in the contradictory wishes of Greek voters as well, who wanted an end to austerity but at the same time demanded by large margins to remain in the Euro. How austerity and the Euro were two sides of the same coin was not understood—either by voters or Syriza's leaders.

4   That 45% compares to Ireland and Italy reductions of only 15% imposed by the Troika.

Chapter Eight

FROM
CONFRONTATION TO
CAPITULATION

One of the tactics of the Troika throughout negotiations was to demand ever greater detail in response to Greek proposals that were repeatedly offered. Lack of sufficient detail was typically used as an excuse to reject the proposals and thereby require the Syriza government to in effect make further concessions in the process of providing it. The government's first proposal was 6 pages. Its second was 11 pages. On April 1, 2015 it offered a third, this time 26 pages. Thinking it was still operating under the Troika commitment to allow it to define the austerity measures—i.e. to 'move the money around'—in the April 1 proposals Syriza reduced its prior measures allowing recovery of some pensions and minimum wages; that is, it reduced the increase in both. It also agreed to accelerate privatizations. In this way it sought to reduce the impact of austerity, while agreeing to continue with austerity. But the Troika would have none of it. Any restoration of pensions or minimum wages from the 2012-14 debt deal was unacceptable.

The ECB did agree to a minimal increase in its Emergency Lending Assistance, ELA, to keep the Greek banks going. It was raised from 71 to 75 billion euros. Greek debt payments of 6.6 billion euros were also scheduled for April-May. But the Troika still refused to release any of the 7.2 billion Euros due Greece under the old debt deal, or make the 1.9 billion interest payment it owed Greece on Greek bonds it had been holding for years.

Varoufakis went on another round of meetings, first to Washington and then with IMF director Christine Lagarde on April 7 to ensure her that Greece would meet its scheduled payment to the IMF. The next round of important meetings was with the finance ministers on April 24 in Riga, Latvia to be followed by the EU leaders summit on May 11. In the meantime, technical meetings with the Troika continued in Paris.

As the parties began to prepare for these crucial discussions on April 24 and May 11, splits began to deepen within Syriza. At least three factions were emerging offering different strategies as to how to proceed. One faction congealed around Energy Minister Lafanzanis, which argued in favor of Grexit and a return to the Drachma currency. Another around Varoufakis, who argued that, since Grexit would cost the Troika $1 trillion, the Troika would eventually fold and Grexit would not be necessary. A third coalesced around Deputy Prime Minister Dragansakis, who favored agreeing with the Troika on whatever best terms Greece might arrange.

By mid-April the ECB, in anticipation of the upcoming critical meetings on April 24 and May 11, threatened to tighten the economic screws once again by limiting the ELA loans to Greek banks and raising the collateral required by Greek banks to receive loans from Greece's central bank based on the ELA. Simultaneously the ECB began buying 60 billion euros a month in bond purchases from other Euro banks and governments (i.e. QE). While the bigger economies of the Eurozone, especially France and Germany, were receiving the lion's share of the ECB's 60 billion a month QE program, Greece was running out of money. Unable to sell Greek bonds on the open market due to the ultra-high interest rates at the time, the Syriza government was forced to require state and local governments to send their cash to the central government—about $2 billion—to cover payments for government workers' wages, pensions, and general government operating costs.

The much awaited Finance Ministers' Riga, Latvia, meeting turned out to be a major disappointment for Greece. It was mostly focused on attacking Varoufakis, during which "ministers took turns berating their Greek counterpart", according to the business press. ECB chairman Draghi voiced his warning after the meeting and German Finance Minister Schauble hinted publicly that Germany was preparing for a default by Greece as its own 'plan B'. Tsipras's meeting with Merkel fared no better than an agreement to keep communicating at their level. One important outcome of the meetings was that the Troika decided it wanted Greek Finance Minister Varoufakis out of the negotiations. It is likely that was a major topic of discussion as well at the Merkel-Tsipras level.

The push for his ouster was likely more intended to split and therefore impact the morale of the negotiating team, than to counter Varoufakis' own positions, which still had not, after all, threatened a Grexit. Varoufakis' position on Grexit was no different from that of Tsipras or the Syriza government, at least publicly. So why demand his removal from the Greek team? In part it was due no doubt to his style, which often led to lecturing Troika representatives—notably on the theme that Greece's proposals would lead to a resurrection of Europe (while implicitly theirs was leading to Europe's demise). Bankers and friends don't like being lectured, especially from academic types like Varoufakis. Troika representatives also likely felt unable to explore confidential 'side deals' with Varoufakis, which is how negotiations largely proceed forward at such levels. They may have felt such overtures might be communicated publicly and prove an embarrassment. In short, he wasn't the type of negotiator whom they trusted with confidential off-the-record communications and thus with whom they felt comfortable. But the greatest motivation for getting Tsipras to remove Varoufakis was that, if successful, his removal would represent a signal from Tsipras that Greece was willing to compromise deeply on its demands. The removal thus would encourage hard-liner resolve among the Troika, while simultaneously undermining bargaining confidence among the Greek government's team.

Troika Economics: 1932 Déjà vu

At the Riga meeting the Troika rejected Varoufakis' proposals based on an economic view reminiscent of the 1932 debates between then economist, Cecil Pigou, and John Maynard Keynes. The Pigou-Keynes debate focused on which strategy was best for recovery from the Great Depression at the time.

Pigou represented the pre-depression period economic thinking that argued the way out of the crisis was to reduce wages in order to stimulate investment. In the abstract, and faulty, economic logic of Pigou, if wages were reduced that would create more cash flow for businesses. That extra cash would then be invested. More investment would create more profits (and more investment) and mean as well more jobs, more wage income, and more consumption in turn. The economy would recover. Employment and wages would rise in the longer run if wages were cut in the short run. In other words, the lack of wage reduction was what was keeping the recovery from the 1930s Depression on hold.

Keynes disagreed and argued Pigou's abstract logic did not conform to empirical reality. Lowering wages did not necessarily stimulate investment even though it might raise business cash and income in the short run. Without effective demand for its products, business would simply hoard the additional short run savings from the wage cuts. But the wage cutting would immediately result in less disposable income for wage earners, and therefore reduced consumption and deeper depression. Cutting wages did not lead to more employment and consumption and economic growth, but just the opposite. And it would therefore mean even less investment, not more; even less growth, not recovery.

The 'Pigou Effect', as it was called at the time, is almost exactly the strategy that Schauble and the Troika were maintaining Greece should adopt. The Troika wanted wage and pension cuts, massive public worker job cuts, reduction of vouchers for food and transport services, higher sales (VAT) taxes, less independent collective bargaining (and therefore union wages), and other similar measures. Schauble in particular believed that, since wage cutting worked in Germany in 2005, it would work for Greece (and other periphery economies). Austerity via wage and income reducing was the logical way to get business costs down, business confidence up, and thus lead to more exports that would require more investment and, in turn, economic recovery. This was original, hard-nosed, 'supply side' strategy. Keynes had clearly debunked the assumptions of Pigou in 1932. Pigou's views were based on logical assumptions that didn't conform to empirical fact (and were therefore actually illogical). But the apparent logic provided a good excuse nonetheless for policy makers to continue to make workers pay with their wages for conditions not of their own making in the first place. The victims of the crisis were assumed to be the cause of it—or at least the cause of failing recovery.[1]

As Varoufakis replied immediately after the Riga meeting with the Troika who called for his ouster, "our partners (Troika) believe that, given time, this agenda will work. If wages fall further, employment will rise. The way to cure an ailing pension system is to cut pensions. And privatizations should aim at higher sales prices to pay off debt." However, "despite a huge drop in wages and costs, export growth has been flat," he noted.[2]

Boosting exports (and thus domestic investment) by means of what is called 'internal devaluation' (reducing labor costs) has been a favored strategy of the Eurozone elites, especially the faction dominated by German bankers and business. Lower wages that reduce wage costs offer the opportunity to reduce prices of exports, allowing the capture of more exports from capitalist competitors. The argument was fallacious, however, since reducing Greek wages neither had nor would have much effect on the overall value of the Euro currency. Euro devaluation would benefit, moreover, mostly German exports. The strategy might work for Germany but not for a small periphery economy like that of Greece. If Greece had its own currency, the drachma, it might have some effect. But so long as Greece remained in the Eurozone, the advantage to the Greek economy of Greek wage cutting—either direct via wages or indirect via pensions and job cuts—was insignificant.

Varoufakis Marginalized

One of the worst moves a bargaining team can make in negotiations is to bow to pressure from the opposition to remove a member from its team. If done, it signals that the party to the negotiations is so weak it is willing to cannibalize itself in exchange for some consideration. It also has the effect of making the remaining team members less confident

and independent. The team falls in line behind the power that
agreed to the pressure to remove one of its members. But
that's exactly what Tsipras and Syriza did when, on April 27,
Tsipras removed Varoufakis from direct negotiations as well
as Varoufakis' other team members. The Troika immediately
applauded the move. Greek stocks rose 4%, bond rates fell
by a similar amount. Deputy Foreign Minister for Economic
Affairs Euclid Tsakalatos replaced Varoufakis.

In order to project an image of toughness in
negotiations despite the removal of Varoufakis, Tsipras
announced immediately after that he might submit the deal
to a referendum of the Greek people if austerity was still
demanded by the Troika.

The Tsipras waffling continued. On the eve of the
May 11 summit, Greece announced it was ready to sell two
ports, concede to the Troika on VAT, and cut some pensions.
It would also 'consult with the International Labor Office
(ILO)' in Geneva before it went ahead with any increase in the
minimum wage—as if the ILO would make a recommendation
that contradicted the Troika. In effect, the Syriza government
now conceded further, backing off of its prior positions further
once again, this time with regard to key austerity measures
like minimum wage, pensions, and privatizations.

Another important consequence of Varoufakis' removal
was that now the Troika's representatives were allowed
direct access, in Greece, to whatever documents and data
they requested—after having been held at bay during the
Varoufakis period as Greek Finance Minister. Now the
Troika could get all the details it wanted.

In a formal sense, Varoufakis was not totally
sidelined. He officially remained part of the Greek government as finance minister and claimed he still had a role in
the discussions, just not at the bargaining table directly
any longer. By mid-May Greece's economic condition

continued to deteriorate further, as the depression deepened and tax revenues continued to slide. Despite having made its IMF payment in May, it was estimated Greece would need another 30 to 50 billion euros in loans—on top of rolling over its 2012 remaining debt—or it could not meet another 6.7 billion euro scheduled loan payments due in July and August. In this environment, although excluded from direct bargaining, Varoufakis issued his own 36 page report, "Greece's Recovery: A Blueprint", and went on another Europe tour to Paris, Rome and Brussels in mid-May.[3] The paper reiterated his views, adding a new item proposing the creation of a 'bad bank', to which to offload Greece's debt to give it room to reduce debt payments. A 'bad bank' was a typical alternative already employed by a number of European economies since Scandinavia employed it in the early 1990s. Instead of considering the idea, the Troika used the Varoufakis report to complain to the Syriza government about who was doing its negotiations—its new team under Tsakalatos or still Varoufakis? The Troika feigned confusion and asked Tsipras to clarify.

Varoufakis henceforth would be limited to throwing proposals 'over the negotiations transom' in a vain effort to influence the bargaining as a quasi-outsider. Disunity was growing within the Greek bargaining camp, as opposition also continued to rise within the Syriza party in the Greek Parliament to what was increasingly appearing as a drift toward conceding to the Troika's position by Tsipras and the new team.

Brexit Before Grexit?

In the midst of the foregoing maneuvers, the United Kingdom held its parliamentary elections on May 8, 2015. The candidate for the Conservative party, David Cameron, offered UK voters the opportunity to vote 'yes' or 'no' on a referendum whether to remain in or leave the European Union, if he were elected.

Cameron pushed the referendum vote offer in order to prevent his party being 'outflanked' on the right by the rising UK Independent Party (UKIP), which was an ardent supporter of UK exit from the EU. The UKIP posed a major challenge to the Conservatives, which the latter barely averted. UKIP won more than 3 million votes,13% of the UK popular vote. It also came second in more than 90 of the 650 contested Parliamentary seats, most of them contested against Conservatives who won.

While the referendum would not occur until June 2016, it likely raised awareness within the Troika that perhaps Greece's potential exit was just the tip of an iceberg of growing discontent with Troika policies (and the Euro monetary system itself) within the Eurozone region. The Greeks were suffering the worst consequences of the top-down, Troika, business-banker neoliberal policies. But simmerings of discontent within the working and small business classes were growing elsewhere in Europe as well.

This writer had predicted in July 2013 that the UK would eventually leave the European Union, based on the negative impact of policies of free trade, austerity, and anemic general economic recovery in the UK since 2010 on working class voters' standards of living.[4] This prediction was repeated immediately after Cameron and conservatives won an absolute majority in the May 2015 elections. As noted by this writer at the time, "it is extremely likely that Britain will vote to leave the EU when the referendum is conducted. The question of a referendum is now not whether, but how soon. Initial talk of a date for the referendum was 2017. But it is more likely to occur in 2016, perhaps even before next summer 2016."[5]

The potential relationship between Brexit and a Grexit had both positive and negative implications. Certainly a Brexit would encourage a Grexit, all things equal. However, a Brexit did not involve the question of the common currency, as the UK continued to control its own currency and thus central bank monetary policy unlike Greece. But the UK, so long as it was a member of the European Union free trade zone, continued to run a serious negative trade balance and deficit. The UK did not have to 'borrow' from the Troika in order to offset the goods-trade imbalance with money inflows. But a Brexit, as the UK would discover in 2016 after it did actually vote for it, would reduce the money capital inflows from abroad necessary to maintain a trade balance and stable currency. The British pound would decline sharply as a consequence. The parallel question for Greece is whether a Grexit, and a restoration of its own currency, the drachma, would mean a precipitous fall in that currency. And would the positive effects on Greek exports under a drachma offset the loss of value in bank deposits and wealth of the minority of Greek businesses and investors doing business under the Euro? The political opposition to a Grexit lay largely in those elements of wealthy Greek business elites that benefited from financial and goods flows to the rest of Europe. They were the great gainers from the Euro, while Greek workers, small businesses, family service and tourist companies, were the great losers.

The Troika's 'Final and Best' Offer—June 2015

With the current extended agreement set to expire on June 30, 2015, negotiations entered the 11th hour. Both sides drifted toward submitting their 'best and final offers' to each other. Behind the scenes, the Troika became more unified and brought bigger guns—in the form of Merkel and other heads of state—to the table. Conversely, internal dissension within the Tsipras new bargaining team—and thus disunity over strategy—grew within the Syriza ranks.

The German central bank chief, Weidemann, pushed hard for the ECB to put a hold on further ELA assistance to Greece's central bank and thus Greek banks. The IMF made it clear that it would not participate in a Troika offer because Greece's debt levels were too high and it could never repay. That condition required the IMF to not participate. The German hard liners used that to insist no Troika assistance would occur without the IMF's participation. Merkel, Hollande, and Tsipras remained in communication throughout the early June weeks and Merkel made it clear there was no possibility of a deal without the IMF involvement. Hollande of France supported her position. The Troika was clearly now coordinating its pressure on Greece with government heads. An important milestone was the meeting of Troika and German-French and other national leaders—including Merkel and Holland—in Berlin in early June. Tsipras and the Greeks were uninvited. From this emerged the Troika 'final and best offer'.

Labor market 'reforms' involving pension cuts, minimum wages, limits on union collective bargaining, ease in enacting mass layoffs, public employment, and the like were all high on its agenda. The Troika proposed no changes in minimum wages, layoffs, or union bargaining without the consent of its monitors. It demanded pension cuts amounting to 1.8 billion euros. This meant ending early retirement and reversing the Greek government's prior restoration in February of the '13th month' pension bonus for the poorest pensioners receiving less than 700 euros a month, a poverty level benefit. Pensioners would also have to pay more for healthcare. The slowing pace of privatizations was also singled out for reversal as a priority demand; the

Troika called for an expediting of sales of ports, airports and railroad systems. Also at issue was how much of a primary budget surplus Greece would have to target: The Troika proposed 1% in 2015, rising in steps to 2%, 3%, and to 3.5% by 2018. The VAT was yet another item of major contention in the negotiations—the Troika calling for a VAT equivalent to 1% of GDP in 2015, which required ending exemptions and standardizing the tax at 23% for most items and a second tier VAT at 11% for food and medicine. It also demanded the end of exemption from the VAT for the Greek islands, for whom tourism was critical.

The Troika was especially disturbed by the Syriza government's partial reversal of austerity measures since assuming office in February. And although Syriza had backtracked on some of the austerity reversals since February, those partial concessions were not sufficient to satisfy it. Troika hardliners in particular demanded reinstatement of all the austerity measures called for in the 2012 deal associated with pensions and other labor market reforms, as well as faster privatizations, as a pre-condition for releasing loans to Greece. As Syriza pointed out repeatedly, Greece had implemented since August 2014 more than $17 billion in loan payments to the Troika through austerity cuts and selling government bonds in the private market—while the Troika had disbursed no loans at all during that period even though they too were called for under the debt agreement.

Just as the Troika had made it a 'quid pro quo' for Greece to agree to extend the 2012 agreement beyond February 28 as a condition of future discussions and negotiations, the Syriza government might have made it a similar 'quid pro quo' demand to the Troika for it to release the scheduled funds, called for under the same agreement, as a condition of future negotiations. But it didn't. And that too weakened its bargaining position, signaling to the Troika it could likely successfully squeeze more concessions from Greece without having to abide by the terms of the 2012 agreement itself. For Greece to have issued its own such 'quid pro quo' it would have had to be prepared to embrace the possibility of Grexit, instead of repeatedly denying it to the Troika. And that possibility was 'off the table' from the start.[6]

Opposition within Syriza and its slim parliamentary majority intensified, as it became evident the Troika was increasingly intent on implementing many of the old austerity measures. The rise of what was called a 'Left Platform' faction of about 30 members of parliament, consolidating around the Lafanzanis group, demanded Tsipras stop payments to the Troika and come up with an alternative plan. The internal opposition intensified further when the Troika, following the Berlin meeting, released its 'final and best' offer, which was interpreted by the Greeks as a kind of 'ultimatum'. The internal opposition grew to around 40 members of parliament.

The growing pressure from the Troika, on the one hand, and internal pressure from the Left Platform group, on the other, translated into Tsipras assuming contradictory positions: in Greece in presentations to Parliament and speeches to the Greek public he assumed aggressive positions with strong anti-Troika rhetoric. However, he simultaneously tried to ensure the Troika publicly and privately that there would be a deal.

In an article in the major French newspaper, Le Monde, in early June Tsipras pointed out how Greek negotiators had just a day before submitted a 47-page proposal that agreed to "move forward" on privatizations despite Greece's concerns, "to implement the major VAT reforms" the Troika proposed, to raise other taxes, "to implement a major reform of the social security system" and raise the retirement age.

Tsipras also noted the Greek proposal agreed to end '13 month' bonuses, cut pensions still further, and that Greece had "accepted to implement labor reforms after consultation with the International Labor Office" in Geneva.[7]

At home, however, Tsipras assumed a 'hard line', calling the Troika's final offer "absurd", "unrealistic", "irrational", and "a step backwards" from the previous positions of the negotiations by the Troika (now called the 'Brussels Group') and Greece. In his speech to Parliament, Tsipras admitted he was unpleasantly surprised by the Troika's official final offer proposals following its Berlin meeting. He was disappointed that the Troika apparently interpreted Greece's previous concessions as a sign of weakness. But in negotiations, repeated concessions by one party, amidst refusal by the other to make any concessions of significance in return, always results in the perception by the aggressive party that its bargaining opponent is weak. And that perception and conclusion always invites greater hardening of positions in the negotiations. What is surprising is that Tsipras was surprised. Tsipras considered the Troika backtracking and ultimatum final offer as either "a bad moment for Europe or a bad negotiating tactic" and believed "those who came up with it will soon retract it". But whose Europe? And 'bad tactic' for whom? For the Troika's Europe and for the Troika's negotiators the backtracking and ultimatum was producing results.

Tsipras concluded his speech by calling on the Parliamentary opposition to express its view of the Troika's proposals, to accept or reject it—in effect calling for a rejection which would provide him the necessary 'left cover' to resume negotiations. He then summarized the remaining, unresolved issues still on the bargaining table—at least in his view if not the Troika's. In his view, they were: the final primary budget surplus figure; the restructuring of the debt with a 'haircut'; protection of pensions and real wages; redistribution of income in favor of the social majority (i.e. taxes on the wealthy who have been avoiding paying their fair share since 2010); reinstatement of collective bargaining and reversal of deregulated labor relations with involvement of the ILO; and a strong investment program for Greece. These were the basis of Greece's forthcoming 'final position'. He ended his speech will a militant declaration that "the Greek government will not bow to unreasonable demands" and assuring all that patience and perseverance in negotiations "will soon bear fruit" and he was "confident that we will succeed".[8]

The speech was not well received by the Troika. Its previously most 'sympathetic wing', the EC, responded with a rebuke of Tsipras by its president, Jean-Claude Juncker. Eurozone social democrats chimed in. If Syriza thought left-leaning social democratic elements would accept Greece's argument that the crisis was not just Greece's but all of Europe struggling to deal with neoliberal policies, he was mistaken. That was yesterday's Europe, not the Europe of the June 2015 negotiations.

Greece's Interim 'Final' Offer

Greece's official 47-page offer in early June already differed significantly from the Troika's on all the major issues of contention—primary budget surplus, VAT, pensions, labor market reforms and privatizations. Its budget surplus proposal was a 0.75% surplus in 2015, rising to 1.5% and 2.5%—well below the Troika's 1% to 3.5%. Its VAT was only 6.5% for medicine, 11% for food, water and energy, and 23% for all other. And exemptions for the islands continued. For pensions, it proposed raising the retirement age to 62 over a decade, while keeping the provisions for the poorest retirees.[9] For collective bargaining, it proposed ILO standards in effect for other European countries; for minimum wage, a one year delay and then restoration to pre-2010 levels; and for privatizations, a euro value of 3.2 billion of sales in 2015-16 and 2.1 billion more by 2020—far less than the Troika's goal of 22 billion euros in privatization sales by 2020.[10]

The Troika's response was that Greece's final offer differed from a private understanding it had with Tsipras the week before. The IMF broke off negotiations and its representatives flew home. Germany began drawing up contingency plans for a Grexit. A scheduled June 18 finance ministers meeting was generally acknowledged as the 'last chance' for a deal.

In a weakly veiled attempt to influence the June 18 meeting, on that same day a new twist—and concession—was offered by Varoufakis. The new twist was called the Independent Fiscal Council. Without stating who would sit on the council, the proposal averred it would function as an 'automatic deficit break', monitoring the Greek budget on a weekly basis. And if Greek government spending or austerity reversals exceeded a primary budget target, it would automatically trigger across the board reductions in all programs and spending. It purported to offer a 'safety valve' for the Troika to ensure Greece would not reverse austerity beyond a certain level. In other words, Greece would abide by the austerity measures, deciding which to implement or reverse, but would be strictly limited in doing so. Varoufakis envisioned that debt buybacks and new loans would accompany the Fiscal Council idea, as well as would a massive investment program funded by the European Investment Bank, the EC's proposed Juncker Plan calling for investment in infrastructure, and the establishment of a Greek development bank. Like virtually all previous

Varoufakis' proposals, it wasn't even considered by the Troika. The idea of a European Investment bank and the Juncker Plan had been shelved long ago by the Troika. And the Troika was not about to allow Greece any leeway in deciding what austerity programs it would adjust or change according to some budget surplus number.

What the Varoufakis proposal did achieve, however, was to create more confusion as to what was the Greek position officially—i.e. was it the early June 47-page document, Tsipras' speech to Parliament, or Varoufakis's latest? Troika hardliners jumped on the situation as indicating lack of serious negotiating and the unreliability of what the Greek government was really proposing.

The June 18 finance ministers meeting in Luxembourg failed to reach an agreement with Greece. A 1.5 billion euro payment to the IMF on June 30 loomed, with Greece announcing it didn't have the funds. The EC called for a general summit of all Eurozone heads of state and finance ministers. Tsipras attended a business conference in Russia, his second visit in June.[11] Meanwhile, withdrawals from Greek banks accelerated, more than 1.5 billion euros on June 19 and 5 billion euros during the week. To prevent a bank run, the ECB increased ELA to Greek banks. Tsipras signaled Greece would make further concessions at the upcoming EU summit, after discussing with his cabinet and then Merkel, Hollande, and EC head, Juncker, by phone.

On the 22nd of June Greece made further concessions, including higher taxes and more limits on pensions, raising the retirement age to 67 and ending early retirement, but no direct pension cuts in 2015-16. Its proposal amounted to a 2015 budget surplus of 1.5%, the figure proposed by the Troika, with an even greater number than the Troika's (2.9% surplus) for 2016. Greece agreed to the Troika's major proposals concerning the VAT, including ending the islands' exemption, except for the tax rate on electricity. Additional taxes were included in the package as well. But Greece held off on the further pension and wage cuts demanded by the Troika, as well as other labor reforms, and added that the concessions required a promise of debt relief as well. The total package amounted to approximately 7.9 billion euros, the majority of which, however, consisted of higher tax revenues.

The initial response by the Troika was positive. Jeroen Dijsselbloem, chair of the finance ministers, described the offer as "a basis to really restart the talks." EC commission president, Juncker, declared "I am convinced that we will come to a final agreement in the course of this week." European Council President, Donald Tusk, called it "a positive step forward." But the Troika hardliners had not yet been heard from. German Chancellor Merkel more cautiously added "There's still a lot of work to be done." Wolfgang Schauble ominously declared he had seen nothing really new, "beyond many trying to create expectations which are not supported by substance." IMF director, Largarde, replied "we are not at all at the end of the route".

The Troika hardliners—Schauble, Largarde, and allies—gathered their forces and just hours before the June 24 finance ministers meeting submitted a five page counter-proposal to Greece's position. Lagarde considered the Greek proposals insufficient for a disbursement of IMF funds and, without the IMF, there was no deal, according to the Germans. The Germans also unequivocally ruled out any debt relief as part of a deal, and wanted the majority of the surplus achieved by means of spending cuts, not tax increases. The hardliners literally crossed out provisions in Greece's proposals, calling for a reduction in taxes for businesses proposed by Greece and for more cuts in pensions—including for the poorest pensioners—and higher sales taxes in lieu of higher corporate taxes. Cuts in public workers' wages were added back in. And, adding further insult to injury, Germany insisted Greece's parliament must approve the hard liners' proposals in toto, as is, before June 30, which meant in just four days.

At an EU summit on the 25th, both Merkel and Hollande pressured Tsipras privately to accept what they called the Troika's "generous" offer. An additional 'carrot', they promised, would be the release of 15.5 billion euros funding in four installments through November 2015—i.e. just about the amount Greece would have to pay the Troika in loan payments coming due. Greece was told it had to accept the deal before the following Monday, June 29. It had a choice to "take it or leave it". The Troika would await Greece's reply over the weekend.

The Road to Referendum

Tripras' response to what he called Troika 'blackmail' and an attempt 'to humiliate the Greek people'—and to what appears to have been a thinly-veiled Troika hardliners' attempt to provoke Greece into an exit—was to announce Greece would hold a referendum on the Troika's latest 'take it or leave it' offer on July 5, 2015. The announcement caused little concern within the Troika.

There had always been a significant faction within the Troika, led by Wolfgang Schauble, to have Greece exit the Eurozone. It had been one of Schauble's suggestions as far back as the 2012 debt restructuring negotiations. In the 2015 negotiations, the Troika had gone further and had undertaken studies of the effects of a Grexit and what steps in the event of a Grexit the rest of the Eurozone should take. During 2015 the Troika was not reluctant to communicate to Greece that the Troika was prepared for a Grexit if it occurred and was not intimidated by such. As in 2012, moreover, Schauble and others suggested it might be acceptable. In a thinly veiled suggestion of Grexit, Schauble would raise the possibility of a 'time out' for Greece; step out of the Euro system for a period then Greece could later decide if it wanted to re-enter. Of course, re-entry would be subject to Troika approval, which was highly unlikely. Once out, the potential way back in was not likely to happen.

The Syriza government did not take Schauble's 'bait', however. The eventual referendum vote was not about Grexit. With Greek public opinion against Grexit, which it interpreted as 'leaving Europe', Tsipras was not about to take the risk of actually proposing a Grexit. It would, however, try to bluff the Troika that it might consider same despite all its declarations to the contrary during previous negotiations. However, it proved an unconvincing tactical move. The Troika called Syriza's bluff. Even stymied it, in advance.

Given the majority public opposition to a Grexit within Greece, the even stronger Greek business opposition, Syriza's slim parliamentary majority and opposition parties, especially New Democracy, waiting in the wings, and the wording of the referendum that ensured the referendum was not at all about Grexit, Syriza was forced to draft the referendum to address accepting or rejecting the Troika's 'last offer'. Rejecting that offer by referendum, Syriza calculated, would give the Tsipras bargaining team one more 'card' to play in the otherwise weak bargaining hand it held. It was to be a message to the Troika, 'see, the Greek people cannot stand austerity any longer, so please give Greece some respite, Troika'. But the Troika didn't care about relieving pressure on Greece. It cared only about ensuring bankers and investors would continue to receive principal and interest payments on Greek debt.

Tsipras and his negotiating team may have thought they were going to get an agreement on June 22nd—and therefore would not have to hold the threatened referendum—based on prior assurances from the EC leaders like Juncker, Djisselbloem, Tusk, and from social democrats like Hollande. But the EC wing of the Troika quickly fell in line behind the German-IMF hardliners two days later when the latter regrouped on the 25th and reasserted demands for still more austerity concessions despite Greece's major concessions on the 22nd. Reportedly, Schauble and the hardliners chastised Juncker and the EC for suggesting a deal was possible to Greece based on its June 22 proposals. The EC quickly backtracked. The events of 22nd to the 25th revealed clearly who calls the shots in the Eurozone—the hardliners, not the remnants and political residue of what was once European social democracy. And now the hardliners had once again asserted their firm control of the bargaining agenda.

There was wide speculation on how the Troika might respond to the referendum call. In 2011 a previous attempt by socialist PASOK leader Papandreou to call a similar referendum in response to Troika austerity cuts had led to his ouster and replacement by a Troika-approved technocrat. Would the Troika, with the help of its pro-Euro opposition party friends within the Greek parliament, now attempt the same? The pro-Troika New Democracy party, and what remained of the PASOK and other smaller pro-Euro parties, quickly jumped on Tsipras and Syriza for announcing the referendum. On the other hand, the referendum quelled for the moment the rising discontent and opposition within Syriza with the concessions that were made to the Troika.

Had the Syriza government worded the referendum as not only a rejection of the Troika's insulting and hard-nosed 'final offer' but as a vote as well to Grexit, it might have provided the Syriza team some real bargaining leverage. Or, it might have strengthened the Troika hardliners position and resulted in a Troika ultimatum to exit. But such questions remain a 'what if' since the referendum was cautiously worded as a rejection off the last offer.

The referendum was specifically worded as follows: "*Should the proposal which was submitted by the European Commission, the European Central Bank and the International Monetary Fund at the Eurogroup of June 25, 2015, which consists of two parts that together constitute their comprehensive proposal, be accepted?*"

The Troika knew already a majority of Greeks opposed the terms of the concessions and austerity. They didn't need a plebiscite to inform them. Their concern was not Greek public opinion. So the referendum as a vote on their last offer, should it pass, changed nothing in so far as their willingness to amend their 'final offer'.

So why did Tsipras and Syriza go forward with it nonetheless, since surely Tsipras should have grasped by now that appeals to the heart or conscience of the Troika would be useless? Perhaps it was a way to allow the Greek people to 'let off steam' and their frustration at not seeing any gains after months of negotiations on austerity concessions and debt relief. Perhaps all it intended to achieve was to allow Tsipras and Syriza say to the Greek people, 'See, we did all we could and you, the Greek people said to the Troika what we've been saying all along, and they just don't care. If the Troika won't listen to the will of an entire nation, there's not much more we, the Greek negotiating team and government can do. We fought the best fight we could, short of Grexit, and we now can only submit to the Troika's superior forces'.

In retrospect it appears that both sides, Troika and Syriza, made tactical errors in the final meetings before the referendum. The Troika made a 'final offer' so onerous and demanding that it enflamed Greek national pride.[12] For the Syriza government, the error was to formulate a vote so weakly worded that it might ensure a majority rejection of the Troika's last position, but which posed no threat to a Troika that cared little about Greek public opinion and was not about to change its position regardless of the vote. Given its wording and Tsipras's constant assurance there would be no Grexit, the referendum was doomed from the beginning as a tactic to try to get the Troika to soften its 'last and final' offer.[13]

The decision to hold the referendum meant Greece would not meet the scheduled $1.8 billion debt payment deadline of June 30 to the IMF. Nor was it certain that the ECB would continue to add incremental increases of ELA loans to Greece's central bank to keep the Greek banks afloat in the interim. If deposit withdrawals continued to accelerate, some form of credit controls to stop the outflow would be needed. Greek bank withdrawals since November already totaled about a third of all bank deposits, or about 50 billion euros.

The US at this point intervened more directly, with Obama and US Treasury Secretary Jack Lew contacting Merkel and Tsipras. The Obama administration wanted some kind of compromise, whereby Greece might be given some debt relief and space in which to stimulate its economy.

In response to the US and other pressures, on the 27th Greek Finance Minister Varoufakis issued a statement indicating that if the Troika extended further loans, it would apply the funds exclusively to financing upcoming debt payments. Greece then requested an extension of the current debt deal for some short term period. This effort too was rejected, as Merkel ruled out any further negotiations until after the July 5 referendum. Not surprisingly, the ECB announced the following day, June 28, it would halt extending the ELA to Greek banks despite a request by Tsipras that it continue until July 5. At this point, facing a bona fide run on its banks, Greece announced its banks would close until after the July 5 referendum and it further imposed controls on withdrawals of over 60 euros at a time. The Greek stock market closed until after July 5 as well.

Troika leaders and Eurozone media mounted a major campaign to influence the vote outcome, not unlike what they had mounted during the Greek elections in 2012 to ensure Syriza's defeat in the parliamentary elections of that year. Syriza's erstwhile 'friend' in the Troika, EC president Jean-Claude Juncker, attacked Tsipras and Syriza in personal terms. Juncker and the Troika went so far as to publicly report, on Greek media, that the Troika's final offer did not propose pension cuts. Within Greece, the pro-Euro parties argued a 'No' vote meant catastrophe; their message was aggressively promoted by Greek TV and media owned by Greek oligarchs who had moved most of their liquid funds out of Greece in the preceding months.

In a letter to the ECB and IMF on July 2, before the referendum vote was even held, Tsipras signaled once again that Greece might accept more concessions if it were part of a two year debt funding agreement and if small changes were made by the Troika in its positions on pensions and taxes. The desperate move to return to the bargaining table only strengthened the Troika's resolve and was again outright rejected. Tsipras subsequently appeared on Greek TV that evening to clarify that a 'No' vote in the upcoming referendum did not mean Grexit but a 'No' vote would improve his bargaining position with the Troika after the vote—a highly dubious point, particularly in view of his clarification.

The IMF next entered the debate with a study indicating Greece would now need 60 billion euros more in new loans over the next three years. It concluded comprehensive debt relief was now needed in the form of extending debt payments from the current 20 to 40 years. But it put full blame on Syriza for the worsening situation, aggravated in particular by the events leading up to, and including, the referendum. The other major development of July 4 was the reported preparations that were begun by the ECB together with Greece's central bank to introduce what was called a 'bail-in', in which depositors with more than 8,000 euros would have to pay to bail out the Greek banks with a 'haircut' of 30% of the value of their deposits. Depositors with balances of more than 100,000 euros had already largely withdrawn their funds. [14]

Referendum and Fallout

The referendum turned out a strong 61% 'No' vote to reject the Troika's last and final offer. Not surprisingly, after the referendum the Troika issued another ultimatum, instead of hurrying back to the bargaining table to make concessions—as Varoufakis repeatedly declared, against all precedent, would happen. As a strong sign to the Troika of his willingness to agree to further concessions, Tsipras fired Varoufakis from all his roles as finance minister shortly after the referendum vote and replaced him with Euclid Tsakalotos. The Troika announced Greece had just two days, until Thursday, to develop another comprehensive proposal, with the necessary additional concessions implied. As EC president Donald Tusk put it in a press conference on July 7th: "I have to say loud and clear the final deadline ends this week". Tsipras was told to submit a more detailed list of austerity commitments and request a two year loan program. All 28 of the European Union heads of state would then meet in an emergency summit on the weekend to consider same.

Relying on pro-European opposition parties—New Democracy, PASOK, and others—Tsipras obtained approval by the Greek parliament for new concessions on austerity to submit to the Troika on July 9.

As a harbinger of things to soon come, Tsipras addressed the European Parliament and reported Greece had requested a bailout from the EC's Stability Mechanism Fund and promised to begin implementing Troika pension and tax measures by the following Monday, July 12. The latest concessionary proposal by Greece adopted virtually all the Troika's June 24th positions: in a 13 page list of concessions, Greece agreed to raise its budget surplus target in 2015 from 0.74% to the 1% demanded by the Troika.[15] The 23% VAT was imposed on the islands and on restaurants, as per the Troika. The Greek proposal for a one-time 12% corporate tax on large businesses was dropped and new yet undefined taxes agreed to in the event of a 'fiscal shortfall'. Pension benefits were cut for the poorest retirees and the retirement age raised to 67 faster. Collective bargaining would be deregulated, as demanded by the Troika from the beginning of negotiations. The only item of minor change was Greece's proposal to cut military spending by 300 million euros in 2015-16, instead of 400 million in 2016. Debt relief was left vague, but it was understood it would not mean a 'haircut' but instead would take the form of extending loan maturities, lowering interest rates, and brief moratoria on rates. Greece would get 60 billion more euros of debt, in exchange for the austerity measures essentially demanded by the Troika hardliners.

Tsipras had accepted almost in toto the same provisions the Greek people had rejected less than a week earlier. His assurances at the time that a 'No' referendum would strengthen his hand in negotiations had totally failed to materialize. But the Greek people had not voted 'No' just to "strengthen his hand"—but to indicate that they wanted

Syriza *to oppose the acceptance of such measures.* In the fabled originating country of democracy, the will of the Greek people no longer mattered.

True to past form, Germany and allied hardliners did their best to prevent the European Union summit over the weekend from agreeing to Greece's latest concessions—in effect their own proposals. Led by Schauble, they demanded that Greece transfer 50 billion euros of state-owned assets into a trust fund to be managed by the Troika, with which to pay down debt. Either that, Schauble argued, or Greece should take a five-year 'time out' from the Eurozone—a kind of backdoor expulsion of Greece from the Eurozone, completely nullifying any Greek threat to use Grexit as a bargaining chip. A 'Grexit' German style! Tsipras' latest concessions were framed as the basis for continuing negotiations (and further concessions), according to the IMF and EC. Greece had yet again been lured into making concessions without achieving any final agreement, or any stop to the negotiating process during which it continued to lose ground. After all, continuing negotiations had worked for the Troika so many times before over the course of the past five months. Its excuse for 'more' was that the referendum and delays by Greece had worsened the economic situation, thereby requiring still more austerity. If Greece wanted debt relief, now called 'reprofiling,' in the form of extending payment periods and reducing interest rates, it would have to agree to still more austerity.

After the July 7-12 concessions by Syriza and Tsipras, it was all downhill in their efforts to bargain. A rear-guard action, a 'mopping up operation' by the Troika, released just enough loans to repay itself the previous loans coming due on July 20 and in August 2015. Capitulation had in effect already occurred. What remained were the details defining the final scope and magnitude of Syriza and Tsipras's collapse and capitulation.

The Troika hardliners, now joined by Merkel and Germany's other dependent small eastern European allies, hid behind charges of 'loss of trust' in Greece as the excuse for squeezing Greece's negotiators still further in coming weeks. But Greece, and Tsipras in particular, had lost much of the will to fight and to take on neoliberal Europe now run by German and northern Europe core bankers, investors, and their political and bureaucratic elites.

Perhaps the interview of Tsipras in the *Financial Times* that appeared July 11, 2015 sums up much of what had transpired to that date. In reply to an interviewer's reminder of Tsipras' activities as a youthful student radical years earlier in his career, Tsipras replied he was surprised at his youthful level-headedness. He added, reflecting on more recent events, "If you start a struggle, it's very important to know when to stop"…"If you don't have the feeling of winning—if you have the feeling of defeat—it's very difficult to fight again."[16] Nor would he again. Greek resistance to neoliberal Europe had been stopped in its tracks. With its elected leaders no longer having the will the fight, the Greek people found little sense in doing so themselves—at least until new developments took place and/or a more resolved contender appeared to lead again.

Why Tsipras and Syriza employed the strategy and tactics they did in their attempt to confront the Troika in the 2015 debt negotiations is a question that demands close analysis. Why Tsipras decided to undertake the referendum vote, get the support of the Greek people, and then immediately within hours give in to all the Troika's austerity demands, remains one of the great political anomalies of the third Greek debt negotiations.

There would be no lack of interpretations for why Tsipras and a majority of the Syriza leadership undertook the 'about face' they did. Those interpretations will be addressed in the concluding chapter. But the abrupt reversal was not the end of capitulation; only the beginning. The Syriza government would backpedal and concede to still more Troika demands and austerity measures over the course of the subsequent year—in a political journey from initial capitulation in July 2015 to eventual transformation to a junior partner in the Eurozone's Troika-administered neoliberal regime.

Endnotes

1   The inversion of logic and reversal of cause and effect relationships of variables is often the stuff upon which economic 'ideology' is based, not economic science. For a deeper analysis of how ideology in economics works, see Jack Rasmus, *'Applications of Ideology in Economic Policy'*, CRITIQUE, vol. 37, 2009.

2   Yanis Varoufakis, *'A New Deal for Greece'*, Project Syndicate, April 25, 2015.

3   Yanis Varoufakia, *'A Blueprint for Greece's Recovery'*, May 16, 2015

4   Jack Rasmus, *'Predicting the US and Global Economic Recovery'*, Z Magazine, July 2013

5   Jack Rasmus, *'Enter Stage Right (Brexit) and Left (Grexit)'*, TelesurTV, May 20, 2015

6   Even if Greece and Syriza had no intention of Grexit, it should never have indicated such so emphatically and repeatedly. Doing so denied it a major source of leverage in negotiations. It was likely concerned that advocating the threat of Grexit would strengthen the hand of the Troika hard liners and undermined what it, Greece, thought were its soft-line supporters within the EC. No doubt those EC sources strongly encouraged Tsipras and Syriza not to do so in order not to undermine their efforts to check the Schaubles and their hard line allies.

7   Tsipras, *'Europe at Crossroads'*, Le Monde, as reported in *Hellenic Republic*, June 3, 2015. Concerning pension cuts, they would come after previous benefit reductions of 20% to 48% since 2010 and despite 45% of Greek pensioners living under the poverty level and another 23% with living standards near poverty, according to data from Eurostat.

8   Alexis Tsipras, *Speech to the Greek Parliament*, June 9, 2015

9   The Troika's proposal was to raise the retirement age to 67, so Greece

was suggesting willingness to compromise at some point between the current 60 years (in some cases) and the Troika's 67.

10   Since 2010 about 25 billion euros in privatization sales had occurred, about half the 50 billion called for in the 2012 debt deal.

11   No agreements or potential loans from Russia were officially announced following Tsipras's meetings with Russia. It is unlikely that Putin was willing to aggravate his tenuous relationships with Germany's Merkel and its importance for bigger issues for Russia by taking sides in the Troika v. Greece negotiations. Nor was China, which was involved in the preliminary bidding for the privatization of Greece's major port of Pireaus under the previous Greek government.

12   Alternatively, perhaps its offer was the product of the Schauble hard-liners faction that wanted to force Greece to precipitate an exit.

13   The Syriza referendum was, to use an analogy, like putting a vote to a union membership in a collective bargaining scenario, to reject management's last offer but not to strike if it, management, refused to come back to the bargaining table and discuss further changes. Rejecting a final offer without taking a strike (Grexit) vote in the process fools no one and is doomed to failure.

14   Kevin Hore, 'Greek Banks Prepare Plan to Raid Deposits to Avert Financial Collapse', *Financial Times,* July 4, 2015, p. 1.

15   Since Greece was now deep in depression again and thus forecast to have a -3.5 deficit in 2015, the 1% amounted to agreeing to a 4.5% budget cutting.

16   'Person in the News', *Financial Times*, July 11, 2015, p. 7.

Chapter Nine

SYRIZA
TAMED

The additional austerity concessions demanded by the Troika on July 12 and agreed to by Tsipras did not constitute a new—third—debt agreement. They were simply demands made by the Troika as a precondition just to start negotiations on a third debt restructuring agreement. If Greece did not first agree to all the Troika's demands in principle, the Troika said it would not even sit down to discuss anything.

Agreeing to its July 12 demands were, as German Chancellor Merkel noted, necessary *to begin* restoring Troika trust that Greece would indeed implement the austerity measures. That meant Greece's Parliament would first have to pass legislation and implement the austerity concessions, not just agree in principle to do so. The Troika's representatives made it clear that no negotiations on debt relief would begin until a third debt deal was negotiated, officially signed off, and legislated.   As the Troika publicly announced, debt relief in any form would thereafter only be "considered", and only "if necessary", but in any event not undertaken until the Troika's first review of Greece's implementation of the measures. That would not happen until November 2015 at the earliest. And of course 'debt relief' per the Troika's view did not mean 'haircuts' or any reduction of total debt levels. At best it meant maybe stretching out the terms of the loans, reducing interest on them, or a short moratorium on interest payments by Greece.

At each 'phase' of negotiations, from July 12 through the end of 2015, Greece would be pressured to agree to additional austerity measures. The Troika always set 'milestones' for Greece to meet. If it missed them, or if the Greek economy deteriorated further in the interim, further austerity measures were sought. Austerity negotiations would thus never really conclude. They were more or less continuous. They were more like *dictats*, where the dominant party—in this case the Troika—told the weaker, Greece, what it had to do as the Troika repeatedly 'moved the goalposts', holding out and dangling the possibility of disbursing loans only if Greece agreed to and implemented the further austerity measures.

On July 20 Greece needed immediately, at minimum, a 7 billion euros new loan to meet a debt payment deadline to the ECB, plus another 12 billion euros for a subsequent payment in late August. Smaller debt payments and deadlines followed. About 30 billion in total was required for the remainder of 2015 for debt and interest payments, once the IMF and other private European investor and bank payments were included. The 30 billion did not include additional funds needed to recapitalize (i.e. bail out) the Greek banks, estimated as at least 25 billion euros. In total, approximately 86 billion euros ($98 billion) was estimated to be needed in a third debt restructuring.[1]

In a report issued on July 14, the IMF publicly declared that even this amount was insufficient. Greek debt is unsustainable, according to the report. Greece could never repay it. And the IMF, per its rules, could not lend if the debt load was considered unsustainable. IMF rules and the issue of sustainability rule functioned as the IMF's 'hammer' with which to drive debt negotiations in the direction it sought: both to pressure the rest of the Troika to include some form of debt relief, and to force Greece to accept still more austerity.

Greece as an Emerging 'Economic Protectorate'

The 2015 debt agreement represented an escalation of the Troika's austerity demands imposed on Greece. This was perhaps best reflected in Schauble's 11th hour last, bitterest pill to be added to the Troika's demanded concessions. It required the establishment of a 50 billion euro privatization trust fund to be financed from the sale of Greek government assets—i.e. ports, airports, railroad systems, utility systems, etc. This privatization fund was to be administrated by the Troika, and located in Luxembourg. Effectively, the 50 billion euro trust fund was a new kind of institutional arrangement enabling the Troika to directly administer the Greek economy. Not only that, Troika administrators would now be given the power to oversee and approve fiscal expenditures in Greece at all levels of the Greek government, including local. And as predicted, the prospect of instituting 'bail-ins', in which Greek citizens' bank deposits might be accessed to pay debt and interest to the Troika or to stabilize Greek banks if the Greek government balked at making the debt payments, raised its ugly head.

By means of such measures, the Troika was in effect profoundly transforming Greece, turning it into a kind of 'Economic Protectorate', and indeed, proposing to steal from individual Greek depositors who bore no individual responsibility for debts arising as a result of the increasing debt resulting from the ongoing debt negotiation process. The original 1999 EU treaty had already removed Greek sovereignty over its banking system. The treaty also put a lid on fiscal discretionary policies for all Eurozone member states and, in Greece's case, imposed a much lower lid to be defined by the budget surplus number. For Greece, however, the creation of the trust fund, the direct management and, if necessary, veto of government expenditures by Troika on-site representatives, and the right to raid depositors' accounts represented a significant deepening of Troika control of the Greek economy. The Eurozone experiment was thus evolving toward even greater centralization of economic control at the expense of economic sovereignty in the case of Greece, and boded the same for other Euro periphery economies as a result of the precedents set in Greece. The increasing loss of economic sovereignty reflected a parallel loss of Greek political sovereignty and representative government. A loss of political autonomy was required to ensure implementation of Troika economic demands.

Party Restructuring as a Precondition for Economic Restructuring

After the initial capitulation of July 12, the Syriza party and the Greek government began a transformation prefatory to the politico-economic loss of autonomy. Syriza had to be institutionally tamed to ensure the Troika's desired results. On July 12 only its leaders and bargaining team had been 'defanged'. Syriza as a political party had challenged the neoliberal Troika arrangements before July 12 and therefore it had to be restructured to function as a junior partner in Troika neoliberal policy.

The firing of Yanis Varoufakis after the referendum vote was a harbinger of things to come. On July 22 Tsipras then discharged other left-wing members of his cabinet who were growing increasingly opposed to the capitulation and austerity concessions Tsipras and his chief negotiator, Takalotos, had agreed to on July 12.

To ensure passage of the required legislation approv-ing the Troika's July 12 demands, Tsipras then split the voting on the measures into two separate Parliamentary votes. A first vote on July 15 addressed tax, budget, and pension austerity measures. Another vote on July 22 addressed farmers, banks and courts. In both cases, a significant percentage of Syriza members, coalescing around the 'Left Platform' faction—i.e. some 36-39 members of Parliament—voted against the Tsipras legislation. Only around 123-126 or so of Syriza members approved the Troika measures, less than the 151 majority needed to pass. But Syriza Tsipras loyalists were joined by their former pro-Euro, pro-Troika party opponents in New Democracy and others to pass the legislation.

Discontent and opposition within the party grew. The Left Platform demanded a debate. They asked, why did Tsipras and the party not consider nationalizing the banks during the recent negotiations to prevent the ECB from squeezing Greek banks and preventing deposit withdrawals and capital flight out of the country? Why did the Syriza government keep paying the Troika debt and interest from February, when the Troika kept refusing, since the previous summer 2014, to distribute any funds as required by the old agreement that was extended? Why did Syriza and Tsipras have no 'Plan B' after the referendum, which the Troika clearly had?[2]

Facing growing opposition and a risk to the passage of a final debt agreement that was required before August 20, in early August Tsipras announced a Special Party Congress would be held in September to approve special rules that allowed the current Syriza leadership to choose which party members might stand for election to represent the party in new national elections set for later that month. This was a party purge in the making.

The Third Debt Deal of August 2015

In parallel, in late July and early August, the Tsipras negotiators continued to bargain with the Troika on the content of a final debt deal. A new Memorandum of Understanding agreement (MOU) on the third debt restructuring was reached between the Troika and the Greek negotiating team on August 19.[3] Many of the provisions of the 2010 and 2012 agreements were incorporated into the August 19 MOU, as were the various new demands issued by the Troika since February 2015 through the July 12 Troika proposals.

The primary yearly budget surplus required of Greece called for -0.25%, 0.5%, 1.75% and 3.5% from 2015 through 2018. The -0.25% proved not much of debt relief, since Greece's GDP in 2015 collapsed by more than $40 billion, from $235 to $195 billion. Under the MOU taxes were raised significantly. Taxation was raised on farmers, on rents, on property, on income, and the VAT sales tax was broadened (covering more low income groups) to generate 1% of GDP in revenues ($1.7 billion in 2015). Some tax loopholes favoring shipping companies were closed.

Sharp cuts in government spending was required by the MOU, especially in the areas of pensions, health care services, public jobs and wages, and general social welfare services.

The pension reductions included the full implementation of the 2010 and 2012 provisions and repeal of the 2015 partial restoration of pensions enacted by the Syriza Parliament earlier in 2015. Early retirement pensions were reduced as well as the practice of 'grandfathering'.[4] Workers might make contributions to the pension funds but the government contributions were frozen until 2021, as were the 'solidarity grants' or year-end pension supplements, which were to be phased out by 2019. The pension age was raised to 67. But that wasn't all. The MOU indicated "more ambitious steps are required" beyond those identified specifically. The social security program and pensions would be 'rationalized', which typically means cost cutting. Pensions and social security were to be integrated into one fund. The pension reductions targeted a 'savings' of 0.25% of GDP in 2015 and 1% of GDP in 2016 and after—the latter figure equivalent to about $1.8 billion a year.

For health care services, individual contributions were raised to 6%. Hospital visit deductible payments were restored. Hospital cost containment (and thus services reduction) was introduced, along with a new Primary Health Care System. A general Social Welfare Review was launched, with the target of achieving 0.5% of GDP in 'savings' (i.e. reduced spending)—or almost $1 billion—by December 2015.

The earlier Troika demand to cut military spending by $100 million in 2015-16 was not specifically referenced in the MOU. And, in sharp contrast to the social spending cuts, military expenditures actually rose by $500 million in 2015 alone, according to the global research firm, *Trading Economics*.[5]

The fact that pubic jobs and wages reductions would result was obscured. The MOU spoke of 150,000 'employment support schemes' to follow, suggesting that the often-noted Troika demand to cut 150,000 public sector jobs was included in the third deal. The 'employment support schemes' were in effect "individualized labor market measures for participants" apparently to assist in job relocation after layoffs. To offset the loss of jobs in part, the MOU called for creating 50,000 part time/temporary jobs for the long term unemployment. For wages, the MOU called for creating a new 'wage grid', with new wage ceilings to be defined by October 2015, the date of the new Greek budget. Thus a lot of the details of the job cuts and wage reductions were left for the Greek government itself to define. What the Troika wanted was an overall reduction of wages as a percent of GDP from 2016-2019. This new objective was to be implemented by June 2016.

Another major section of the MOU addressed the bank bailouts. Twenty-five billion euros at minimum were required to recapitalize (restore losses and withdrawals) the Greek banks. In addition, the massive load of non-performing business loans burdening the banks' balance sheets had to be resolved. The Troika would provide the 25 billion initially to the banks, but that would be added to the overall debt of Greece (the Greek people) to be repaid. Two additional very specific references illustrated the priority given by the Troika to the bank bailout. The Greek parliament could not introduce any fiscal policy, or other policy, that may "undermine the liquidity, solvency, or future viability of the banks". And the government, furthermore, could in no way regulate or any longer interfere with the management and operation of the banks, "which will continue to operate strictly in accordance with market principles". Greece had not only lost its sovereignty over its central bank with the 1999 creation of the Euro and ECB; now in 2015 it lost any semblance of control over its own domestic banking system as well.

Fiscal policy control by Greece's elected government was now all but circumscribed as well. The proposal for a 'Fiscal Council' was added as part of the fiscal reforms embedded in the MOU. Originally proposed by Varoufakis in an attempt to entice Troika lenience by offering it a voice in Greek fiscal decisions, the Fiscal Council now became a vehicle by which the Troika could dominate and veto any fiscal decision as its technical advisers, members of the council, might see fit. The MOU called for special legislation by November 15 to establish the Fiscal Council.

The attack on workers' job rights and union rights

in the MOU assumed the form of the call for an immediate review to strengthen management rights to enact mass layoffs, curbs on industrial actions (e.g. strikes) and limits on union collective bargaining. The specific measures concerning these subjects were to be worked out by Greece in coordination with another European institution, the International Labor Office in Geneva. However, no eventual measures to be defined would be permitted to conflict with the fiscal goals of the MOU.

Other job-related labor market changes included a general Education System Reform to be completed by April 2016, including further rationalizations—i.e. job reductions. And an opening up of the professions, by ending licensing and other restrictions, in order to increase competition for professional jobs and thereby reduce salaries.

A final major element of the MOU addressed privatizations and sales of government assets and public works in order to raise cash. Fifty billion euros was targeted for the Schauble-German-demanded Privatization Fund, added at the last minute by the Troika on July 12. As the MOU stated, "a new independent fund will be stablished ... to manage valuable Greek assets ... under the supervision of the relevant European institutions". Half of the 50 billion fund was earmarked to repay the Troika for its loan to recapitalize the Greek banks "and other assets". The remaining 25 billion had to go to general debt repayment. In other words, three-fourths was earmarked for banks either directly in Greece, or indirectly via distribution from the EC to its Euro bank lenders.

In terms of specific projects, the MOU indicated "by 2015 the authorities will take irreversible steps to privatize the electricity transmission company" as well as "irreversible steps for the sale of the regional airports at the current terms with the winning bidders already selected", as in fact many bidders already had been for a number of public companies under the 2012 privatization program. The sale of the two main ports, Piraeus and Thessaloniki, were to be undertaken by end of October 2015, as were the 20 pending privatizations identified as of July 2015 as well.

The Parliamentary Election of September 20, 2015

Immediately after concluding negotiations on the new debt deal with the Troika, Tsipras announced his resignation and called for new Parliamentary elections on September 20. The Troika immediately announced it would disburse its first loan to Greece in more than a year—a 13 billion euro package provided by the European Stability Mechanism (ESM), and arranged by the Troika. The 13 billion was just sufficient to make the retroactively instituted debt payments to the Troika due in August and for the rest of the year.

A new party based on Syriza's former 'Left Platform' MPs was formed, led by former Syriza minister of energy, Lafanzakis, called the 'Popular Unity'. At first it appeared Popular Unity might ride a wave of discontent with Tsipras and the rest of the 'rump' Syriza now purged of its leftist elements. Greek polls showed 70% of the electorate believed the August 2015 3rd bailout was worse than the previous deals. Other polls showed 79% were disappointed with Tsipras.

But in the snap elections of September 20, Syriza won 35% of the vote. New Democracy came in second with 28%. The voter turnout, at 56% of those eligible to vote, was the lowest in modern Greek history. In terms of Parliamentary seats, Syriza ended up with 145—just 5 short of a simple majority. New Democracy had 75. The rest of the parties, including PASOK, the Communist KKE, and fascist Golden Dawn party won seats in the mid to low teens.

Popular Unity, which called for Grexit, failed to get any seats. Tsipras' purge of the left had succeeded. Syriza could now form a coalition again with the nationalist 'Independent Greeks' to form a government. And New Democracy and other pro-Euro parties would support it on votes involving the Troika's demands.

Following the election, the Troika again and still had not released any funds. It now demanded that the new Greek government first draft and pass a new Budget supporting the August 20 debt deal's austerity measures. In early October Tsipras again addressed the nation. This time his speech sounded like the pro-Troika PASOK and New Democracy governments of the past: Greece needed to recapitalize its bank, reduce its debt, cut spending and raise taxes, and push ahead with austerity while trying to 'soften' it. Growth was predicted around the corner, in the first half of 2016.

A minor tussle between the new government and the Troika emerged in November around the issue of the pending 13 billion euros distribution to recapitalize the banks. The Troika wanted it all directed to cover banks' non-performing business loans; the government wanted some of it directed to aid homeowners' mortgage loans, also non-performing. In the end, 10 billion was allocated to cover business loans and 2 billion to help homeowners avoid foreclosures. Schauble opposed the home-owners assistance, insisting it should all go to bailing out Greek banks' business loans. He remarked, "it doesn't make sense to recapitalize the banks if banking rules don't allow banks to collect their claims".

General Strikes and Grexit

In mid-November a 24-hour general strike occurred. A second followed a couple of weeks later. But by then the damage had been done. The austerity was virtually irreversible. One wonders why such direct action was not called well before, during the events surround July 12, for example, or even in August? Syriza of course would not call for industrial action when it had already capitulated on the political front. Greek unions, it appears, were not sufficiently unified to do so.

Successful general strikes, history shows, require a simple and clear singular demand. That demand could only have been an exit from the Euro. Furthermore, rolling, one day general strikes, such as undertaken by the Greek unions on their own, eventually become an annoyance, resulting in the fading of public support. A sustained general strike, however, is a different matter. But sustaining such a tactic requires political unanimity and Syriza, with its bare majority in Parliament, and its leadership now fragmented and in retreat, was not about to support such direct industrial action.

Could Greek unions have taken the lead in July or August to champion a sustained general strike as part of a Grexit strategy? Not likely either. Like Syriza, Greek unions were faced with the fact that a clear majority of Greeks themselves did not want Grexit. There was insufficient public support for a Grexit throughout the negotiations period. Both Syriza, and the unions, were thus boxed in. A majority of the Greek people—not a massive majority but a majority nonetheless—wanted to be 'European' more than they wanted an end to austerity. Or at least they didn't realize the connection. Put another way, they incorrectly conflated remaining in the Euro currency union as a precondition for being European. Money fetish and national identity had become one and the same. The role of ideology was thus a particularly strong factor. And neither the Syriza party or government, its Tsipras-Varoufakis leadership, or even Greece's unions did much to break the ideological connection and to properly prepare the ground with the voters for a Grexit.

The government passed its 2016 budget in early December 2015, by a slim margin of 153 to 145 votes by Parliament, incorporating most of the Troika's demands. It called for 5.7 billion in public spending cuts, including 1.8 billion from pensions and more than 2 billion euros in tax hikes.

Feints, Rear-Guard Actions, & Longer-Term Agreement

For the next several months, well into 2016, Syriza held onto a slim 3 or 4 MP majority in the Parliament. While the Greek government had agreed in the August MOU to the Troika's various demands and concessions, and provided for the same in its upcoming budget, each of the austerity measures still had to be legislated in order to take effect; specifically more than 48 separate measures were identified in the August MOU. Neither the budget nor MOU were the final act sealing the negotiation. Legislative approval was.

The Syriza government's strategy as it entered 2016 was reduced to trying to delay legislation, when possible, or otherwise tweak and redefine the austerity measures to blunt their effect. By January, about 70% of the 48 measures had been fully implemented, according to Tsipras. That left the remaining 30% around which the Greek government could try to maneuver—sometimes delaying Troika-demanded legislation, other times replacing a spending cut here with a tax hike there, substituting a different interpretation of a section of the MOU, or some other tactical rear guard action.

Resistance to the Troika's proposals for cutting pensions was a prime example of such maneuvering. Although it held only 5% of Greece's total government debt, the IMF insisted on cutting pensions by another third in 2016, even though pensions had been reduced by 40% already since 2011. The IMF had still not officially accepted the August 2015 MOU as sustainable debt arrangements—for reasons associated with debt sustainability noted previously. And an IMF debt payment by Greece was coming due in April-May 2016. Another element of Syriza's new strategy was to interest the Troika in a longer-term comprehensive, multi-year debt agreement extending beyond the current deal's 2018 end date.[6]

In February 2016, the IMF sought to clarify its exceptionally hard-line stance on further cuts to Greek pensions. It argued that in order for Greece to meet its 2018 budget surplus target of 3.5% it would have to cut spending equivalent to 4.5% of GDP and that Greece could not do that without major further cuts to pensions, according to the IMF, insofar as the IMF itself rejected a further raising of income or other taxes to achieve the 4.5% cost reductions. To lower the 3.5% and 4.5% and thereby reduce the need for further massive pension cuts, Greece would have to have significant debt relief, the IMF then argued. But the Germans, as always, would have nothing to do with that. Thus Greece was still caught, as it had always been, between IMF sustainability rules that required either significant debt relief (or more austerity) and the German refusal to budge on the issue of debt relief. Germany ensured this dilemma continued, moreover, by insisting on the inclusion of IMF lending as a precondition for its own lending to Greece, directly or through the EC's new ESM fund.

The IMF, like Greece, was clearly looking for a way out of the German-imposed dilemma. Greece was suggesting a longer term agreement, in exchange for the debt relief that might provide the IMF a way around its rules. But as before, Germany and its conservative allies among the EC finance ministers had tied the negotiations knot tightly and was not about to allow it to unravel.

The IMF's Secret Concerns in Negotiations

In the midst of this scenario, Wikileaks released a transcript on April 2 of a private teleconference in March between IMF Europe representatives on Greek debt and upcoming Greek debt payments of 3.5 billion euros due in July.[7] The secret transcript revealed the frustration of the IMF representatives, caught between the EC and the Greek negotiators. The EC believed the Greek debt was sustainable; the IMF did not. The IMF wanted either more austerity or debt relief; the EC wanted less austerity but its German faction remained adamant on no debt relief. Greek negotiators were hesitating to agree with the IMF's mission to Greece on further pension reform, VAT, further wage cuts, and IMF proposals to cut business taxes instead of raise them—although, according to one of the IMF participants in the teleconference, "what is interesting though is that they (Greece) did give in … they did give a little bit on both the income tax reform and on the … both on the tax credit and the supplementary pensions."[8]

In the secret teleconference discussions, Poul Thomsen, IMF Europe Director, expressed extreme concern that the negotiations would drag on. The EC, he felt, was totally focused on the pending UK 'Brexit' vote. But if Brexit happened, it could coincide with the last hour negotiations with Greece in July on the next debt payment. Brexit, moreover, might even encourage more Greek interest in Grexit once again. The timing was bad. Some kind of precipitating event was needed now, those on the teleconference suggested, to get Greece to wrap up early the discussions on pensions, taxes and wage cuts—i.e. before a Brexit and another possible Greek blow up. The thrust of the discussion was that it might be necessary to push Greece into a near default in order to conclude negotiations in April-May, well before a possible Brexit.

Another possibility was to somehow leverage the growing Middle East immigration crisis to get Germany to move off of its position and agree to Greek debt relief. As Thomsen put it to the other IMF representatives on the teleconference, the IMF might say to Germany, "Look, you Mrs. Merkel you face a question, you have to think about what is more costly: to go ahead without the IMF—would the Bundestag say 'The IMF is not on board'?—or to pick up the debt relief that we think that Greece needs in order to keep us on board?' Right? That is really the issue."[9]

Upon learning of the teleconference on April 2, Tsipras called an emergency meeting of his ministers and shot off a letter to IMF director Christine Lagarde, accusing the IMF of planning brinkmanship, being an untrustworthy negotiating partner, and negotiating in bad faith. The IMF, Tsipras argued, was trying to push Greece into bankruptcy.

The Wikileaks release prompted the IMF to issue an immediate denial. But what the secret teleconference proceedings clearly revealed is the growing divisions within the Troika as to how to proceed with managing the Greek debt deal, which was still not totally wrapped up. The IMF not only differed with the EC and Germany on the solution to unsustainable Greek debt, but was clearly growing impatient with its role. With only 5% of total Greek debt approaching resolution, it increasingly appeared to want out of the continuing morass of Greek debt deals and negotiations. The IMF had growing claims on its involvement elsewhere, in the Ukraine and in likely soon emerging crises elsewhere in emerging markets. Its EME participants were growing more vocal complaining about all the attention and rule-bending it was doing with regard to Greece. The IMF vs. EC/Germany differences, according to the business press, "remains the clearest sign to date that the fund wants to leave Greece's

86 billion euros rescue to the EU and wash its hands of a programme that has led to a torrent of criticism."[10]

The IMF-EC/Germany Split

Germany may have wanted to keep the IMF 'in' to use its rules as an additional leverage point in negotiations with Greece, but the IMF assessment of Greek debt was that it was unsustainable in the long term. The current MOU called for 3.5% budget surplus in 2018 and thereafter; the IMF argued to reduce it to 1.5%, to cut investment taxes, and to sharply reduce pensions. The current 2016 weak Greek economy required, according to the EC, a surplus of 3%; the IMF estimated it would require 4.5%—an obviously impossible goal. Only then might Greek debt become sustainable. But Greece resisted both the tax cuts for business and the pension reductions, and Germany insisted on the 3.5% surplus called for by the August 2015 MOU. According to Schauble, the IMF's debt relief proposal was "an unnecessary distraction" and an "attempt not to do what irrefutably must be done."

The further cuts in pensions, business income taxes, and wages was the IMF 'stick'; the reduction of the surplus to 1.5% was the 'carrot'. Which would the Tsipras government choose? was the question.

The IMF was the first to blink. It retreated, by late April indicating it was open to a "menu of options" that might achieve debt relief, such as debt maturity extensions and what was called 'reprofiling' (rate reductions or moratoria). The German-led finance ministers group meeting concluded Greece would need to implement additional austerity measures worth about 3.6 billion euros, or 2% of its GDP. If Greece agreed, only then would the Troika begin discussing debt relief.

Greece blinked next. It proposed the 3.6 billion euros be achieved by across the board cuts including all departments (and taxes) instead of focusing all the cuts on pensions and wages. The Troika, now reunited, quickly rejected the idea. Tsipras again appealed to the more liberal forces in the EC and was just as quickly rebuffed—also again. However, Schauble, for the first time indicated willingness to entertain debt relief so long as it was not in the form of a 'haircut' and involved no changes to the austerity measures. But what he exactly meant by that—whether extending loan terms, moratoria on interest or principal, lower rates of interest on debt, or whatever else—was not explained at this point.

As it had repeatedly done earlier, the Tsipras parliament in early May passed legislation increasing austerity-related measures, now calling for 5.4 billion ($6.16 billion) euros of same, more than the Troika had originally indicated.[11] The cuts include pensions. Strikes and protests once again erupted throughout Greece. The IMF followed with a letter to EC finance ministers that cuts equal to another 2% of GDP, another 9 billion euros, were needed if the EC did not agree to debt relief. Greece had agreed to concessions—twice. And still the loans promised in the August MOU were not forthcoming, due to the IMF-EC/German standoff. Greece was projected to be bankrupt by July if there were no resolution to the IMF/ EC differences. Withdrawals from Greek banks were again rising, up by 12% since March. Meanwhile, Germany was blocking any release of loans to Greece, this time not because of Greece but because of the IMF/EC dispute. But in this intra-Troika tussle, the IMF was bound to lose. Most of the IMF's governing board consisted of European and USA representatives, and none were inclined to allow the IMF to precipitate another Greek debt crisis with a Brexit vote pending on June 23rd.

Rumors were that the EC might 'buy out' the IMF's position by paying off the IMF's loans to Greece and swapping them out for new EC loans from the ESM fund. Another option discussed was to front-load some of the austerity measures and finally pay Greece the 1.9 billion euro profits from Greek bonds held by the ECB in return. There was also the option of the 19 billion euros left over from the 25 billion allocated to recapitalize Greek banks. Not all that 25 billion was now needed since the banks were able to raise money from private markets again. Some of that might also be allocated to 'buy out' the IMF's role. None of these options were activated, however. Germany insisted the IMF remain part of the Troika debt deal. The likely option that began to emerge after a meeting of Schauble and the IMF's Largarde at the G7 meeting in Japan was an agreement by Schauble to allow debt relief—but only in 2018, after Germany's parliamentary elections in 2017. And then only on the understanding that Greece in the meantime had met all the austerity requirements fully.

The final outcome had to wait until the IMF met with Germany on May 24. The Troika finally declared that Greece had met all the requirements and austerity measures raised by the Troika on July 12, 2015 and after. Greece would now get a 10.3 billion euros ($11.5) loan, and the first installment of 7.5 billion euros ($8.4) would be released in late June in time to pay it back to the Troika for debt payments coming due in July. So far as Greek 'debt relief' was concerned, the finance ministers of the EC agreed to a 'road map' for debt relief. This meant relief would begin only in 2018, when the current 2015 debt deal ended and then only "if needed". "Relief" then would take the form of deferrals on interest rates and payment to Greece of profits on Greek government bonds held by the ECB. Dijsselbloem of the EC added that leftover funds from the ESM bailout fund might be used to repay "other official loans, for instance from the IMF." The IMF was thus clearly the loser in the tussle with the German-led faction of the EC as was, of course, Greece, as always. The 'way out' for the IMF was to announce it still had to assess the measures and hadn't made a final decision to participate in the May 2016 'mini-debt' deal with Greece. The IMF position was to simply delay its decision until it conducted another Greek 'debt sustainability' analysis later in 2016. In the interim, it didn't say it wouldn't participate and didn't say it would. It just issued a statement of its intent to join the bailout, and that was good enough for the EC and Germany. The IMF thus lent its credibility to the deal, if not officially becoming part of it. As one Eurozone official publicly put it: "If it looks like we are kicking the can down the road, that is because we are."[12]

Once again, the $11.5 billion loan disbursement was just a temporary resolution, first to get Greece through its debt payments due in July and then to cover subsequent debt repayments through October 2016.

Debt Restructuring by Another Name?

The capitulation of the Syriza government in July-August 2015 and its continual 'back peddling' through the first half of 2016—agreeing to yet additional austerity and allowing itself to be manipulated further by the IMF-EC hardliner dispute—does not mean the Greek debt crisis is over. The IMF and EC simply 'agreed for the interim' to get beyond the immediate Brexit issue. The IMF would make a definitive decision only at its September 2016 meeting whether to join the new revised debt agreement with Greece.

The fundamental issue behind the EC-IMF dispute is whose rules will prevail. The EC hardliners pressed for their interpretation of EC rules whereby no 'haircut' form of debt relief was permissible. With German elections in 2017 there was no way Schauble and Merkel would agree to a 'haircut', if that meant debt forgiveness of principal or even of interest (profit) in the long run. Conversely, IMF rules demand that it cannot participate if the Greek level of debt was 'unsustainable'—meaning too large to ever be repaid which, of course, Greece's debt cannot be, short of absurd estimates of 4% and more Greek GDP growth for literally decades to come.

Throughout summer 2016 IMF Director Lagarde assumed the public position that "for debt to be sustainable, this requires a restructuring. In our view this could happen without a nominal 'haircut'."[13] How this might be possible the IMF has not yet revealed, but Lagarde's statement satisfied the German-allies hardline faction's view of its rules in the meantime. The IMF will have to define and decide what it means by September 2016, however. And in the interim, the Europe economy—and with it, Greece—appears headed for another contraction and bout of major financial instability in the wake of the Brexit effects, the growing crisis of Italian banks, and continuing slowdown of global trade and therefore of Europe exports.

It is noteworthy that in the midst of this scenario, as of late July 2016 the US appears to be taking a more active role as mediator between the IMF and EC/German hardliners' positions. The Turkish coup and US concern about Greece's geopolitical importance prompted US Treasury Secretary Jack Lew to announce a planned visit to Greece and meet with Tsipras. Throughout the 2015 debt negotiations the US had leaned, not surprisingly, toward the IMF position and urged German hardliners to consider more relief for Greece. As a prelude to his visit to Greece, Lew expressed his concern over the still uncertain economic effects of Brexit and the threat of Italian banks precipitating a new bank crisis in Europe—indirectly chiding Europe for not having addressed both Brexit and the Italian bank issues sooner. The US thus may mediate the EC/German and IMF differences in the closing weeks of summer 2016, and before the IMF meets in September. Lew optimistically noted that "there been broad agreement that there does need to be (Greek) debt restructuring", adding that "the specifics will obviously matter a great deal."[14] Indeed they will. As will the course of the Greek, European, and global economies, as events and conditions in the UK, Italian, and the broader global economy portend problems ahead

Observations on the Third Debt Agreement of 2015-18

The capitulation by the Syriza government in July 2015 was a complete retreat. Agreeing to Troika austerity demands at that time marked only the beginning of a series of capitulations to additional Troika austerity measures—in the formal MOU in August, in the discussions involving bailouts of homeowners' mortgage debt in November, in the Greek government's budget for 2016, and in the May 2016 mini-deal. This was political 'concession bargaining' in its most blatant form. Once bargaining becomes focused on concessions, as in union contract negotiations, it almost always leads to even more concession demands. Here too, the same bargaining dynamic took hold early and accelerated after July 12.

Further, the process set in motion with the Syriza capitulation of July 12 inevitably led to the de facto destruction of Syriza as the party it once was, heading a progressive government intent on challenging the German-dominated Eurozone neoliberal consensus. A political consequence of the Syriza acceptance of Troika austerity measures was the political restructuring of Greek party and electoral politics. Political restructuring was both the outcome of the economic restructuring, and, at the same time, the necessary precondition to enable the economic debt restructuring and the emerging 'economic protectorate' in Greece to move forward.

Syriza as a party and a government became a fundamentally different institution after its collapse in negotiations. It moved significantly 'rightward', past the center even, and assumed a role of a junior partner in the Euro Neoliberal project. The purge of its 'left' enabled Tsipras and company to continue in office and rule from the 'center-right'. The Troika's objective had always been to destroy Syriza one way or another. It may have hoped that a premature and unprepared Syriza Grexit decision might accomplish that goal. Perhaps even a Germany-enforced Grexit. But neoliberal forces could not have wished for anything better than for Syriza to self-destruct as indeed it did. Tsipras and what was left of Syriza thus abjectly traded its Thessaloniki program for a few more months in office.

If the Syriza strategy before July 12 was incorrect and doomed to fail, then its strategy post-July 12 was even more fundamentally in error. Before the capitulation, that strategy rested on the false assumption that more progressive elements in the EC might be leveraged to get a better deal from the IMF and ECB elements of the Troika. The Syriza belief that it might reawaken European social democracy as its ally was a nostalgic fantasy. Syriza and Tsipras' strategy after July 12 was no less naïve. It was based on the idea that 'we fought the good fight and lost, so let's see what we can resurrect from the collapse. Let's at least salvage the most important anti-austerity measures, like pensions and prevention of complete privatizations and some jobs, from the Troika's obsession with austerity.' Salvaging something by means of rear-guard parliamentary maneuvers proved fruitless in the end, however. The Troika could not be fooled. They were pros at this kind of thing. And despite Syriza efforts to salvage something—anything—from the chaos that followed capitulation, it failed.

Again in 2016 the Greek government more or less repeated its failed strategy of trying to appeal to one faction of the Troika against the other. Once again it self-imposed more austerity in the hope of some debt relief that might give it room to shift the austerity emphasis a little and give itself room to stimulate some growth. But how, by imposing more austerity on itself, could it still hope to endear itself to the soft wing of the Troika and thereby get some debt relief? No matter. The IMF-EC/German split rendered Greece a minor third party in the negotiations that concluded in May 2016.

Then there were the external events that accompanied the negotiations of spring 2016: the pending Brexit UK referendum and the surging refugee immigration through Greece into mainland Europe.

One of the more interesting questions surrounding the 2016 negotiations is why the Syriza government did not strike a harder bargain with the IMF and Troika, given the obvious leverage available to it with the Brexit vote and more particularly, with the waves of refugees seeking passage to the rest of Europe. The IMF was clearly worried about the possible convergence of a Brexit with Greece's July debt payments. A Brexit might reinvigorate interest among the Greek people in favor of Grexit as well. Instead of quickly conceding to more austerity and then unilaterally legislating it, per the Troika's demands, in April in the hope of some ephemeral commitment to debt relief 'maybe', 'someday', 'if necessary', etc.—the Syriza government might have stalled until July. Even without resurrecting the idea of Grexit, simply stalling would certainly have strengthened Greece's bargaining position and allowed it to 'rescue' some austerity provisions, like pensions. The prospect of a Brexit would certainly give Greek negotiators some leverage in bargaining.

In addition to playing a possible 'Brexit card', the escalating flood of refugees from the Middle East, most of whom came through Greece, might have also provided some leverage in negotiations. Why Greece did not use cooperation on control of refugee flow as a bargaining chip at the time was interesting, to say the least. Turkey had done so, extracting major financial concessions from the Eurozone countries. Greece apparently extracted no concessions whatsoever for its cooperation with other Eurozone countries.

But Syriza by the spring 2016 was a spent force, with little or no internal energy, resolve, or willingness to risk or launch a new and more aggressive negotiating strategy. The Syriza-Tsipras July 12, 2015 capitulation, the onerous austerity terms of the August MOU, and the repeated backtracking in response to Troika additional austerity demands thereafter, had clearly temporarily demoralized the Greek people. A period of exhaustion and sense of political helplessness prevailed in the immediate aftermath. That made it easier for the 'rump' Syriza government after the purges and September elections to deliver on the Troika's demands and to continue, and even deepen, the austerity.

But that demoralization was temporary. By November 2015, protests and resistance began to slowly emerge once again. In 2016 they continued to grow, in the face of further austerity concessions by the Greek government. Nor are they likely to go away, especially if the Greek and/ or Eurozone economies weaken further in 2016-17. The UK 'Brexit' referendum and the growing 'euroscepticism' throughout the region can only continue to feed a nascent popular resistance to Greece's debt burden. It is impossible for that burden to 'go away'.

As Euroscepticism fuels party and movement protests and alternatives, from both the 'left' and 'right' throughout Europe in 2017 and beyond, it will perhaps provide examples to follow for Greeks discontented with the Troika debt deals and their endless austerity. The evolution of Euroscepticism may yet radically change the Greek misconception that to remain a part of Europe, i.e. to be 'European', it is necessary to retain the Euro currency, to let the ECB run the Greek banking system, and let Troika representatives exercise veto power over Greek fiscal policy. But to remain European Greece need not allow itself to transform into an 'economic protectorate' of the neoliberal, German-led faction of bankers, investors, and their political elite of bureaucrats and politicians that now clearly run Europe's economy and control the pan-European political institutions that have been created to ensure its interests—the EC, ECB, ESM, European Parliament, and so forth.

The notion that in order to remain in Europe and 'be' European means necessarily to remain in the Euro monetary system—a notion still held by such a large proportion of Greeks—reflects a form of pan-European 'nationalist ideology' that has been cleverly promoted and manipulated by neoliberal interests since1999. That notion of 'European' identity has been created in their interest, no less than have the economic and political structures they have also created to defend and advance their interests. Behind the new nationalist ideology of 'Europeans', behind the new pan-European political and economic institutions, at a more fundamental level, lie these economic interests.

What the 3rd Greek debt negotiations reveal is that the Syriza party and government, and a sizeable majority of the Greek people themselves, resisted for a time the Troika's plan to advance its own economic interests at the expense of theirs. They rejected and fought against austerity. So

214 | LOOTING GREECE

too was it clear that the political institutions of the Troika represented the locus of attack on Greek elected and representative political institutions—i.e. parties, government and parliament. The fight was against austerity and against the Troika.

214 | LOOTING GREECE

too was it clear that the political institutions of the Troika represented the locus of attack on Greek elected and representative political institutions—i.e. parties, government and parliament. The fight was against austerity and against the Troika.

However, what held back the negotiations strategy and that fight against austerity and the institutions of the Troika was Greece's inability to shed the ideological notions that supported those interests and institutions. In the end, neither the Greek people nor Syriza could bring themselves to reject the neoliberal notion of what it meant to be 'European'. Neither Syriza nor a majority of the Greek people wanted to leave the Euro. And that was the great strategic error that eventually led to the imposition of yet another, third, debt and austerity regime of 2015-2018.

Endnotes

1   The 86 billion was more than the 73 billion in the 2010 first bailout, but less than the 154 billion in the 2012 second debt deal.

2   See the preceding chapter 8 for possible reasons why Tsipras called the referendum in the first place, and then ignored it.

3   The following references are from *The Memorandum of Understanding Between the European Commission Acting on Behalf of the European Stability Mechanism and Hellenic Republic and Bank of Greece*, Athens and Brussels, August 19, 2015.

4   'Grandfathering' refers to allowing those already qualifying, and in this case having recently retired early as a result of Syriza's partial rollback of prior limits on early retirement, an exemption from the new rules.

5   See *Tradingeconomics.com*, for Greece/Greece Government/Military Expenditures

6   According to Poul Thomsen, IMF Europe director, '*Greece: Toward A Workable Program*', IMFdirect blog, February 11, 2016.

7   IMF participants to the conference included Poul Thomsen, director of the IMF's European department, Delia Velkouleskou, Head of IMF Representative Mission to Greece, and Iva Petrova of the IMF. For the transcript, see <https://wikileaks.org/imf-internal-20160319>

8   Velkouleskou comment, Wikileaks transcript, March 19, 2016, see <https://wikileaks.org/imf-internal-20160319>

9   Thomsen quote, Wikileaks transcript, March 19, 2016, <https://wikileaks.org/imf-internal-20160319>

10   Jim Brundsden and Kerin Hope, IMF Debt Comments Prompt Athens Anger', *Financial Times*, April 4, 2016, p. 2.

11   The New Democracy-led opposition voted against the Syriza government measures.

12   The split between the IMF and the rest of the Troika was therefore not over. It will arise again, this writer predicts, perhaps even before the end of 2016. The May 2016 agreements represent not only a 'debt relief roadmap' for Greece, but also a course and direction for eventual IMF exit from Greek debt negotiations, the next step of which may emerge around the IMF's Fall 2016 debt sustainability analysis for Greece.

13   Gillian Tett and Barney Jopson, 'Lew Seeks to Stir Rethink Over Greek Debt', *Financial Times,* July 21, 2016, p. 2.

14   Tett and Jopson, 'Lew Seeks to Stir Rethink Over Greek Debt', *Financial Times*, July 21, 2016, p. 2.

Chapter Ten

WHY THE TROIKA PREVAILED: INTERPRETATIONS AND ANALYSES

An Overview of the Greek Economy 2015-2016

Since the Syriza capitulation of July 6-13, 2015, and the August 20, 2015 signing of the third Greek debt agreement, Greece's economy has collapsed into depression territory once again, recording negative growth rates for three consecutive quarters from October 2015 through June 2016. Throughout 2015 the country's GDP fell by no less than $40 billion, from $235 to $195 billion, with the trend continuing into 2016.[1]

Government spending at this writing, in second quarter 2016, is down by a third from what it was July-October 2015, largely as a result of new austerity measures. The only exception was government military spending, which rose in 2015 by about 12%, roughly $600 million, over the previous year.

Despite the continued decline in government spending, the Greek government's debt to GDP ratio has barely changed, declining from 180.1% in 2014 to 176.9% in 2015, despite the allocation of about a third of the $98 billion in Troika loans earmarked in the August 2015 debt deal.[2]

As loans and Greek debt grow, Greek government spending falls by around the same amount as it implements austerity. The Greek government borrows less to finance government operational costs and social benefit programs—while it borrows more to pay for interest and principal payments on old debt or to replenish money capital flowing out of Greek banks to elsewhere in the Eurozone. This has been the story ever since the first 2010 debt agreement. Greece's debt to GDP ratio was 172% in 2011, an indicator of how Troika 'help' is not helping.

Whether the 2015 deal's debt of $98 billion, or the past six years' of more than $400 billion, the Troika continues to pile debt onto Greece. The more debt it provides to Greece the more austerity it demands. Spending declines, and borrowing to stimulate the Greek economy slows—with the result that in net terms the debt to GDP ratio remains largely unchanged. Debt from government spending on Greece's own domestic economy is replaced by debt for payment of principal and interest to Troika and Euro banks.

While little to nothing of the $400 billion plus Troika credit has gone to recovery of Greece's economy, that $400 billion went somewhere. But that somewhere wasn't ultimately to Greece—except perhaps in the form of a detour through Greece's government and its central bank's files of electronic money en route from the accounts of the EC, ECB and IMF back to the Troika and European banks and investors in the form of principal and interest payments on Greece's ever-rising debt.

The Greek Debt Crisis as a Banking Crisis

The Troika's policy of issuing more debt to cover interest and principal on old debt—paid for with austerity by the Greek people—has been a threefold failure: it hasn't reduced Greek total debt, or even made Greek debt sustainable; it has imposed on Greece a six year long depression with no end in sight; and it has failed to restore what is essentially an insolvent Greek banking system.

With each debt deal the Greek banks have been in effect 'recapitalized' (i.e. provided money capital) by tens of billions of euros since 2010. However, they have then quickly collapsed back into insolvency again (if they in fact ever left it). With each debt crisis, successful waves of bank withdrawals by businesses and wealthy Greek investors, and subsequent capital flight from Greece, followed. The result was a repeated loss of bank capital as deposits dwindled. Each debt crisis period also meant rising non-performing loans by Greek businesses. Greek banks' earnings also collapsed with the deepening economic decline. Together, the loss of capital, rising loan losses, and declining bank incomes meant Greek banks further insolvency. Greece does not suffer from a liquidity problem, which is how the Troika is treating it, but rather has been facing what is in essence an insolvency crisis (i.e. technically, a bankruptcy) of the Greek banking system since 2008. And insolvency cannot be corrected with simply more liquidity, as the subsequent eight years have proved.

In 2016 Greek bank instability has continued to worsen once again. Net negative money outflows from Greece have again been rising, occurring every month except one since July 2015—thus portending renewed problems in the Greek banking system as it continues to struggle with perhaps as much as $100 billion in non-performing bank loans.

It is essential to understand that the repeated Greek debt crises are really a reflection of a larger banking system crisis in the Eurozone that has existed since 2008.[3] Greece is but a microcosm of a much larger, unresolved problem lingering since 2008 throughout the region. While the problem in Europe is generalized, it appears periodically in eruptions in a given bank or member economy. Last year it was Portugal's Banco Novo. This year it is cropping up in Italy, with its reported more than $400 billion in current non-performing bank loans. Next year may be Deutsche Bank. Or Austria's Raffeisen Bank, with its overexposure to Eastern Europe and Ukraine lending.

There is perhaps as much as an estimated $2 trillion in non-performing bank loans throughout Europe. Troika policy throughout the Eurozone is to provide liquidity as a stop-gap solution, as if it were facing an insolvency problem. Just as the ECB has been throwing QE liquidity at the entire Eurozone, the Troika has been throwing liquidity at Greece since 2010 as a stopgap instead of addressing the more fundamental insolvency of Greece's banks. But here's a critical difference: the ECB cannot resolve Greek bank insolvency unless Eurozone bank insolvency is addressed; both are connected fundamentally in what is one banking system. One cannot be resolved without the other.

So the Troika continues to 'kick the can down the road,' force-feeding more liquidity and debt into Greece as a short term alternative. To allow the Greek banks to collapse would risk precipitating a general Eurozone banking crisis. For the same reasons, the Troika cannot allow Greece to eliminate its accumulated debt via a 'haircut' or other direct debt relief. It simply cannot 'forgive' Greek debt because to do so would precipitate similar demands for expunging debt from other members of the Eurozone—Italy, Spain, Portugal and even France. Debt relief on that massive scale, given the basic insolvency of Euro banks, could easily snowball into a bona fide, Europe-wide banking crisis of historic dimensions. So the charade keeps the vicious cycle turning—with the Troika insisting on more liquidity (debt) to keep the insolvent Greek (and Eurozone in turn) banking systems afloat, paid for by Greek austerity.

This bank solvency crisis underlying Greek debt scenario is supported by studies that show that virtually all the debt loaned to Greece by the Troika ultimately returns to Eurozone (and Greek) banks and investors. The Troika is but the conduit for this recycling.[4] Greek principal and interest payments are in effect subsidizing not only Greek banks but the Euro banking system itself. Interest and principal payments by other 'debt burdened' economies in the Eurozone—whether recent past (Greece, Italy, Spain, Ireland, Portugal), present (Italy, Portugal), or future (France and others), are functioning similarly—i.e. subsidizing a regional banking system that is far more fragile, unstable, and in some ways actually insolvent, but is being covered up by phony bank stress tests, massive ECB liquidity injections, and other accounting gimmickry.

Greek debt crises are but the appearance of a more basic Eurozone bank insolvency condition. So long as Greek (and Euro banks) remain insolvent, or at best near insolvent, pushing liquidity into the system solves nothing except to buy time before the next crisis inevitably erupts.

The Big Picture

Two historic developments of the global capitalist system lie behind the three Greek debt crises to date.

The first is the growing fragility in the global financial system, which has been explained at length in this writer's recent book, *Systemic Fragility in the Global Economy*. One of the fundamental themes of that study is that global capitalism has been transforming since the 1980s to a system increasingly focused on financial asset investment, and relatively less on real investment in equipment, structures, plant, inventories and so on. As the shift to financial asset investment and financial securities speculation has grown, real investment has slowed. The consequence is fundamental changes in industry and labor markets, slowing wage growth amidst accelerating capital incomes from finance, consequent growing income inequality, declining rates of productivity, and a drift toward deflation in real goods and services, while inflation and price bubbles in financial assets become more frequent and widespread.

This 'financialization' is evidenced by a combination of factors—institutions, markets, and agents: the emergence of new financial institutions, sometimes called shadow banks, otherwise referred to as capital markets, along with a spread of highly liquid financial markets globally, and an explosion of new forms of credit-creating financial securities traded in those markets by those institutions. An even more fundamental, critical element is the emergence of a new global finance capital elite as agents who manage these institutions, who sell the new securities created for purposed of generating profits via the expanding financial asset markets rather than via the real economy. The 1970s collapse of the prior Bretton Woods international financial system and its replacement by central banks has led to an explosion of liquidity and debt. The central banks have turned on the money capital spigot ever since. Changes in technology have also given risen to new non-money forms of credit that have been exacerbating the liquidity-debt explosion. This set of factors plays an increasing role in driving the shift to financial investing and deepening its political influence to enable the shift to financial asset investing to continue. The agents-products-markets-institutions nexus constitutes a unique definition of 'financialization'. This financialization evolution has been driven and dominated by the US and UK, where most of the new elite 'agents' are concentrated. This financialization evolution clashed with another, taking place in Europe.[5]

The second historic development is the origin of the Eurozone itself, commencing with its 1999 European Monetary Union (EMU) agreement that introduced the Euro as the common currency among a subset of European Union economies. Along with the Euro a rudimentary form of central bank, the ECB, was established—as well as related, weak basic 'rules' concerning fiscal matters among the Eurozone member economies. In an historic sense, this second development clashed with the first financialization driven from the US and UK, which underwent a major crisis in 2008-09. The 'clash' was between the US-UK shift to financial asset investing, with highly developed capital markets and a shadow banking system increasingly integrated with traditional commercial banks, on the one hand, and on the other, a Eurozone system focused on production and export of real goods and services between its members, with an undeveloped central banking system, a commercial bank dominated financial system, weak capital markets, and a currency (Euro) attempting to challenge the dominance of the US dollar and British pound. The Eurozone development—which had started to undergo a late and weaker form of financialization—came out on the short end of the clash.

When the 2008-09 global financial implosion occurred, the Eurozone—with its weak central bank and capital markets, lack of a central fiscal union, and strict limits on national fiscal spending—could not even provide necessary liquidity to put a floor under its banking system collapse. The crash overwhelmed the Eurozone. The US central bank, the Federal Reserve, had to provide Eurozone national central banks with up to a trillion US dollars (in swaps for the Euro) as emergency aid to prevent a Euro banking implosion. ECB and Troika bailouts in the form of new EFSF, ESM, LTRO and other such liquidity funds only came later, in hesitant steps and insufficient volume to correct the fundamental insolvencies, only putting a floor under the collapse. To date the Eurozone banking system still has not been successfully restructured.

Eurozone Structure and the Greek Crisis

The structure of the Eurozone system itself is at fault. The ECB was never—and still is not—a true central bank in the sense of a Federal Reserve or Bank of England or Bank of Japan. It lacked the power independent of coalitions of national central banks to determine what monetary policies to undertake; it was prohibited by EMU rules to provide liquidity or bail out member governments in debt (requiring the creation of special funds by the EC to do so), it lacked sufficient private bank supervisory powers, it could not provide deposit insurance, and so on. Rather, it was a currency union plus a weak banking union functioning without a fiscal union in any sense, except for some general, unenforceable rules about members' allowable deficits as a percent of their GDP.

Beneath this central banking and fragmented fiscal structure lay a private banking system that was essentially unable to compete with the new 'financial system' emerging from the US, and UK, economies since the 1990s, with its more profitable focus on financial asset investing, derivatives-based and securitized and arcane financial products. This 'shadow' banking system, or 'capital markets' system, expansion was largely undeveloped throughout continental Europe and the Eurozone in 2008-2009, and remains relatively so compared to the US-UK to this day. Thus an unstable central banking institution overlay an uncompetitive and fragile Eurozone private banking system.

The Greek debt crises—and the deeper underlying Greek and Eurozone banking crises—are the outcome of the clash between these two historical developments: the emergence of the Eurozone with weak banking union, weak private banking system, lack of fiscal union to adjust monetary imbalances among its members when necessary, and a new currency at a distinct disadvantage outside its home Euro region—and the expansion of the shadow bank-capital markets, financialized system driven by the globally ascendant US-UK finance capital elite. The consequence was that the US-UK were able to more quickly recapitalize their banking system, put a floor under their real economies, and generate a positive—albeit weak by historic comparisons—economic recovery. The Eurozone has unable to resurrect either its banking or its real economy, which continues to grow fragile and stagnate to this day.

The Eurozone has been dominated by a traditional commercial banking system, and only recently has been struggling to develop its own capital markets /financialization alternative to that traditional banking system, albeit with significant difficulty. In the US-UK the capital markets have meanwhile been increasingly dominating the traditional commercial banks in function, size of assets, and influence. Commercial banks that remain successful in the US-UK are those that have adapted, changing their structure and practices in order to become 'hybrid' shadow banks themselves. Their other option has been to retreat to regional and market niches where they may still survive competitively for a while.

The clash between the two developments was evident during, and in the aftermath of, the 2008-09 financial system meltdown. The US and UK more quickly and successfully bailed out their respective financial systems than did the Eurozone. The more traditional commercial banks in the Eurozone—the primary source of lending to non-bank businesses in that region—were unable to recover from insolvency conditions after 2008-09 as quickly, or in many cases, as in Italy and elsewhere, were not able to recover at all. In addition to Italian banks, certain French, Portugal, Austrian banks are still technically insolvent. And conditions continue to deteriorate even for German banks like Deutsche Bank and Commerzbank.

The Eurozone is a system that emphasizes the exchange of goods and services—i.e. exports and imports—and the Euro currency was designed as an element to accelerate the exchange of exports-imports within the Eurozone. But the rudimentary central banking structure, the original ECB, created with the Euro, as well as the lack of any fiscal union, has meant that financial flows from intra-Eurozone trade evolved into gross trade and financial imbalances between the Eurozone's respective members.

The Eurozone, in other words, lacks a private banking system that is able to redirect and rebalance the money capital flows that tend to concentrate within Germany and northern core economies at the expense of the periphery. The Eurozone's private banking system is incapable of redistributing those imbalances. To date, it has failed even to provide sufficient lending to non-bank businesses within its national economies. With the private banks unable to re-allocate capital to the periphery where it is desperately needed, that task is left to the ECB. But the ECB lacks the tools and the authority to do so. The re-balancing could be achieved by fiscal policy. But the lack of a fiscal union means that no central government—even Germany's—can offset the inevitable imbalances by providing spending to periphery member economies in the form of offsetting investment.

The Eurozone and EMU created a system in which the benefits of currency union became concentrated in Germany and northern European economies—at the expense of the Eurozone periphery economies, most notably Greece. The ECB only began to try to re-stabilize the Eurozone's traditional commercial banks when it was first provided with bailout funds after 2010.[6] But the initial 2010 bailout fund proved insufficient when the second 2011-2013 Europe recession hit. Additional, larger bailout funds were therefore created and consolidated. However, the ECB today still lacks other necessary central bank tools, such as independence of decision making from national finance ministers and central banks, authority to purchase governments' debt, private bank supervisory powers, deposit insurance, etc. So it just keeps throwing more and more liquidity at the private system in hopes that an ever greater volume of liquidity will somehow solve system insolvency and get the banks to lend sufficiently to non-bank businesses which will then invest and generate real economic growth and recovery.

The Eurozone is not a country. It is a federation of countries and economies. The ECB is not a true central bank; it is the institutional expression of 19 national central banks, a coalition of which, led by Germany, dominates the ECB's Governing Council (of 19) and its more important Executive Board (a subset of the 19). The ECB does what Germany wants in most cases, with a few exceptions. The power behind the ECB is a coalition of finance ministers led by Germany. Since Germany has done well in this arrangement of a weak, easily dominated token central bank, it prefers not to have the ECB's powers expand into those of a bona fide central bank. Germany has been the main beneficiary of the imbalances in goods and money flows created by the Eurozone and EMU. It doesn't want to change this current arrangement.

The German-led coalition does not want the Eurozone to evolve toward a more fiscal union. That would mean a more powerful (non-German) central government, with authority to tax and spend to correct the imbalances in trade and money that inevitably result from a currency union without a banking union. The minimal rules on fiscal spending that exist—i.e. a limit on national economies' budget deficits as a percent (3%) of GDP—reflect the extent of the fiscal union preferred by the German coalition. But failure to change it means continuing debt crises in Greece, and periodic eruptions of the same throughout the Eurozone whenever the Eurozone economy in general slows, or the specific economy in question slows, or a banking insolvency issue arises in one country or throughout the system.

To summarize: the Eurozone's traditional private commercial banking system cannot restore the imbalances. The ECB is not structured to do so and, in any event, is repeatedly checked by the coalition of German-led national central banks on the ECB governing council whenever it tries. Finally, there is no fiscal apparatus to offset the imbalances. Here too the situation is actually made worse, as the German coalition insists on Eurozone member states adherence to EMU rules that limit national budget spending and deficits.[7]

The Eurozone is thus a system in which its weaker members are destined to lack the tools to deal with debt crises so long as they remain members of the system. The promise of the Eurozone initially, i.e. to raise all economies by means of stimulating more inter-trade of goods and services between them, has not been realized. Nor can it be, so long as the region is unable to develop a Euro private capital market on a scale similar to that of the US-UK; or to evolve to a true central banking-endowed union where the ECB can make decisions without regard to its member national central bank preferences; or even less likely, to reform to introduce some kind of central government tax and investment project spending authority.

Syriza initially called for creating such a Euro-wide investment program funded by the Eurozone's member states that would theoretically enable periphery member economies like Greece to stimulate GDP growth and thereby 'grow out of' its debt crisis. Similar ideas had been raised by the remnants of social democracy in Europe in recent years. But the German coalition successfully checked the efforts, and essentially scuttled Syriza attempts to resurrect them during the 2015 negotiations. In contrast, agreeing to lock Greece into the Euro meant never even challenging the ECB and its control of Greece's central bank and therefore Greece's entire banking system. Nor did Syriza ever consider challenging the big Eurozone private banks' ownership and control of Greece's four largest private banks. So Syriza went into negotiations with no demands to take back Greece's banking system and monetary policy, and it instead attempted to gain some minimal space for a more independent fiscal policy by seeking allies with social democracy forces at Euro-government levels and with what it erroneously believed were sympathetic elements within the EC. Herein lay its fundamental strategic error.

Syriza's Fundamental Error

To have succeeded in negotiations with the Troika, Syriza would have had to achieve one or more of the following—expand the space for fiscal spending on its domestic economy, end the dominance and control of the ECB by the German coalition, restore Greece's central bank independence from the ECB, or end the control of its own Greek private banking system from northern Europe core banks. None of these objectives could have been achieved by Syriza alone. Syriza's grand error, however, was to think that it could rally the remnants of European social democracy to its side and support and together achieve these goals—especially the expanding of space for domestic fiscal investment. It was Syriza's fundamental strategic miscalculation to think it could rally this support and thereby create an effective counter to the German coalition's dominant influence within the Troika.

Syriza went into the fight with the Troika with a Greek central bank that was the appendage, even agent, of the ECB in Greece, and with a private banking system in Greece that was primarily an extension of Euro banks outside Greece. Syriza struggled to create some space for fiscal stimulus within the Troika-imposed debt deal, but it was thoroughly rebuffed by the Troika in that effort. It sought to launch a new policy throughout the Eurozone targeting fiscal investment, from which it might benefit as well. But just as the ECB was thwarted by German-core northern Euro alliance countries, the German coalition also successfully prevented efforts to promote fiscal stimulus by the EC as well. The Troika-German coalition had been, and continues to be, successful in preventing even much stronger members states in France and Italy from exceeding Eurozone fiscal stimulus rules. The dominant Troika German faction was not about to let Greece prevail and restore fiscal stimulus, therefore, when France and Italy were not. Greece was not only blocked from launching a Euro-wide fiscal investment spending policy; it was forced to introduce 'reverse fiscal spending' in the form of austerity.

Syriza's insistence on remaining in the Euro system meant Grexit was never an option. That in turn meant Greece would not have an independent central bank providing liquidity when needed to its banking system. With ECB control over the currency and therefore liquidity, the ECB could reduce or turn on or off the money flow to Greece's central bank and thus its entire private banking system at will—which it did repeatedly at key moments during the 2015 debt crisis to influence negotiations.

As one member of the Syriza party's central committee reflected on the weeks leading up to the July 5 capitulation, "The European Central Bank had already begun to carry out its threats, closing down the country's banking system".[8]

The ECB had actually begun turning the economic screws on Syriza well before the final weeks preceding the referendum: It refused to release interest on Greek bonds it owed under the old debt agreement to Greece from the outset of negotiations. It refused to accept Greek government bonds as collateral necessary for Greek central bank support of Greece's private banks. It doled out Emergency Lending Assistance, ELA, funds in amounts just enough to keep Greek banks from imploding from March to June and constantly threatened to withhold those same ELA funds when Troika negotiators periodically demanded more austerity concessions from Greece. And it pressured Greece not to impose meaningful controls on bank withdrawals and capital flight during negotiations, even as those withdrawals and money flowing out of the country was creating a slow motion train wreck of the banking system itself.[9] The ECB, in other words, was engineering a staged collapse of Greece's banking system, and yet Syriza refused to implement any possible policy or strategy for preventing or impeding it. Why?[10]

Syriza's Objectives

An effective political movement must have the following elements: correctly identified objectives; an effective grass roots—not just parliamentary—organization with which to achieve those objectives; a strategy defining how the party and its social movement will realize those objectives; and tactics that support and advance the strategy. Syriza was deficient to various degrees with regard to all the above. But it starts with incorrectly identified objectives.

Debt relief, debt restructuring, and limits on austerity were the expressed primary goals of Syriza throughout the 2015 crisis and negotiations. These objectives were not achievable, however, given the essential structure of the Eurozone/EMU at the time.

A true banking union and some reasonable form of fiscal union would be necessary, as would a Greek banking system that was not a subsidiary of other core Euro private banks. The Eurozone structure would have to be fundamentally changed to achieve either. But neither Syriza nor Greece proved capable of bringing about those changes, independently or with social democratic allies in Europe. The dominant forces—the German coalition—were benefiting nicely from the imbalances and debt crises that the structure created, and they preferred to keep arrangements just as they were. The ECB was firmly in the coalition's hands, while the European Commission, EC, offered minimal resistance to the German-Coalition forces, which was always able to eventually get its way. So too the IMF, despite complaining Greece's debt could never be paid, in the end always deferred to the EC-German coalition interests

Other interim objectives that Syriza might also have adopted but didn't might alternatively have been: to reconstitute its central bank and private banking system independent of the ECB by nationalizing them; to create a parallel currency alongside the Euro within Greece—i.e. without a Grexit—and immediately, upon assuming the government, institute controls on bank withdrawals and capital flight from the country by businesses and the wealthy. Other primary objectives might have included raising a serious threat to leave NATO if the Troika continued to refuse to disburse previously agreed to funds and interest on Greek bonds that Greece was owed by the ECB. The Syriza government might also have offered more attractive terms to Russia and China in exchange for loans and investment than it apparently did—for example, by remaining committed to, and not reversing, its intention to oppose further Eurozone sanctions on Russia. Or announcing it was awarding China the rights to buy into Greece's Piraeus port, to the exclusion of other Eurozone economic interests. It might have publicly requested to join China's newly launched Asian Industrial Investment Bank or joined the BRIC countries' trading zone, or made similar serious efforts toward economic independence. Primary objectives in part determine which strategies thereafter can be followed, and even the effectiveness of those strategies. But Syriza hamstrung itself strategically from the very beginning by choosing objectives that would not even remotely threaten the Troika's economic or political interests.

The possibility of Grexit itself should have remained an option Syriza publicized, even if it had no intention of undertaking it.

Varoufakis in particular believed Schauble and the Germans would never throw Greece out of the Eurozone, and that a Greece-initiated exit would result in massive financial losses for the Eurozone economy and banks. In spite of that view, Varoufakis himself was not a proponent of Grexit and instead proposed what he called his 'Plan X', a complex and convoluted contingency plan based on 'a euro-denominated electronic system' of repayments.[11] In other words, they kept trying to change the system overall—a gargantuan task unlikely to be successfully leveraged by such a minor player as Greece—rather than fighting with the tools they actually had.

Could a Grexit Have Succeeded?

Since Syriza's primary objectives were debt relief and restructuring, plus some limits on austerity, pursuit of these objectives necessarily excluded adopting Grexit as an actual objective.[12] Conversely, were Grexit to happen, debt relief and austerity limits would become non-issues.

Since Grexit itself was never a primary objective, a Syriza strategy for achieving it was never developed either. Which raises the point, could Greece have successfully exited the Euro? According to Varoufakis, Tsipras and the Syriza leadership was terrified of the prospect of a Grexit. They clearly did not know how to plan for it and never initiated planning. As Varoufakis himself admitted shortly after Syriza's July 5 capitulation, "we would have to create a new currency from scratch...Grexit would be the equivalent of announcing a large devaluation more than eighteen months in advance: a recipe for liquidating all Greek capital stock and transferring it abroad".[13] A not very confident view of the Grexit option, and by one of the Syriza bargaining team's more aggressive members, whose view likely reflects the general thinking by Tsipras and other Syriza leadership at the time.

Yes, of course, Grexit and the creation of a new currency would have resulted in a devaluation of the new currency. But isn't that just what Greece needed to compete more effectively in terms of exports, which would stimulate production for exports and thus the economy in turn? The Euro was preventing Greece from competing on a level plane since it ruled out Greek devaluation. It forced Greece to engage in 'internal devaluation'—i.e. to cut export costs by wage and labor cost-cutting. Austerity, in short. Devaluation of the new currency would therefore not have been all 'bad', contrary to Varoufakis' fears.

A new currency need not even have replaced the Euro entirely. Greece could have functioned for a while with a dual currency. It could have then told the Troika: either distribute the loans and interest owed Greece, or we will pay you with the new currency instead of Euros. Take it or leave it.

The German hardliners then possibly would have tried to throw Greece out of the Eurozone. But such an act would have been illegal since the 1999 Treaty has no such provisions. Syriza could have also announced that Greek taxes would henceforth be payable in the new currency. That would have raised the demand for the new currency and thus its market price and value. Turning in euros to Greek banks for the new currency would also have increased the government's holdings of Euro reserves. Greece's central bank, with more Euros on hand, might then have intervened in currency markets to buy the new currency with Euros to keep the former from devaluation too quickly or too far. Greece's central bank could then also have also issued new bonds on the currency. The central bank at this point would be working on behalf of Greece's growth, in other words, instead of on behalf of the ECB.

Varoufakis' concern that a new currency and Grexit would have meant a flood of money capital stock from Greece is also exaggerated. That flow could have been checked by early and stringent capital controls, special taxation, and measures regulating capital outflows from Greece.

Varoufakis' third concern was that the transition to a new currency was exceedingly complex, involving changes in software among all Greece's trading partners affecting payments, as well as issues with forward contracts (options and swaps). But as others have noted, the payments issue could be accomplished within a few days, and since Greece was involved with relatively little long term derivatives trading, that changeover could be done in as few as 30 business days.[14] Derivatives and futures trading added little to Greece's real GDP and economy, so who would care if that issue is not resolved quickly, except perhaps professional investors and bankers?

Syriza Strategies

What then about the respective strategies employed by Syriza and Troika forces? Which proved more effective in the end?

Apart from its 'grand' strategy of eliciting help from Europe's somnolent social democratic parties and political elites, Syriza's primary strategic thrust was to maneuver with liberals within the European Commission for concessions on austerity and debt relief. But EC officials, like Jean-Claude Juncker and others, ran alternately both hot and cold in their support for Greek proposals. They spoke indirectly in favor of Greek suggestions, only to backtrack quickly once German coalition hardliners in the EC council of finance ministers pushed back. So Syriza's strategy of leveraging support within the EC was doomed to fail in the end.[15] It was one thing to talk to politicians and administrators, and another to deal with bankers, who actually held the power.

At the same time as it was attempting to leverage support within the EC, Greece took pains to avoid criticizing or provoking open conflict with the IMF or ECB. Greece always assured it would meet payments to these two wings of the Troika when they came due, the exception being its last minute late June default to the IMF. Greece's debt relief proposals targeted the EC and its lending to Greece provided through its EFSF and ESM funds—not the ECB or IMF fund sources. The problem was the EC funds were provided proportionally by the Euro member countries, and Germany was the largest provider so it had the largest voice. It also had significant allies in the EC—as it had in the ECB—among smaller East Europe, Baltic, and other northern core country members of the Eurozone. Germany controlled the purse strings, so it always had the last word within the EC as to EC response to Greek proposals for relief and austerity. Germany almost always said 'no' to liberals in the EC inclined to seek a solution with regard to Greek debt. The events between July 5 and July 13, when the German coalition over-ruled the EC 'liberals' and demanded even more austerity is perhaps the most noted example of the German coalition's ultimate influence over the EC in critical matters. The coalition exercised a frequent majority over ECB decisions as well. Germany also exercised significant influence within the IMF, as would become apparent in the spring of 2016, when it insisted Germany would not provide any funding support of any kind to Greece if the IMF did not 'sign on' to the deal. Despite the IMF's deep concerns about Greek debt sustainability and its desire to exit the Greek deals, the IMF nonetheless bowed to German pressure and remained in the Troika.

Syriza leadership believed it could soften Troika adamancy with regard to debt relief or austerity by assuring it that Greece had no intention of Grexit. But that strategy elicited no softening of Troika demands. Syriza leadership issued conflicting messages concerning Grexit from the very beginning through the referendum vote. While Grexit was always a possibility, albeit remote, the leadership—in particular Tsipras—made repeated private assurances to the Troika that Grexit was not a real consideration. The Troika was never 'fooled' by the possibility Greece would exit. It knew it would not—not least, because Syriza never engaged in any planning for such a project. This was especially obvious in the wording of the July 5 referendum, which purposely did not indicate that a 'no' vote was a vote for Grexit. To vote 'no' was merely to vote to reject the Troika's last proposal and nothing more.

The referendum vote was also a strategic error by Tsipras and Syriza, insofar as they gave it no teeth. The Syriza leaders had made it abundantly and repeatedly clear from the beginning of negotiations that they were negotiating with the Greek government, not its people. Whatever the outcome of the popular vote, the Troika insisted it would not change its final offer. If the referendum vote was simply to say to Syriza's bargaining team 'go back to the bargaining table' and get something better, the Troika clearly would not agree to do so. To retreat from its prior position in response to the referendum, or to go back to the table and offered new proposals after the vote, the Troika would in effect be signaling to Greece its, the Troika's, final offer was not actually final. Of course the Troika's 'final offer' was never really final in that it kept 'moving the goalposts' on Syriza and demanding even more austerity and concessions as bargaining progressed, and then kept doing so even after Syriza's July capitulation, the final August agreement, and thereafter well into 2016.

While the Troika's negotiators not only rejected the referendum and remained unmoved by its results, the Troika hardliners used the vote as an opportunity to demand even more austerity from Greece as a condition for a debt deal. A worse offer was of course bargaining in bad faith. But so what, when the Troika knew Tsipras and Syriza's bargaining team were 'on the run' and they were clearly winning. So what, if it was bargaining in bad faith. What higher authority or source could impose penalties for such bad faith bargaining? By making its offer worse, the Troika was in effect telling the Syriza government, 'if you play the populist referendum card we will make it worse for you in the end'. And they did. If Syriza and Tsipras had no plan to take action based on a 'no' vote outcome, they should not have held the referendum. And they had no follow-up plan 'B'. Following the 'no' vote—which clearly should have been anticipated, and seemed the basis for holding it at all—Syriza and Tsipras were nonetheless in a confused state as what to do next. They sacked Varoufakis, replaced other cabinet members, then drafted a response to the Troika that wasn't even considered. The Troika came back with even more onerous proposals than it had offered the week earlier.

What Syriza did with the referendum was analogous to labor-management contract negotiations. In effect it asked its 'membership' (Greek people) to vote to reject the 'company's' (Troika) last offer but did not ask it to give them the authority to call a strike (Grexit). The Troika knew there was no 'strike' (Grexit) forthcoming, so the referendum was actually worse than an empty gesture. It showed Syriza was boxed in, incompetent and had no idea what to do. It signaled Syriza was at best bluffing—which should never occur at late stages of negotiation—or else pleading for some last minute, token concession from the Troika by a show of Greek majority rejection of the Troika's last and best final offer. If pleading, it only confirmed the Troika hardliners conviction they were winning, Syriza was about to collapse, and their hardline bargaining strategy was producing dividends and should 'double down' instead of grant some token, minimal concession to get a deal.

Perhaps Tsipras and his team had already given up. According to this interpretation of events, the referendum was a cover for Tsipras, who fully expected a 'yes' vote to occur. And if so, he would resign, the Syriza government would fall, and he and his party and government would be absolved from responsibility for the more severe austerity deal that would surely result. No such luck.

Tsipras's immediate response was to fire Varoufakis as finance minister and restructure his cabinet, deepening his capitulation to to the Troika's last offer in total contradiction to the result of the referendum. Instead of preparing an alternative set of proposals, meeting with the Troika, and pressing his interpretation of the vote as his authority to Grexit, the Tsipras team instead threw in the towel—only to be surprised by even more austerity demands by the German hardliners in the EC, to which the soft EC forces quickly succumbed. So here wasTsipras, coming to accept the Troika's previous week 'last and final offer,' only to be confronted with an even more onerous offer. But such is the nature of negotiations when one party collapses prematurely; the other party often imposes even harsher terms to 'teach them (and any similar interested parties) a lesson' for next time.

Syriza also made several strategic 'errors of omission' throughout the negotiations. It feebly attempted to play the 'Russian card' after Tsipras went to Moscow on several occasions. Nothing was officially reported of these meetings. It may have been that Putin was not about to aggravate Merkel by siding with such a wavering partner as Greece, especially after Tsipras reversed his position on the question of Greece approving Russian sanctions early in Greek debt negotiations. In any event, courting Merkel was perhaps more important for Putin than dealing with a fickle Greek government proceeding timidly in general with the Europeans. But it may have also been that Tsipras was reluctant to offer serious concessions to Russia in exchange for funding. Greece could have renewed a threat to veto further Eurozone sanctions on Russia, or even threatened to exit from NATO, but didn't. That would certainly have gotten US attention and perhaps led to US pressure on the EC to make more reasonable concessions to Greece. But

Tsipras quickly backed off from playing any 'Russian card' after his second visit to Moscow in May 2015 and nothing more was heard of the matter. Similarly, one can only guess what the US and NATO response might have been if Greece declared it was suspending all planned further expenditures in its proposed budget until 2018 and the end of the current debt agreement.

Another possible source of political leverage ignored by Syriza was the accelerating refugee crisis in Europe at the time. Much of the immigration to Europe from Syria and the Middle East was coming through Greece. Europe was in the process of negotiating with Turkey to stem the tide of refugees by granting major financial and other concessions to Turkey. Greece could certainly have done the same with the Troika. But there is no hard evidence that it even tried to leverage this important development.

Tsipras and Syriza's economic strategy in negotiations was no less wanting than its political. From the very beginning of assuming office it allowed bank withdrawals to continue without serious intervention, mostly undertaken at first by businesses and wealthy Greeks. The ECB was effectively encouraging withdrawals by providing minimal day to day support for Greece's central bank and as a consequence for its private banks, keeping the banking system on the edge of total collapse, while threatening to withdraw support altogether. That made depositors even more worried and encouraged further cash withdrawals from Greek banks and capital flight out of the country. The ECB thus functioned as the 'big hammer' behind the negotiations, threatening to bring down the system and Greece's economy totally in turn.

Syriza failed to respond to this extreme economic blackmail, until just before the referendum when at last it imposed limits on withdrawals and minimal capital controls, shutting the barn door when most of the horses had fled. An effective economic counter strategy might have included nationalization of the banks, and replacement of Greece's central bank leadership with those less sympathetic to the Troika and ECB to ensure it followed policies more independent of the ECB. This would of course have deeply angered the Troika and upset negotiations early in the process, but what worse was there to expect than what actually played out? Such determined moves might also have sent a message to the Troika hardliners that Greece was prepared to 'play hard ball' as well, and it might have eventually softened the Troika's position. It certainly would have flushed out, and called into question, the hardliners' threat to push Greece toward Grexit and determined if that hardliner threat was real or, as Varoufakis consistently maintained, was always a bluff. But Syriza's economic strategy from the beginning was always undeveloped, and destined to remain ineffective so long as the ECB held the 'trump' card, barring Grexit, of bringing the Greek banking system to its knees whenever it wanted. If destined to lose, they still could have played a much better game.

Troika Strategies

During the first (2010) and second (2012) Greek debt crises negotiations the Troika was at a greater disadvantage than during the third (2015). In 2010 it faced significant overhang from the 2008-09 crash and serious problems in the Euro-wide banking system. It also lacked sufficient bailout funds with which to stabilize Greece, and the subsequent sovereign debt crises that soon erupted after Greece in Ireland and elsewhere. Happily for the Troika, there was a very compliant and cooperative Greek government at the time.

By 2012 the Eurozone economy had collapsed into

a second, double dip recession region-wide. Banking problems within the Eurozone had in some cases and locations actually worsened—in France, Belgium, and especially in Italy and Spain. The Troika was preoccupied once again with even bigger problems outside Greece, although the threat of contagion from the Greece crisis to the others (and vice-versa) was also real. Once again, however, token resistance from the Greek government, this time the center-left PASOK and its replacement, the center-right, New Democracy, gave the Troika a pass. Another plus: the Troika by now had established significant bailout programs and funds, both for the banks and for governments.

By the 2015 third debt crisis and negotiations the Troika was in a far stronger bargaining position than it had been in 2010 and 2012. The bailout funds were larger and now consolidated. There was no double dip recession, and actually some moderate growth throughout the core of the Eurozone. Even former weak links like Spain had recovered somewhat, as a consequence of harsh 'internal devaluation' wage-cutting measures that boosted Spanish exports. The ECB had also launched its QE liquidity program, guaranteeing Eurozone bankers 60 billion euros a month for the next year and a half. The ECB had struggled against German coalition opposition to introduce a QE. That meant it was not likely ready to challenge the coalition again over Greek debt negotiations. In general, the Troika was in a stronger position. In contrast, it now faced a more committed opposition with the Syriza government than it had with the PASOK or New Democracy—at least 'on paper' according to election period rhetoric, and so it seemed, during the first month of the new Syriza government. But that negative factor was far outweighed by the Troika's new advantages.

The Troika's strategy from the beginning, from which it never wavered, was to insist that Greece honor the pre-existing 2012 debt restructuring deal, at least until its formal expiration February 28, 2015. Thereafter, while it continued to negotiate by pursuing further accommodations by Syriza, it effectively closed negotiations for changes on its end by insisting on the continuation of what was essentially the same terms and conditions it offered in the 2012 deal, so far as debt arrangements and austerity was concerned.

Its first strategic victory was when it convinced the Syriza government to extend the terms of the 2012 agreement through June for four more months. That concession by Syriza must have convinced the Troika its strategy was correct. If it just refused to relent, it could get Syriza to concede. Its strategy was also to refuse Greece any loan disbursements under the old agreement, even though the agreement was extended and thus it was eligible. More loans would have put the Syriza government in a stronger bargaining position and made it able to hold out longer. The inverse of this strategy was to actually reduce Syriza's funds on hand, which was accomplished by the ECB refusing to pay Greece the interest on the Greek bonds it held—also required under the old agreement—and to change the rules regarding bank collateral so that the central bank of Greece could not borrow from the ECB as well. Even the very short term access to ECB funds in the form of the Emergency Lending Assistance program was rationed very strictly by the ECB so the Central Bank of Greece faced a slow but progressive collapse of the private Greek banks during the negotiations period. That was designed to put pressure on the Greek government to concede further during negotiations, which it did. As the Greek banks deteriorated they needed more liquidity injections in order to recapitalize. That meant more loans as part of a new debt deal. But more loans meant more Greek government debt and that meant Troika demands for still more austerity.

The Troika strategy therefore was, through the tool of the ECB, to slowly squeeze the economic life out of Greece and in the process demand, and get agreement, on more austerity—even if it meant destroying the economy that it was purporting to rescue. That was a signal to Greek negotiators that it was better to agree sooner to Troika terms because deteriorating conditions were bound to result in even worse Troika terms. So the Troika strategy also included destabilizing Greek banks, in an incremental, step by step process. As bargaining progressed, the Troika in effect continued to 'move the goalposts', giving Syriza negotiators less and less room to maneuver.

Troika strategy also made good use of playing one member of the Troika against Greece to get concessions, which other Troika members then did not agree to, which required Greece then to negotiate with the others and grant still more concessions to get the agreement of the other members. It was a kind of 'offense in depth'. The liberal forces in the EC played the role of keeping Greece's strategy focused on hopes for softening, while the German coalition hardliners could then dash those hopes. A lot of this kind of 'whipsawing' also went on away from the bargaining table, as both Tsipras and Varoufakis made constant 'tours' of Berlin, Paris, Brussels, and even Rome to seek unwritten understandings which on occasion they received unofficially from Paris and elements in Brussels. The understandings would then collapse in the face of German coalition opposition, and meanwhile precious time was passing and expenditure of effort. The EC liberals plus German hardliners thus played a kind of 'hard cop-soft cop' game with Syriza, as a conscious strategy. So too did the Holland government and the Merkel government, with Paris 'soft' and Berlin 'hard'. In this way, the Syriza team bargaining resolve was slowly broken down.

According to Greek finance minister Varoufakis, the resolve 'at the top' in Greece—meaning Tsipras—weakened considerably as early as late April. As he put it at the time, Greece had three choices: Grexit; accept the Troika's position and demands; or continue to disobey the Troika while suggesting agreement on terms. According to Varoufakis, neither the EC liberals and the ECB would allow Grexit and would eventually bend and renegotiate better terms. However, he noted that Tsipras belief in the third way—Varoufakis' strategy—had faded. As he put it, "I could see he was crumbling".[16]

Another strategy of the Troika was to have Varoufakis removed from the Greek negotiating team, which they accomplished in late April. These kind of moves tend to have significant, if unseen, effects and usually signify a major shift in bargaining strategies and/or tactics. Varoufakis remained in the background after that, attempting futilely to influence Syriza negotiations 'from afar' by publishing proposals and suggestions in the media. He was eventually completely removed on July 5 when Tsipras began cleaning everyone out of his cabinet who might resist his decision to capitulate to the Troika on its terms immediately after the referendum vote.

The Troika also had significant allies within Greece itself and its strategy included leveraging these whenever possible in negotiations. These included the Greek central bank, the leadership of the opposition parties in the Greek parliament, and the mainstream Greek media which remained consistently pro-Euro and Troika deal and also terrified of a possible actual Grexit initiated by Syriza. The Troika's strategic manipulation of these internal forces within Greece attained a peak during the week of the referendum. Troika representatives appeared repeatedly on Greek TV, the corporate newspapers ran editorials and feature stories about how a 'No' vote would result in economic collapse, the leaders of the two main opposition parties—New Democracy and PASOK—publicly criticized Syriza and recommended a 'yes' vote and Greek bankers advocated the same. Despite the efforts of friends of the Troika, however, Greek voters decided in favor of rejecting the Troika's last offer by 62%.

Although it is difficult to prove, it is very likely that another of the Troika's strategic objectives was to either thoroughly 'tame' Syriza by transforming it, or to precipitate a Greek parliamentary crisis and force new elections—replacing Syriza with a more compliant government more like New Democracy and PASOK in previous debt crises. This was at least part of the strategy of the German coalition and hardliners like Schauble. In the end it proved successful. Out of the capitulation of July 5-13 came a new Syriza, purged of its internal left opponents at the government level. The purge was followed by parliamentary splits, which were then institutionalized with the new elections to Parliament in September 2015.

In summary, the Troika had numerous allies, both within Greek society, its economy, and the Greek government and it strategically used them effectively. Syriza had virtually none outside Greece, which alone was probably sufficient to result in its eventual capitulation. Its internal allies were the majority of the Greek people, but Syriza failed to prepare and mobilize that base of support when it counted— i.e. in the wake of the referendum—let alone to formulate or even contemplate a plan for Grexit.[17] Its general strategy was confined to a narrow negotiating table strategy. The Troika 'triple-teamed' and 'double-triple teamed' the Syriza negotiators. The former also proved more experienced and clever in debt negotiations. The difference in negotiating skills shows up in a comparative appraisal of their tactical errors.

Tactics—Troika vs. Syriza

Syriza's first major tactical error was to concede to the Troika's demand to extend the current debt agreement beyond February 28, for which Syriza won no concessions in turn. Furthermore, it was not just a strategic but also a tactical error to make constant reassurances to the Troika that Grexit was not a possibility. Even if it had no intention of Grexit, it should not have taken that card off the table during negotiations. Throughout the negotiations, Tsipras sent conflicting signals and messages. He spoke in very conciliatory tones when before the Troika, and then sounded militant and aggressive when speaking to the Greek parliament or Syriza party members. The statements and speeches often directly contradicted each other.

Syriza's initial position at the start of negotiations was that it didn't want new loans from the Troika, and it would even refuse them. It then quickly reversed itself and declared it should be provided the loan disbursements under the old agreement. As small debt payments kept coming due from March until June, it made the payments without demanding, as a condition of payment, that the ECB first release funds due Greece and pay it the interest on its bonds it had agreed to. Whenever a critical opportunity arose to inject tactical demands, the Syriza team seemed to let it slip by. Conversely, it made repeated unilateral concessions on austerity demands by the Troika without any quid pro quo. The Troika consistently insisted there would be no discussions even on the topic of debt relief until the final agreement was signed; Syriza should have insisted there would be no final agreement until the topic of debt relief was discussed. By making repeated unilateral concessions with nothing conceded by the Troika in turn and by not raising equivalent quid pro quo proposals when the Troika did, Syriza violated basic tenets about tactics in negotiations—to counter and fight back.

In submitting to the demand for the removal of key members of its bargaining team, Varoufakis, yet another serious tactical error was committed. Tsipras and Varoufakis often failed to coordinate their bargaining statements and positions, which at minimum likely confused the Troika and also probably convinced them that the members of the Syriza team were highly inexperienced.

There is arguable evidence, however, that Varoufakis himself was not a very tactically effective negotiator or representative of the government in any event. Anecdotal examples abound of how his style aggravated and angered his Troika counterparts, from the first visit of the EC's, Djisselbloem to Greece, who was reportedly publicly slighted by Varoufakis, to the latter's various presentations to Troika finance ministers in Brussels. Finance ministers and high level government functionaries generally take offense at being 'lectured to' by academics, regarding the latter as people they pay to give them advice or political cover; they are not used to being told they are stupid or are destroying Europe, even if in fact they are. Varoufakis' publishing on his website the text of his presentation to the EC following his initial meeting with them was also a tactical error. Negotiating in public, via the press and media, is almost always a tactical mistake. Varoufakis' demeanor and style often signaled, or even directly communicated the opinion that the EC and Troika just did not understand what was necessary for Europe. There is nothing to be gained in negotiations by specifically insulting the other side's representatives, even as one employs bargaining tactics that themselves are insulting to the opposing side. By so doing, Varoufakis gave the EC an excuse to go over his head and complain to higher ups (e.g. Tsipras), and that no doubt intensified the already growing divisions and uncertainties within Syriza's negotiating team. All this did not help the Syriza's bargaining position, although it certainly made little, if any, difference in the final outcome of events which in retrospect seem (though as I have pointed out not necessarily so) fore-ordained.

Varoufakis would admit well after the events of 2015 that he indeed considered the Troika's representatives less than his equals. In his interview with Peter Spiegel, he re-marked on why the EC grew so angry with him. Apart from denying the reports on the Djisselbloem matter, Varoufakis replied sharply to the EC representatives gathered in Brussel —"I called them incompetent and they were incompetent"[18]— proving perhaps only that lectures are best kept to venues of academic halls and not in debt crises negotiations.

Not least, as previously mentioned, the Syriza government committed a major tactical error in how it worded its referendum vote. The referendum was in effect a social 'strike vote', and to call for a rejection of the Troika's final offer without simultaneously calling for authority to strike, is a major tactical faux pas. Simply saying no to a final best offer will not get the opposition back to the table and make another offer. If it knows beforehand that no action will follow the strike vote-referendum it will just sit tight on its last position. Syriza had to have another Plan B that it immediately started to implement following the referendum—perhaps an announcement to nationalize the Greek banks in the state of economic emergency. But it hadn't prepared a Plan B and the Troika no doubt knew it.

Tsipras then laid one tactical error on top of another: he immediately sent back to the Troika a letter of acceptance of its final position— having just completed a referendum in which the populace rejected that same position.[19] Greek vot-ers were shell-shocked and demoralized, and the opposition potential within Syriza temporarily immobilized. Tsipras would be able to gather what centrist forces remained and check open opposition by the declaration that Greece needed to remain united for the upcoming formal negotiations on the terms of the debt deal, which was eventually signed August 20, 2015. But recovery from the tactical error of the referendum and the abrupt capitulation of the Syriza team and government would take time—if it would happen at all.

The Troika also made tactical errors. Its June 2015 harsh, hardliners' final proposal only inflamed Greek public opinion. Its harsh terms and insulting delivery galvanized Greek opposition in the streets. And it likely shifted support within Syriza to towards holding the referendum, although Syriza's adamant refusal to Grexit ensured the referendum was too cautiously worded, which put Syriza in a box—given its lack of Plan B—when the vote turned out 'no'.

The Troika's consistent 'hardline' bargaining attitude throughout the negotiations—often crossing the line into what constitutes 'bad faith' bargaining—may have assisted it in gaining the upper hand in the short run, but it will no doubt have consequences for the longer run concerning the Eurozone's relationships with Greece. The harsh treatment of Greece no doubt also reverberated elsewhere in Europe. Others, growing increasingly 'eurosceptic', may recall in the future as they exit the Euro the kind of treatment they might expect to receive in a similar crisis from Troika bureaucrats and politicians. It is never good to win too great a victory at the bargaining table. Contrary to the view that it 'teaches the opposition' a lesson, it more often means that instead they learn a lesson about the kind of aggression and militancy that is necessary to win next time. It erases the misconceptions and illusions as to what is necessary to win; the soft-cop diversion is unlikely to be pursued next time around. Contrary to 'taming' the opposition with a harsh settlement, it may make them even more determined and similarly ruthless in a subsequent conflict.

The Troika's successful tactics were various: i.e. forcing Syriza to grant concessions unilaterally without offers in return; getting it to extend the agreement through June; using the ECB to progressively squeeze and destabilize the banks and collapse Greece's economy; 'moving the goalposts' of austerity measures; whipsawing Syriza's team from various directions; forcing removal of Syriza team members from negotiations; employing 'hard cop-soft cop' approaches; refusing to even discuss debt relief until a final agreement was signed—the list is long and suggests that the Troika were not only in a stronger objective position in 2015 compared to its Greek opposition, but that its negotiators were more experienced and effective in such negotiations.

The Individual Factor in Syriza's Defeat

Among analysts and critics of the events of the third debt crisis there is a line of argument that attributes the major reason for the capitulation to the Troika by the Syriza government to the Syriza leadership, in particular to Prime Minister Alexis Tsipras. Tsipras's immediate abandonment of the referendum vote and decision to almost as quickly agree to the Troika's last and final proposals is cited as the primary cause of the capitulation. The defeat is thus a direct cause of failure and betrayal by Syriza's leadership, according to this perspective.

This view leads naturally to a host of secondary queries about Tsipras and Syriza's top leadership. Was it due to Tsipras's personal psychological collapse? Did Tsipras seek a way to move back to the center, ally with pro-Euro forces and parties, and then jettison his left critics within his own Syriza party in order to opportunistically retain his role as prime minister and head of government? Did he come to identify more with his Troika adversaries over the course of five months of intense contact and discussions with them? Was it gross inexperience in negotiating with the seasoned bureaucrats and masters-of-deceit politicians that inhabited the halls of the Troika institutions and governments and engaged in these kinds of maneuvers on a career basis? Was he simply naïve about Greece reforming the entire, firmly neoliberal Europe, with a vision of a resurrected social democracy that was a nostalgic historical fantasy, far removed from the current political zeitgeist? Was it a lack of courage and resolve?

This view that the Greek defeat is primarily attributable to the failure of individual leadership ignores the fact that while individuals and leaders may play an important role in the outcome of events, it is the conditions and context within which they act that are ultimately determinative. Tsipras caved in and accepted what the Troika offered. But would he have acted differently, say, if he and Syriza were leading the country in 2010, or even 2012, when the Troika was at a much greater relative disadvantage? If Syriza and Tsipras led the government in 2010 or 2012 the relationship of forces with the Troika would have been much more equal. Syriza instead of the obsequious New Democracy or PASOK leadership could easily have led to a much different outcome in those earlier debt negotiations. But if that is so, it means the individual factor is not the sole or primary determinant of outcome. Tsipras was not destined to 'betray' regardless of conditions. Under different circumstances he may not have done the same.

One may say the same about Yanis Varoufakis, the Syriza finance minister. His personality no doubt had an effect on the course of negotiations with the Troika. But his personality traits and actions most likely would not have fundamentally changed the final outcome of the 2015 debt negotiations—i.e. the Syriza capitulation of July 2015, and the subsequent further descent into austerity thereafter imposed by the Troika and accepted with minimal resistance by the new 'rump' Syriza party and government after the splits and new elections.

Aside from all the objectives, strategies and tactics employed by both sides—Troika and Syriza alike—the conditions in Greece and the Eurozone in 2015 would have likely led to the same choices and outcome which they did, no matter the leadership—until conditions and the orientation of the Greek people themselves made Grexit a realistic alternative, at least as a tactical threat.

Organization and Public Consciousness Factors

While incorrect objectives, failed strategies, ineffective tactics and unstable individual leadership all played a part in Syriza's eventual capitulation and subsequent retreat, institutional forces have contributed to that final outcome as well. These included the composition of Syriza as a party, the Syriza government's consistently razor-thin majority in the Greek parliament, and the social class composition of Greece itself.

Although it originated as a coalition of parties and social movements about a decade ago, Syriza by 2015 had become basically a parliamentary party. This transition primarily occurred after its electoral success of 2012 and its 2014 elections to the European Parliament. In the course of this shift and transformation, "its leadership more and more took on an autonomous stance" in relation to its grassroots members, according to former party central committee members.[20] The periodic one- or two-day strikes initiated by Greek workers, before and after the capitulation, had been organized mostly by their unions, not by Syriza. Mass protests and marches had been largely spontaneous, or else called out by smaller groups and parties. As a parliamentary party, Syriza took its cue largely from its parliamentary or government leaders, rather than from decisions of its grassroots rank and file. Syriza's leaders were content to engage the Troika and its allies within Greece on the negotiating stage, but not via the streets.

In the 300-member Greek parliament Syriza never had a solid majority, which was another important institutional factor. It had to ally with smaller parties, and even then could muster only a majority of 3 (around 153 votes), for key issues. This was the case before the capitulation as well as after.

The composition of Syriza as a party also mitigated against militant action. As one commentator and critic more-or-less accurately described it, "Syriza is a party led by affluent upwardly mobile professionals, academics and intellectuals. They rule over (but in the name of) the impoverished working and salaried lower middle class, but in the interests of the Greek, and especially, German bankers."[21] Syriza's senior leaders were thus a reflection of the party's own class composition, 'armchair leftists ("Marxist seminarians")' with little experience in or taste for mass struggles.

Syriza party leaders and senior parliamentarians of this character meant Syriza would never undertake a clean break with the Troika and pursue an independent national economic policy. Given its primary parliamentary focus, and its narrow majority in that regard, it could hardly be expected to undertake bold initiatives against the Troika, which of course it didn't.

There is also the social-cultural composition of Greek society itself as an institutional factor. Its once-significant ship-building, mining and related industries have declined in output and employment. Traditional industrial working class ranks have declined in turn, as they have significantly elsewhere in the 21st century as well—with their jobs either replaced by technology or offshored by business to emerging markets. Small service- and tourist-related businesses, farmers, and other pro-market groupings constitute the majority of the social composition of Greece in 2015. In the referendum vote, it was estimated 70-80% of the vote rejecting the Troika's last proposal occurred in definable Greek working class neighborhoods. Conversely, a similar 70%-80% in business and professionals neighborhoods voted to accept the Troika's proposals.

This social composition as a whole tended to view remaining in Europe as primary, and was strongly opposed to a Grexit. Remaining in Europe was identified with remaining in the Euro system, as uninformed and unnecessary as that conclusion may have been. The party reflected this social composition, as its leaders reflected the party in turn. With deep ideological illusions as to what remaining in Europe meant, this social composition likely contributed to the Tsipras-Syriza decision to capitulate in July 2015. This again raises questions as to the significance of the role played by individuals in determining the final outcome of events like the Greek debt crisis. Was Tsipras predisposed toward betrayal, as some argue, whether due to personal psychological reasons or just due to crass opportunism? Or was Tsipras trapped from the very beginning by a Greek electorate that wanted to identify itself as 'European' no matter what the economic and austerity costs; that didn't want austerity but was insufficiently willing to challenge the preconditions that guaranteed that austerity?

Greek working class elements suffered economically the most from the debt agreements and the associated austerity measures imposed by the Troika. In contrast, the wealthy, small businesses and professionals were able to send their money abroad with ease. They could shift the burden of austerity-driven VAT, property, and even income tax increases onto the Greek consumer in large part. They favored privatizations of Greece's pubic assets, since it portended an inflow of foreign capital that might stimulate their business, whereas a new currency, should Grexit occur, would mean a major devaluation of their capital and thus a major capital income loss.

The very social composition of Greece created a bias against radical action like Grexit, and in favor of accepting the Troika's austerity measures. The majority of Greeks may have wanted the Greek negotiators to return to the bargaining table and get a better deal when they voted "No" in the referendum. But they didn't want Grexit. And without support for that option—in the party, the party's parliament faction, and within Greece itself—capitulation was inevitable in July 2015. If not then, then later; if not by referendum, then by other means.

Thus unclear objectives, ineffective strategies and tactics, the mindset and character of leaders, public consciousness, and institutional factors—all played an important role is the Syriza government decision not to opt for Grexit, not to mobilize popular resistance more aggressively, and to eventually capitulate.

Is a Fourth Greek Debt Crisis Inevitable?

The answer is an unequivocal 'yes'. Another crisis is predicated on the level of Greek debt and payments coming due, on the one hand, and Greece's continued inability to pay principal and interest, on the other.[22] If Greece's economy continues to falter in 2016-17, the availability of an income flow with which to repay the debt will decline.

And if Europe's economy slows, which it will, that means that increasingly so too will Greece's.

Since the concluding of the 3rd Debt agreement with the Troika in August 2015, Greece's annual GDP has declined for three consecutive quarters—by -1.7%, -0.7% and -1.3% through the first quarter of 2016, the last for which data is available.[23] Both consumption and investment have been driving the GDP decline, as well as net exports from which income might be earned from which to make payments on scheduled Troika debt. Declining export income suggests more borrowing will be necessary at some point. Given declining GDP and external income, Greek government debt has also continued to rise from August 2015 levels by more than 10 billion euros, to a total debt as of April 2016 of more than 322 billion euros. Greek government debt in 2016 is projected to rise still further and exceed the 180% of debt to GDP record it attained in 2014.

With Eurozone growth slowing toward stagnation, and Germany's imports—Greece's major trading partner—slowing as well, the prospects of Greek GDP and exports growth recovering in 2016-17 are slim to none. A slowing Eurozone economy translates to a still further decline in Greece's economy. That means as larger Greek debt payments come due in 2017, Greece will have less ability to make those payments once again. The need to borrow and incur still more debt is on the horizon.

The willingness of the Troika to provide further credit (debt) to Greece, and on what terms, is another determinant of how soon another Greek debt crisis arises. Once Greece lacks the ability to make payments—as is surely in the cards—the Troika will have to add more debt to enable it to make payments. That in turn will translate into still more austerity. Requiring more austerity from Greece was already evident this past spring 2016, as the IMF and EC together maneuvered to impose still more debt on Greece, as described in a preceding chapter.

Another related development that may result in another round of Greek debt increase, perhaps even before year-end 2016, is the IMF's potential withdrawal from the Troika on the matter of Greek debt financing. The IMF has repeatedly stated Greece's unsustainable debt violates its IMF rules. The IMF cannot lend technically to countries unable to repay that debt. Consequently the IMF has still not officially or formally approved of the Greek debt deal amendments of this past spring 2016. However, it will decide on that issue in its September 2016 meeting. It is a distinct possibility therefore that within the next six to twelve months the IMF may withdraw from the Troika Greek debt arrangements. If so, then the EC will likely pay off the IMF's share of Greek debt, and subsequently add that payoff to Greece's total debt in turn. The event may provoke yet another Greek debt crisis, or at minimum a 'mini-crisis' similar to the spring 2016 debt amendments. In the process of the debt restructuring to accommodate an IMF withdrawal, the Troika may demand Greece deepen its austerity measures still further, as it did this past spring 2016, precipitating yet another debt restructuring confrontation.

Still another wild card is the recent developing bank crisis in Italy and the need for further Troika bank bailouts in that country and potentially elsewhere. Signs of contagion from Italy's bank problems to the rest of the Europe banking system have begun to emerge, just as contagion effects on the Euro-wide banking system from the recent UK 'Brexit' are also arising. The Italy and Brexit problems could easily spill over again to Greece's highly fragile banking system. Recent Eurozone bank stress tests show significant weakness in key banks in France and even Germany, and once again in Ireland and elsewhere. The contagion effects from another

European bank crisis will almost certainly result in a further deterioration in Greece's debt situation. That would require further lending from the ECB to Greece's central bank and the Greek government.

Since July 2015, net negative money outflows from Greece have occurred every month except one, portending renewed problems in its banking system as it continues to struggle with more than $100 billion in non-performing bank loans.[24] There's nothing more likely to precipitate a renewed debt crisis than a new banking crisis, driven by non-performing bank loans. But this time the crisis and need for debt renegotiations may include Greece as part of a larger Eurozone-wide problem, centered in Italy but spreading contagion beyond.

There's also the question of political contagion, not just banking contagion. Greater political instability in the Eurozone system in the coming months may exacerbate that Greek political resistance. Movements for 'exits' from the Eurozone are growing, as well as general public 'euroscepticism'. An important Italian government sponsored referendum on restructuring Italy's political system is due for a vote in October 2016. It may stimulate and legitimize other referenda. Resistance to Troika fiscal rules is also growing in a number of Euro countries, as well as the awareness that the ECB has failed by means of monetary policies to generate normal economic recovery for the past eight years. National elections are due in 2017 in Germany and France, and a strong possibility exists that the anti-Euro National Front in France may prevail and, if so, introduce a French referendum on the subject 'Frexit'. Significant impetus to other exits would follow. A potential unraveling of the Eurozone, at least in part, is thus not impossible. Should referenda and 'exits' occur elsewhere, it would almost certainly revive movement in Greece for a reconsideration of 'Grexit' in the event of another Greek debt crisis arising. Conversely, a reconsideration of Grexit itself could precipitate another 4th Greek debt negotiation.

Independent of political instability and contagion, there's the possibility of austerity reaching such a point in Greece where the population on which it is imposed rebels once again, with or without a new party leading them. That too can precipitate a renewed debt crisis. The Greek people are currently 'shell-shocked' from the events of 2015-2016. However, resistance is rising, slowly, led by elements outside Syriza. Austerity is once again driving Greece's economy back into depression—this time on an economy already ravaged by years of austerity-driven decline.

Recognizing and acknowledging that another Greek debt crisis is inevitable is hardly a radical conclusion. As one very mainstream economist has concluded, "The modern Greek tragedy is not over...there will be more acts".[25] It doesn't take brilliant economic analysis to realize that the Eurozone structure was broken from the very beginning, and now shows signs of actual dissembling. Without monetary solutions, and deprived of fiscal solutions, of its own, "some kind of write-down, restructuring, or default is inevitable". However, more debt alone solves nothing, and actually exacerbates all. The Eurozone may not have been initiated with the intention of imposing a new kind of financial imperialism upon its economically weaker members, but that's in fact what has evolved. And those more powerful economic states, like Germany and its allies, don't want to change what has been quite profitable and beneficial to it, even though their gain has been at the expense of others. But such is also the nature of imperialism.

More countries in the Eurozone are questioning a system that provides them few benefits, while concentrating most of the benefits in Germany and a few other northern 'core' Euro economies. If they are getting little out of it, why remain in it? Not only is another 4th Greek debt crisis inevitable, so too will be an eventual 'Grexit'. As others note, "the Greek problem will never be resolved so long as Greece remains in the Eurozone."[26] However, the precondition for both may be the further unraveling of the Eurozone and other 'exits' elsewhere in the region. The Eurozone may leave Greece, before Greece actually leaves it.

Syriza's leaders naively hoped to achieve success by reforming Euro neoliberalism with more Euro social democracy, But what may happen in fact is a crisis of Euro neoliberalism as the Eurozone system based on it unravels, to be replaced by something quite different from Syriza leaders' nostalgic vision of a past era that is impossible to retrieve.

Endnotes

1   These and subsequent data on Greece's economy today are from the *tradingeconomics.com* website.

2   The 176.9% figure for all of 2015 is no doubt higher as of mid-2016, as renewed GDP contraction has been occurring.

3   Banks remain unstable elsewhere globally as well, but the condition is significantly generalized in the Eurozone, as well as throughout the broader European region. British banks like Barclays remain fragile, and increasingly so in the wake of the Brexit June 2016 referendum. Along with Deutsche Bank, Germany's Commerze bank shows signs of growing difficulty. The US bank, Citicorp, once among the world's largest, and Bank of America, were technically insolvent after the 2008 crash and remain very fragile to this day. US and Europe bank 'stress tests' that periodically give banks a 'pass grade' are in various ways designed to ensure most banks, despite their condition, are reported to the public as 'safe' in which to invest and purchase stock—which is the primary objective of bank stress testing.

4   Once again, the EMTS study referenced in preceding chapters, and other similar published commentary by insiders, including former Finance Minister, Yanis Varoufakis.

5   A third historic development concurrent with the two discussed here, but less directly relevant to our argument, is the rise of China and other key emerging markets tied to it as providers of commodities. Just

as the first development overwhelmed the Eurozone experiment since 2008, the third 'China model' has been progressively succumbing since 2013 to the global financialization forces set in motion by the US-UK as well.

6   This was the EFSF, European Financial Stability Facility, established late that year. It provided initially, however, a 'mere' $440 billion in bailout funds, a 'drop in the bucket' of what was needed to restore banking system and sovereign solvency. To it was added a larger European Stability Mechanism in 2013, which was a stop-gap measure just sufficient for the second Europe crisis of 2011-2013. The ECB's 'QE' program is an example of a still further liquidity provisioning program for banks and non-bank businesses. But it too will fail.

7   Which the larger economies, like France and Italy, continually ignore marginally and Germany tolerates. But not so for the smaller economies, like Greece, that are held to a higher, and more austerity standard.

8   Dimitris Konstantakopoulos, 'Greece: Revolt Betrayed', *Counterpunch*, July 6, 2015.

9   Why Syriza hesitated and did not impose stringent capital controls from the very beginning is evidence of its policy of placating the ECB during the negotiations, while focusing on support within the EC. On more than one occasion Syriza leaders made it clear they had no intention of not making ECB and IMF debt payments as they came due. Efforts to get the Troika to agree to 'debt relief' always focused on the EC loans, not the IMF or ECB. As negotiations continued, the ECB nonetheless tightened the screws on the Syriza government and Greece's central bank in various ways previously noted.

10   Again, it was Syriza's fundamentally flawed strategy of focusing on gaining concessions from what it thought were sympathetic social democrat elements in the EC and select Euro governments, while showing its intent of cooperating with the ECB and IMF. It was a 'divide and conquer' strategy that never achieved any division among the Troika, that maintained internal solidarity among its elements throughout negotiations and after.

11   Yanis Varoufakis, Interview with Alex Sakalis, *OpenDemocracy* blog, October 25, 2015. In the post-capitulation period during which this interview was conducted, Varoufakis continued to adhere to the view that a pan-European resurgence of social democracy was required to extricate Greece from Troika debt. He had launched a new movement toward such, thus recommitting to Syriza's previous failed strategic error of seeking alliances and support from declining social democratic forces in Europe as the key strategic focus.

12   As negotiations proceeded throughout 2015 Syriza pared down the limits on austerity it initially proposed, so that by July the bar to acceptable austerity was set quite low. That bar was lowered still further throughout 2015-2016.

13   Varoufakis interview with *The Guardian*, July 7, 2015

14   See 'The Intricacies of Greece Adopting a new Currency', *Financial Times*, July 1, 2015, p. 22.

15   This intra-EC initiative and maneuver by Syriza may be viewed as a reflection of its 'grand' strategic error, previously noted, of trying to rally government level social democratic forces (France, Italy) to its position. The latter focused on obtaining fiscal space with which to stimulate its economy; the former—the intra-EC—focused on obtaining debt relief and austerity reduction that indirectly might enable the same.

16   Peter Spiegel interview with Varoufakis, *Financial Times*, March 26, 2016, Life Section, p. 3.

17   Reportedly, some left elements within Syriza's party central committee were attempting to develop some kind of Grexit plan at the time but it was never made public.

18   Peter Spiegel interview with Varoufakis, *Financial Times*, March 26, 2016, Life Section, p. 3.

19   This immediate reversal is the basis of the interpretation that Tsipras was surprised by the "No" vote, having expected a "Yes", which would have allowed him to resign. But now, having apparently lost resolve to continue the fight some weeks previous, his answer to why capitulation was 'we fought the good fight against superior forces'. Little Greece stood up to the behemoth Eurozone alone and can be proud. All we can do now is to try to minimize the pain of austerity. I will continue in office with that objective.'

20   Interview with Syriza former chief economic adviser, Jannis Milios, *Global Research*, January 29, 2016

21   James Petras, "Lies and Deceptions on the Left: The Politics of Self Destruction", *Global Research*, March 22, 2015.

22   Compared to 2015, the level of debt repayments to the Troika coming due in 2016 have been exceptionally light.

23   Per the National Statistical Service of Greece, as reported by TradingEconomics.com as of August 2016.

24   Compared to Italy's more than $400 billion in current non-performing bank loans, and perhaps as much as $2 trillion in similar NPLs throughout Europe.

25   Alan Blinder, 'The Greek Solution Solved Nothing', *Wall St. Journal*, Juy 17, 2015, p. 11.

26   Blinder, p. 11.

A NEW FINANCIAL IMPERIALISM EMERGES

The recurring Greek debt crises represent a new emerging form of Financial Imperialism. What, then, is imperialism, and especially what, when described as financial imperialism? How does what has been emerging in Greece under the Eurozone constitute a new form of Imperialism? How is the new Financial Imperialism emerging in Greece both similar and different from other forms of Imperialism? And how does this represent a broader development, beyond Greece, of a new 21st century form of Imperialism in development?[1]

The Many Meanings of Imperialism

Imperialism is a term that carries both political-military as well as economic meaning. It generally refers to one State, or pre-State set of political institutions and society, conquering and subjugating another. The conquest/subjugation may occur for largely geopolitical reasons—to obtain territories that are strategically located and/or to deny one's competitors from acquiring the same. It may result as the consequence of the nationalist fervor or domestic instability in one State then being diverted by its elites who are under domestic threat, toward the conquest of an external State as a means to avoid challenges to their rule at home. Conquest and acquisition may be undertaken as well as a means to enable population overflow, from the old to the new territory. These political reasons for Imperialism have been driving it from time immemorial. Rome attacked Carthage in the third century BCE in part to drive it from its threatening strategic positions in Sicily and Sardinia, and also to prevent it from expanding northward in the Iberian Peninsula. Domestic nationalist fervor explains much of why in post-1789 revolutionary France the French bourgeois elites turned to Napoleon who then diverted domestic discontent and redirected it toward military conquest. Imperialism as an outlet for German eastward population settlement has been argued as the rationale behind Hitler's 'Lebensraum' doctrine. And US 'Manifest Destiny' doctrine, to populate the western continent of North America, was used in the 19th century as a justification, in part, for US imperialist wars with Mexico and Native American populations at the time.

But what may appear as purely political or social motives behind Imperialist expansion—even in pre-Capitalist or early Capitalist periods—has almost always had a more fundamental economic origin. It could be argued, for example, that Rome provoked and attacked Carthage to drive it from its colonies on the western coast of Sicily and thus deny it access to grain production there;[2] to deny it strategic ports on the eastern Iberian coast from which to trade; and eventually to acquire the lucrative silver mines in the southernmost region of the peninsula at the time. Nazi Germany's Lebensraum doctrine, it may be argued, was but a cover for acquiring agricultural lands of southern Russia and Ukraine and as a stepping stone to the oil fields of Azerbaijan,

Persia and Iraq. And US western expansion was less to achieve a population outlet than to remove foreign (Mexico, Britain) and Native American impediments to securing natural resources exclusively for US use. US acquisitions still further 'west'—i.e. of Hawaii, the Philippines and other pacific islands—were even less about population overflow and more about ensuring access to western pacific trade and markets in the face of European imperialists scrambling to wrap up the remaining Asian markets and resources.

Imperialism is often associated with military action, as one State subdues and then rules the other and its peoples. But imperialist expansion is not always associated with military conquest. The dominating State may so threaten a competitor state with war or de facto acquisition that the latter simply cedes control by treaty over the new territory it itself had conquered by force—as did Spain in the case of Florida or Britain with the US Pacific Northwest territories. Or the new territory may be inherited from the rulers of that territory. Historically, much of the Roman Empire's territory in the eastern Mediterranean was acquired this way. Or the new territory may be purchased, one state from the other—as with France and the Louisiana Purchase, Spanish Florida accession, and Russia's sale of Alaska to the US.

In other words, imperialism does not always require open warfare as the means to acquisition but it is virtually always associated with economic objectives, even when it appears to be geo-political maneuvering or due to social (i.e. nationalist ideology, domestic crises, population diversion, etc.) causes.

Colonies, Protectorates, and Dependencies

Another important clarification is the relationship between imperialism and colonialism. A colony is a particular way—not the only way—inn which an Imperialist state might rule over and manage an acquired state and its economy. A colony is a particular political form. As Hobson, one of the original theorists of imperialism, accurately explained, a colony is a form of imperial rule in which the imperialist state has full control over the legislature, the government and bureaucracy of the dominated state.[3] Moreover, the extent of colonization may vary. There are colonies which have their own representative legislatures, but no government except the appointed governor of the Imperial state. There are also colonies with their own representative legislature and representative government, but where the Imperialist state exercises veto power over legislation and government decisions.

In contrast to a colony, a protectorate is where a bilateral agreement exists between the imperial and the dominated state in which the latter cedes certain authority to the former. The dominated state may retain full formal independence in the sense of selecting its own representative legislature, government and bureaucracy, but agree to the imperial state determining certain of its policies such as foreign policy or military policy. Institutions managing foreign-military policy in the dominated state may be simply coordinating agencies ensuring implementation and consistency with the imperial state policies. It may be argued that Scotland today is a political protectorate of Britain. So too Catalonia, of Spain. And Puerto Rico, of the US.

And as Hobson further explained, 19th century states like Canada and Australia had representative institutions but no imperial state governor or right to veto. They had even by late 19th century their own military and political policies. Nonetheless, these States' economies were significantly integrated with that of the imperial state, the United Kingdom. So what were they, if not colonies? They may have been politically independent, but were they economically dependent? At the time, they may not have been political protectorates, but could be argued to have been economic protectorates.[4]

A dependency refers to dominated economies whose growth is dependent on the trajectory of growth in the imperialist economies. The dominated economies are so structured by the imperialist that they are unable to grow independently. Dependency is a purely economic structure. There are no forms of political control, as in protectorates and degrees of colonization. But there is economic influence and control exercised by the Imperialist economies over the dominated. This control is exercised largely by controlling the flow of money capital and investment into the dominated economies. Investment into the latter—sometimes called FDI (foreign direct investment)—only takes forms that benefit the Imperialist economies.

While economic dependency has been associated mostly with states that were once colonies and economic protectorates in the pre-1970 decades, a new trend is emerging in states with smaller economies located near major imperialist economies. Greece today shows signs of similarity to the kind of economic dependency that was once associated only with post-colonial, post-protectorate economies. However, as will be argued, Greece today also represents an emerging new form of economic protectorate. The Euro regime, even before the debt crises eruptions of 2010-2015, had imposed relationships of dependency upon Greece. Since 2010, however, Greece has evolved from a dependency to an economic protectorate.

Capitalism as a system is constantly restructuring and remaking itself. Imperialism is a basic element of it, but it does not expand and deepen at the same pace at all times. It ebbs and flows. Old forms of imperialism accelerate, penetrate, become established and then decline, then give way to new, and often even more 'efficient' forms. Late 19th century European imperialism, focusing on Africa, was similar in many ways, but also different from 18th century British imperialism or 17th century Spanish and Dutch imperialism.[5] There was very little 'self-government' associated with the new imperialism of that period. Its political form was nearly always full colonization with the associated political institutional control.

Greece is not a colony of the Troika, but it is increasingly dependent on the Troika financially (i.e. in terms of credit and debt) and passed over the threshold to an *economic* protectorate since 2010.

Greece as an Economic Protectorate

An economic protectorate exists when the dominated State cedes control of certain of its economic institutions, policies and economic assets to the imperialist. Following the third Greek debt agreement of 2015, that is what Greece became. The 'imperialist state' in this case is the Eurozone's supra-national institutional bodies—the Troika of the European Commission, the European Central Bank, the IMF, and the pan-European court system ruling on their decisions, etc. And to the extent that the Troika institutions[6] define the economic policies of Greece's central bank, dictate allowable economic policy to the Greek legislature, set the budget, government spending and taxing parameters of the Greek government—then the Troika is defining and determining the economic policies of Greece. Greece has ceded this economic control to the Troika under duress, so it cannot be considered to have done so voluntarily. The debt agreements have been 'negotiated' in name only, in only a formal sense. The demands and proposals of the Troika have become virtually all the final terms and conditions of the debt agreements. There is little of Greece's original proposals in the agreements. So the agreements are the result of 'one-way' negotiations or, in other words, they were not really negotiations at all since that would imply some reasonable degree of compromise by both parties.

An economic protectorate has thus been imposed upon Greece. Greece has become an economic suzerainty of the Troika, a de facto economic vassal state of the Eurozone.

Not only has the Troika defined Greece's economic policies. It directs the policies of its central bank, making it an appendage of the ECB. Greece's central bank does what the ECB asks, even to the point of criticizing its own Greek government and agreeing with the ECB's policies that negate the Greek central bank's role of supporting its own Greek banking system.

In exchange for Troika credit and debt, Greece's Parliament cannot introduce legislation that may contravene the debt agreements or the budget policy set by the agreements. Nor can Greece's legislature pass any fiscal measures—nor can government agencies initiate fiscal measures—that the Troika considers may in any way inhibit the attainment of the budget targets it, the Troika, has defined. Reportedly, representatives of the Troika remain on site and are responsible for ensuring no legislation or executive action contravenes the debt agreement and its objectives.

Greece's government must maintain spending within the parameters defined by the Troika-determined debt agreements. Greece's government cannot decide unilaterally whether to cut spending, or on what, or whether to cut or raise taxes, and on whom. It is told what programs it must implement to reach that budget target. The Troika de facto veto power reportedly extends down to the local government level, to ensure that local administrators implement the debt-imposed austerity as defined in the terms of the agreement.

In short, Greece now has no independent central bank and thus no independent monetary policy. It has no currency of its own that it might devaluate in order to stimulate exports and growth. Its limited fiscal authority of action has been taken away, as it is no longer allowed to determine its budget, spending programs, and taxation policies. Greece no longer has independent economic institutions of any significance. It has ceded them to the Troika. Greece's parliament and government may exercise non-economic decisions and initiatives; but these are subject to veto by the Troika should Greece attempt to exercise economic initiatives.

Wealth Extraction as an Imperialist Objective

Whether via a bona-fide colony, near-colony, economic protectorate, or dependency the basic economic purpose of imperialism is to extract wealth from the dominated state and society, to enrich the Imperialist state and its economic elites. But some forms of Imperialism and colonial arrangements are more 'profitable' than others. Imperialism extracts wealth via many forms—natural resources 'harvesting' and relocation back to the Imperial economy, favorable and exploitive terms of trade for exports/ imports to and from the dominated state, low cost-low wage production of commodities and semi-finished goods, exclusive control of markets in the dominion country, and other ways of obtaining goods at lower than market price for resale at a higher market price.

Wealth extraction by such measures is exploitive—meaning the Imperial economy removes a greater share of the value of the wealth than it allows the dominated state and economy to retain. There are least five historical ways that imperialism thus extracts wealth. They include:

Natural Resource Exploitation

This is where the imperial economy simply takes the natural resources from the land and sends them back to its economy. The resource can be minerals, precious metals, scarce or highly demanded agricultural products, or even human beings—such as occurred with the slave trade.

Production Exploitation

Instead of relocating the resources and production in the home market at a higher cost, the production of the goods is arranged in the colony, and then shipped back to the host imperial country for resale domestically or abroad. The semi-finished or finished goods are more profitable due to the lower cost of production throughout the supply chain.

Landed Property Exploitation

The imperialist elites claim ownership of the land, then rent it out to the local population that once owned it to produce on it. In exchange, the imperialist elites extract a 'rent' for the use of the land.

Commercial Exploitation

Here the imperialist elites of the home country, in the form of merchants, ship owners, and bankers, arrange to trade and transport goods both to and from the dominated economy on terms favorable to their costs. By controlling the source of money, either as currency, credit, or precious metals, they are able to dictate the arrangements and terms of trade finance.

Direct Taxation Exploitation

More typical in former times, this is simple theft of a share of production and trade by the administration of the imperialist elite. The classic case, once again, was Imperial

Rome and its economic relations with its provinces. It left the production and initial extraction of wealth up to the local population, while its imperial bureaucracy, imposed locally, was simply concerned with ensuring it received a majority percentage of goods produced or traded—either in money form or 'in kind' that it then shipped back to its home economy Italy for resale. A vestige of this in modern colonial times was the imposition of taxation on the local populace, to pay for the costs of the Imperial bureaucracy and especially the cost of the imperial military apparatus stationed in the dominated state to protect the bureaucracy and the wealth extraction.

The preceding five basic forms of exploitation and wealth extraction have been the subject of critical analyses of imperialism and colonialism for more than a century. What all the above share is a focus on the production and trade of real goods and on land as the source of the wealth transfer. The five types of exploitation and extraction disregard independent financial forms of wealth extraction. Both capitalist critics and anti-capitalist critics of imperialism, including Marxists, have based their analysis of imperialism on the production of real goods. This theoretical bias has resulted in a disregard of the forms of financial exploitation and imperialism, which have been growing as finance capital itself has been assuming a growing role relative to 21st century global capitalism.

'Reflective' Theories of Imperialism

Marx never referred to imperialism per se, but did address colonialism—in Ireland, India, and China. He thus focused on its political forms of enforcement. The economic objective in all cases was extraction of surplus value and wealth from these colonies, but he described this extraction in terms of production exploitation and/or commercial-trade exploitation. The focus was always on real goods or physical commodities, their production and trade. Exploitation by financial arrangements was not considered primary, or independent of production, because financial relations were always a consequence of production. This was a 'reflection theory' of growth, of crises, as well as of imperialist exploitation.

Marx's own explorations of banking and finance in his final unpublished notes, in his posthumous publication of *Capital*, volume III, edited selectively by Engels, were left undeveloped. Marx left contradictory messages in his latest notes on whether 'finance was subordinate to industrial production' or not. Engels in 1890 solidified the assumption that finance was a mere reflection of production (and therefore imperialism always extracted wealth by the former and not via financial relations). As Engels put it in a letter of October 27, 1890 to a Swiss journalist, finance plays a subordinate role to real production. However, like Marx, he left the door open with a qualification: "As soon as trading money becomes separate from trade in commodities it has a development of its own, special laws and special phases determined by its own nature". So classical Marxism of Marx and Engels remained cautious about whether financial capital and Imperialism could act independently of industrial capital and production. How to compromise the two views?

This somewhat reluctant recognition that perhaps finance capital independent of industrial capital (production) and merchant capital (trade) might develop its own form of imperialist exploitation per se was recognized as well by J. Hobson in his classical book, *Imperialism*. In his closing remarks in chapter VII, summarizing the economics of imperialism, Hobson addressed the topic of 'Imperialist Finance'. He raised the idea of public debt as "a normal and a most imposing feature of Imperialism". He was referring foremost to the use of public debt by the Imperialist state to pay for the costs of military occupation and administration of the colony. But he also recognized that other kinds of public debt were possible in the imperialist-colonial relationship. Public bonds and loans were a profitable business for bondholders and finance capitalists in general, as "state guaranteed debts are held largely by investors and financiers" worldwide and not only in the Imperialist country. Hobson concluded that imperialism by its very nature is integrally connected "to the moneylending classes dressed as Imperialists and patriots".[7] What the possible connections between public debt and the moneylending imperialists were, exactly, was not described; nor were the relationships between industrial capital and finance capital in the pursuit of imperialist expansion. Was finance subordinate to industrial capital, as most Marxists seemed to suggest; or was it potentially independent as well?

The classical Marxist bias toward production first—and finance as merely a reflection of production—has its ultimate roots in classical economics' preoccupation with production, productive labor, and growth. Classical economics, from Adam Smith on, poorly understood banking and finance.[8] And Marxist economists, as inheritors of much of classical economics' conceptual framework, repeat the same production and real goods bias of classical analyses. They therefore view financial effects as a consequence of industry and production.[9] Imperialist wealth extraction must consequently also reflect production and trade of real goods, and not financial forces.

After Engels, most notable Marxists adopted this view. Marxist Rudolf Hilferding, in the early 20th century, attempted a compromise between the two views on the role of finance in Imperialism. According to Hilferding, in the 19th century Marx and other bourgeois economists viewed the world in terms of industrial capital and financial capital. The convergence of the two in the late 19th century resulted in what Hilferding called 'finance capital', which was industrial capital that had turned to financial capital independently, bypassing banks. Industrial capital had expanded so greatly, forming 'trusts' and raising money capital as 'joint stock companies', and becoming monopolies, that industrial capitalists now were able to raise their own capital and were able increasingly to bypass traditional banks as sources of capital. Industrial capital and finance capital had thus merged. Industrial capital was monopoly capital and monopoly capital had become an ascendant force within Finance Capital. Monopoly finance capital became the driving force of the new Imperialism in the early 20th century, according to Hilferding.

As Lenin would write in 1916, adopting the views of Hobson and Hilferding a decade earlier, imperialism was 'The Highest Stage of Capitalism'.[10] The big banks were the driving force of the new imperialism. But that was because they were organically connected to heavy industrial capital and were enabling—i.e. financing—the latter's Imperialist expansion. The big banks had assumed control of the big industrial companies and fostered the concentration of capital into monopolies. They then financed industrial expansion into colonial territories. But Lenin still held the view that finance was 'subordinate to industrial capital', albeit with a twist. Big banks had become big industrial capital but the forms of exploitation were still primarily production based. The Hilferding-Lenin view was in effect a view primarily of German banking and German industrial capital at the time. Independent forms of financial exploitation were not considered. The Marxist 'finance capital is subordinate to industry capital' view did not permit it.

Not all Marxists at the time held to the 'subordinate'

view, however. In her book, *The Accumulation of Capital*, written shortly Hobson and Hilferding and before Lenin, Rosa Luxemburg addressed the subject of International Loans and lending by finance capital directly to the dominated state. The loans and bonds provided were made to finance the import of capital equipment by the local capitalists. "Though foreign loans are indispensable for the emancipation of the rising capitalist states, they are yet the surest ties by which the old capitalist states maintain their influence, exercise financial control, and exert pressure on the customs, foreign and commercial policies of the younger capitalist states."[11] Luxemburg here appears not to be thinking of the financial relations of an Imperialist state to a colony, but to another less developed or small capitalist state dependent on loans and credit from a more economically powerful imperialist cousin. Could the nature of the imperialist relationship differ with the development of the dominated state? Could more independent forms of financial exploitation characterize the imperialist-small capitalist state? Luxemburg raised indirectly some interesting questions that Hilferding and Lenin ignored.[12]

The view that finance is subordinate to industrial capital became embedded in Marxist analyses of imperialism thereafter.[13] John Smith's recent attempt to update Imperialism analysis to the 21st century has been much heralded in US Marxist circles. The update, however, is more a case of 'new wine in old bottles'. Smith's book is wedded to the traditional Marxist tradition that Imperialism is about real goods and related services, and the analysis is virtually devoid of consideration of financial forms of imperialist exploitation.[14]

Like the preceding bias toward reflective theories of Imperialism, where finance capital is subordinate to, or subsumed by, industrial capital, Smith dismisses any real independent role to finance as a driver of imperialism or determinant of capitalist crises in the 21st century.[15] For Smith, industrial capital and exploitation of productive labor is still the driver of imperialism (as well as of capitalist crises). Finance is subordinate to this process, relegated to assisting capital in imperialist economies to engage in 'predatory overseas expansion', where it is compelled to go due to the development of monopoly capital, declining rates of investment, and falling rates of profit in real production in the Imperialist core. Finance in this (post-Marx) Hildferding-Leninist view is not a cause but a "symptom" and "side effect" of the 21st century "transformations in the sphere of production, in particular its global shift to low-wage countries".[16] This is the old version Marxist view that it is the exploitation of labor value in producing real goods that drives the financial side of capitalism. Commenting on the global financial crisis that began to emerge in 2007, and erupted in 2008-09, Smith succinctly summarizes his classical reflective theory view: "the crisis is ultimately rooted not in finance but in capitalist production,"[17] that what may appear as a financial crisis, or financial forms of imperial exploitation, is but a reflection of more fundamental production forces.

Alternatives to Hilferding-Lenin

To be fair, not all contemporary Marxists agree that finance is just an enabler of Imperialist expansion and ultimately just the handmaiden of monopoly capital. A more open-minded view is David Harvey's *New Imperialism*, a work that explores alternative explanations of mperialism beyond reflective theories of Imperialism.[18] Harvey suggests perhaps finance capital and financial exploitation today represents a kind of late 20th century rapacious 'primitive capitalist accumulation' in the Marxist sense of that term. If so, then financial imperialism, as a process of primitive accumulation, can occur outside the basic capitalist labor exploitation process. In Marx's analysis, primitive accumulation pre-dates basic capitalist exploitation, even as it may also coexist alongside the latter at the same time. That suggests that financial exploitation, and thus Financial Imperialism, may not be a mere extension or appendage of exploitation from production. It is not 'reflexive'. Financial Imperialism may have a dynamic of its own, interacting with traditional production-based exploitation and Imperialism, but nonetheless represent a force of its own and driven by its own causal forces.[19]

In yet another important challenge to the Hilferding-Lenin view of Imperialism, contemporary German Marxist economist, Michael Heinrich, concludes that "the relationship between financial markets and industrial production is not constant in either a quantitative of qualitative respect. This relationship can be different in different countries, and can also change in the course of capitalism development."[20] Heinrich specifically challenges the Hilferding-Lenin view that the merger of industrial and bank capital, creating 'trusts' and monopolies, leads to declining profits in the advanced economies, thereby forcing them to expand abroad in search of more profitable, cheap labor. That capitalist state in the advanced economies assists this expansion—thus Imperialist policies emerge. Imperialism is the economic necessity of monopoly capitalism. Industrial capital integrates finance, and mobilizes the state on its behalf, to offshore its capital to developing markets where wages are less and exploitation and profits thereby high. As Heinrich correctly notes, however, more money capital has been 'exported' between the advanced capitalist economies, than from the latter to emerging markets in the 20th century.

Imperialism in Lenin's time does not represent the 'highest' or 'final' stage. Heinrich suggests the need "to formulate a theory of Imperialism outside Lenin's framework" as an important task.[21] That would necessarily mean a perspective that breaks from the notion that Imperialism is not just about production nor finance just an appendage of production.

The reflective view of what drives Imperialist expansion and exploitation is not limited, however, to the Marxists. There is a long tradition in mainstream economics that attributes supply-side, or production forces, as the main determinant of growth, of capitalist crises, as well as of the dynamic toward imperialism. The most famous in this regard is perhaps Joseph Schumpeter.[22] Another line of analysis is offered by the neo-Ricardian, Piero Sraffa, who viewed the financial system as a mere superstructure facilitating monopoly control of industry and directing it into regions of higher profitability, including presumably colonies and emerging market economies.[23] There is no lack of variations on the theme that it is the production of goods—and more specifically the slowing of that investment and production and therefore profitability from traditional capitalist production—that drives capitalism inherently toward seeking greater profitability by imperialist expansion. That expansion is what enables capitalism to maintain its profitability and growth.

That the forces underlying capitalism drive it toward extracting wealth from external regions is not the question. Imperialist expansion has always sought colonies and protectorates, or to make other regions dependent upon it. It has—and continues to this day—to exploit and extract wealth by means of producing with lower cost labor outside its 'core', by manipulating the terms of trade for exports and imports exchanges with the regions into which it expands, by stripping ownership of land from the indigenous inhabitants and then charging them land rent to use their own land, by theft of natural resources, and by imposing taxes on the indigenous populations to pay for the costs of the imperialists' policing them. These are all historic forms of exploitation, all of which still continue today to some degree in various places globally.

Classical 19th century British Imperialism extracted wealth by means of production exploitation, commercial-trade, and all the five basic means noted above. It imposed political structures to ensure the continuation of the wealth extraction, including crown colonies, lesser colonies, protec-torates, other dependency relationships, and even annexation in the case of Ireland and before that Scotland. The British organized low wage cost production of goods exported back to Britain and resold at higher prices there or re-exported. It manipulated its currency and terms of trade to ensure profit from goods imported to the colony as well. Its banks and currency became the institutions of the colony. Access to other currencies and banks was not allowed. Monopoly of credit sources allowed British banks to extract rentier profits from in-country investment lending and trade credits. They obtained direct ownership of the prime agricultural and mining lands of the colony. They preferred and promoted highly intensive and low cost labor production. Production and trade was structured to allow only those goods that allowed Britain investors the greatest profits, and prohibited production and trade that might compete with Britain's home production. But the colonial system was inefficient, in the sense that was costly to administer. The cost of administration was imposed on the local country in part, but also on the British taxpayer.

Twentieth century US Imperialism proved a more efficient system. It avoided direct, and even indirect, political control. State legislatures, governments, and bureaucracies were locally elected or selected by local elites. There were few direct costs of administration. The local elites were given a bigger share of the exploitation pie, as joint production and investment partnerships in production and trade were established with local capitalists as 'passive' minority partners who enjoyed the economic returns without the management role. Only when their populace rebelled did the US provide military assistance, covertly or overtly, either from afar or from within as the US set up hundreds of military bases globally throughout its sphere of economic interests. The US and local militaries were tightly integrated, as the US trained local officer ranks, and even local police. Security intelligence was provided by the US at no cost. The offspring of the local elites were allowed to enter private US higher education establishments and thereby favorably socialized toward US interests and cooperation. Foreign aid from the US ended up in the hands of local elites as a form of windfall payment for cooperation. US sales and provision of military hardware to the local elites provided built-in 'kickback' payment schemes to the leading politicians and senior military ranks of the local elites. Local military forces became mere appendages of the US military, willing to engage in coups d'etat when necessary to tame local elites that might stray from the economic arrangements favoring more local economic independence beyond that permitted by US interests.

US multinational corporations were the primary institution of economic dominance. They provided critical tax revenues to the local government, employment to a share of the local workforce, and financial credits from US globally banking interests. The US also controlled the dominated states' economies through a series of new international institutions established in the post-1945 period. These included the International Monetary Fund, established to address local management of currency and export-import flows when they became unbalanced; the World Bank, which provided funding for infrastructure project development; and the World Trade Organization and free trade agreements—bilateral or regional—which enabled selective access to US markets in exchange for unrestricted US corporate foreign direct investment into dominated state economies, financed by US financial interests.   These investment and trade arrangements were tied together by the primacy of the US currency, the dollar, as the only acceptable trade currency in financial and goods exchanges between the US and the local economy.

This new 'form' of economic imperialism—a system of political dominance sometimes referred to as 'neo-colonialism'—was a far more efficient and profitable (for US capitalists and local capitalist elites as well) system of exploitation and wealth extraction than the 19th century British system of more direct imperial and colonial rule. And within it were the seeds of yet a new form of imperialism based on financial exploitation. As the US economy evolved toward a more financialized system after 1980, the system of imperial dominance associated with it began to evolve as well. Imperialism began to rely increasingly on forms of financial exploitation, while not completely abandoning the more traditional production and commerce forms of wealth extraction.

The question is: What are the new forms of imperialist exploitation developed in recent decades? Are new ways of extracting wealth on a national scale emerging in the 21st century? Are the new forms sufficiently widespread, and have they become sufficiently dominant as the primary method of exploitation and wealth extraction, to enable the argument that a new form of financial imperialism has been emerging? If so, what are the methods of finance-based wealth extraction, and the associated political structures enabling it?[24] If what is occurring is not colonialization in the sense of a 'crown colony' or even dependent 'neo-colony', and if not a political protectorate or outright annexation, what is it, then?

These queries raise the point directly relevant to our current analysis: to what extent does Greece and its continuing debt crises represent a case example of a new financial imperialism emerging?

Greece as a Case Example of Financial Imperialism

There are five basic ways financial imperialism exploits an economy—i.e. functions to extract wealth from the exploited economy—in this case Greece.

- Private sector interest charges for financing private production or commerce
- State-to-state debt aggregation and 'interest on interest' wealth extraction
- Privatization and sale of public assets at fire sale prices plus subsequent income stream diversion from the private acquisition of the public assets
- Foreign investor speculative manipulation of government bonds
- Foreign investor speculation on stock, derivatives, and other financial securities' as a result of price volatility precipitated by the debt crisis

The first example represents financial exploitation related to financing of private production and trade. It is associated with traditional enterprise-to-enterprise, private sector economic relations where interest is charged on credit extended for production or trade. This occurs under general economic conditions, however, unrelated to debt crises. The remaining four ways represent financial exploitation enable by state-to-state economic relations and unrelated to financing private production or trading of goods.[25]

One such form of financial exploitation involves state-to-state institutions, public sector economic relations where interest is charged on government (sovereign) debt and compounded as additional debt is added to make payments on initial debt.

Another involves financial exploitation via the privatization and sale of public assets—i.e. ports, utilities, public transport systems, etc.—of the dominated state, often at 'fire sale' or below market prices. Privatization is mandated as part of austerity measures dictated by the imperialist state as a precondition for refinancing government debt. This too involves state-to-state economic relations.

Yet a third example of financial exploitation also involving states occurs with private sector investor speculation on sovereign (Greek government) bonds that experience price volatility during debt crises. State involvement occurs in the form of government bonds as the vehicle of financial speculation.

An even more indirect case, but nonetheless still involving state-state relations indirectly, is private investor speculation in private financial asset markets like stocks, futures and options on commodities, derivatives based on sovereign bonds, and so on, associated with the dominated State. This still involves state-to-state relations, in that the investor speculation is a consequence of the economic instability caused by the state-state debt negotiations.

Finance capitalists 'capitalize' on the debt crises that create price volatility of financial securities, making speculative bets on the financial securities' volatility (and in the process contributing to that volatility) in order to reap a financial gain from changes in financial asset prices. And they do this not just with sovereign bonds, but with stocks, futures options, commodities, and other financial securities.

All the examples—i.e. interest on government debt, returns from fire sale prices of public assets, investor speculative gains on sovereign bonds, as well as from financial securities' price volatility caused by the crisis—represent pure financial wealth extraction. That is, financial exploitation separate from wealth extraction from financing private production. All represent 'money made from money', in contrast to money made from financing the production or trading of real assets.

Before describing in more detail each instance, and how they occur in Greece, here are some general comments on financial imperialism.

Financial Imperialism does not displace other traditional forms of imperialist exploitation based on production, commerce, or any others of the five methods noted previously. Financial imperialism adds to, and therefore intensifies, traditional exploitation. Financial forms of imperialism may function as an integral part of the traditional forms. But they may also arise and exploit independent of traditional forms as well—as in the case of financial asset speculation and even privatization of real public assets.

In its most basic sense, finance is about extending money and credit in the expectation of receiving a greater value of money and credit in return. Debt is the equivalent expression of credit. The lender extends credit and the borrower accepts it, thus incurring a debt equal to the credit. The total debt to be repaid is always more than the original credit-debt extended, as 'interest' on the debt is added to the initial value of the extended credit. The residual difference between the total debt and principal is the interest charged on the debt.

Private Sector Interest Transfer

In its basic form, financial imperialism and exploitation is about interest flows that originate from the production and commerce of goods. That is, interest payments from credit extended for production and trade.

A foreign bank or financial institution or (jointly owned or foreign) business engaging in foreign direct investment (FDI) into Greece, extends credit to a Greek business to build and/or operate production facilities. The bank or financial institution or foreign business then eventually repaid the loan (principal) plus a rate of interest. The interest charge is ultimately paid for by the Greek worker-producer and/or Greek consumer, as the debt is factored into the wage paid the worker or added onto the price of the product. If the full debt in the in form of interest is not retrievable by shifting its interest cost to wages or prices, then the industrial capitalist (Greek and/or foreign) may write off the interest cost as a deduction from taxes. The Greek taxpayer thus assumes the residual burden of interest. Or, all the above occur—the worker, the consumer, and the taxpayer all pay part of the interest on a basic, private sector financial investment. In private financial exploitation, the imperialist multinational corporation often functions as a monopolist or oligopolist, so it is easily able to shift the burden of interest payment to the local workforce, or to the market price of its product, or to the foreign or Greek taxpayer.

What this process represents is a private sector set of economic relationships, not state-to-state relationships. It represents private sector credit, debt and interest payment. It is a traditional form of financial exploitation involving production and commerce. It is not yet state-to-state financial exploitation, which is an essential feature of the new financial imperialism.

As it concerns interest payments on credit extended to production and commerce, the flow of payments is quite simple: the enterprise receiving the credit repays the bank on a set schedule of principal and interest payments with certain associated terms and conditions. If the bank is not a Greek bank, the interest payment flows from Greece to the core Euro bank. The interest payment may be to a jointly owned Greek bank, part of which is then redistributed in turn to the Euro bank by the Greek bank. This works until such time as a financial or economic crisis interrupts and prevents the interest payment being made by the enterprise and/or by the Greek bank to the core Euro bank. The latter now faces potential losses from defaulted loans to the enterprise and seeks to ensure the payments occur. Arrangements are pursued that permit the Greek government (or central bank) to provide funds to bail out the Greek enterprise or Greek bank so that it is able to continue to make its scheduled interest payments to the core bank.

Initially this is possible by the Greek government issuing bonds, the proceeds from which are used to bail out Greek banks and enterprises about to default, or defaulting in fact, on scheduled interest payments to Euro banks. But when the economic downturn is severe, as was it was in 2008-09, issuing government bonds may be difficult (or too expensive) and therefore the amount raised is insufficient to cover deficits and bailouts. Diverting government revenues from other sources from the Greek budget is an alternative. But the economic contraction's severity makes it difficult to redistribute declining tax revenues to bail out Greek enterprises and banks facing default. Unable to sell sufficient bonds, or redistribute declining tax income internally in sufficient volume, to bail out its own Greek banks and enterprises—and itself also in need of more borrowing to cover deficits as its economy collapses from the crisis—

the Greek government turned to borrowing from the only source then available to it as a member of the Eurozone: the Eurozone's Troika institutions. The Troika was willing to lend to ensure Greek banks and businesses did not default on Euro bank and business loans. But it was only willing to lend the minimum necessary—after Greece squeezed everything it could first from issuing its own bonds and raising taxes and cutting spending (i.e. austerity).

But the Eurozone as constructed in 2010 had no central fiscal authority, and poorly developed funds, from which Greece (and other periphery economies) could borrow. There was no contingency built into the Eurozone from its inception to handle such situations. ECB to national central bank rules limited the credit the ECB might lend Greece's central bank. And government-to-government lending was just then being constructed 'on the fly' by the EC and poorly so. By 2012 it was still a cumbersome, bureaucratic and highly politicized process. The manner in which debt negotiations took place further exacerbated Greek government debt levels, as did austerity policies.

In summary, the need to ensure scheduled principal and interest payments established in the private sector prior to 2008, in the midst of the 2008-09 crisis that wasn't of Greece's making, led inevitably to Greek government borrowing from the Troika and its institutions. Private interest on private debt was thus offloaded onto government balance sheets as Greek banks and businesses were bailed out by Greek central bank and Greek government borrowing from the Troika. Private sector interest payments were ensured in the short run, but only by replicating the private payments as debt on Greek government balance sheets for which interest was also to be paid to the Troika. Private debt became government debt, and private interest payments to Euro banks and businesses became mirrored in Greek government debt and Greek interest payments to the Troika.

State-to-State Debt and Interest Aggregation and Transfer

Financial imperialism is not just a matter of a bank lending to a private enterprise, which eventually in turn repays principal and interest to the bank. That is the kind of financial exploitation that occurs at an enterprise or 'micro' level. In the case of financial imperialism, however, overlaid on this basic 'micro' relationship are complex 'macro' relationships: i.e. imperial state institutions lending to dependent governments; imperial central banks to governments and their central banks; central banks repayments to imperial institutions; dependent governments to all the above; and so on.

Credit, debt, and interest have always been an element of traditional forms of imperialism based on production and commerce (trade). What's fundamentally different in the case of financial imperialism is that the interest charged is not just on the principal credit extended for the production and transport of a particular private good or service. Interest ends up being charged on interest, as debt is incurred to pay for previous debt. With financial imperialism the primary institution is no longer just the enterprise or the private bank that funds the enterprise goods production and/or trade. Financial imperialism involves state-to-state exchange and interest payments. In the case of Greek debt, the role of the imperial state is played by the entire structure of Eurozone Troika institutions—the European Commission, the European Central Bank (ECB), the IMF, the various funds established for lending by the Troika to Eurozone member governments and their central banks, and ultimately the national central banks and governments that determine the policies of the Troika itself.[26]

In 21st century financial imperialism the imperialist state/structure plays the role of aggregator of private bank credit, which it then extends as its own credit (Troika) to the dominated state's (Greece) institutions. Greece incurs Troika credit as debt, and then in turn extends the credit to its banks and non-bank enterprises. These private enterprises, bank and non-bank, may include foreign enterprises and banks doing business in the country as joint enterprises or as solely owned local enterprises and banks. The loans and credits provided are then recycled as private payments to enterprises and banks in the imperialist economy beyond Greece. Thus the private money as private credit is recycled completely—from imperialist banks, investors and enterprises through Imperialist state institutions to Greek government institutions, to Greece's private sector, and from there back to the originating 'core' Euro banks and investors.[27]

When a major financial crash and extended recession occur, this financial flow is seriously disrupted. Greece's private sector—banks and business—cannot make payments on their private debt and default. Their default then threatens losses for the originating creditors in the imperialist economy. If the banks and investors in the imperial 'core' are also experiencing potential or actual default—as was the case in 2008-09 in the Eurozone banking core and then again during the 2011-2013 second recession—the need to ensure debt repayment from the local debtors by some alternative means becomes especially important. In addition, if the northern core Eurozone banks, already in trouble, are deeply invested in the major Greek banks, then the bailout of the Greek banks is necessary as part of a bailout of the Eurozone core banks.[28]

But if both Euro core and Greek banks are simultaneously in trouble as they were in 2008-09, from where would the payments come? The Greek private sector debt would have to be assumed by the government sector in order to make the payments, in effect transferring Greek private debt to the balance sheets of government institutions. This is how the Greek debt run-up originated—as a transfer of private debt to government balance sheets. But it was only the beginning of the Greek government's debt buildup. As was the case with all governments during the 2008-09 crisis, the deep recession meant a collapse of tax revenues just as social payments to support household spending and small business rose simultaneously. This meant government deficits escalated and therefore government debt. Overlaid on these two important sources of rising Greek government debt, were the austerity measures imposed by the Troika from 2010 onward. The double dip recession of 2011-13 in the Eurozone further exacerbated Greek deficits and austerity conditions.

How the Troika handled the debt negotiations also contributed significantly to the buildup of Greek government debt.[29] The Troika insisted repeatedly on Greece raising debt (issuing bonds) in private markets first, before lending to it, even though, due to the crises, the interest on the new bonds sold on the private market rose to extreme levels. Global shadow bank (hedge funds, etc.) speculators during each crisis drove up the bond rates further, thus further increasing Greek debt. There were additional factors as well. By delaying providing loans to Greece as the crises each deteriorated the Greek economy—which the Troika did on each of the three occasions—the Troika in effect allowed the debt totals to rise further than otherwise might have been the case. But even this was not all. As the debt crises and negotiations ran their course, withdrawal of deposits by businesses and wealthy investors from Greek banks required even more loans from the Troika to re-stabilize (i.e. recapitalize) Greece's private banks. This meant the Greek government had to borrow even more from the Troika to bail out its own banking system, after the Troika purposely permitted—and actually encouraged—it to crash during debt negotiations as a way to pressure Greece to accept Troika terms.

So Greek government total debt—and rising interest payments on the escalating debt—is attributable to six basic causes:

- transfer of private sector debt to government balance sheets,
- rise of government deficits associated with the 2008-09 crash and subsequent double dip Euro recession of 2011-2013,
- excessive speculation on Greek government bonds by private investors and vulture funds,
- ECB action during crises that ensured excessive Greek bank withdrawals and capital flight requiring additional ECB lending to Greece's central bank to recapitalize Greece's banking system,
- austerity policies of the Troika that drove Greece into depression, raising deficits and debt,
- Troika insistence that debt be piled onto debt, in lieu of debt relief, to ensure Greece would make payments on old debt with new debt.

The rising interest on the Greek government debt is paid from Greek national production. Just as in basic financial exploitation, where the worker-consumer-taxpayer ultimately bears the burden of payment of interest on private debt, government debt and interest is fundamentally the same—except that payment occurs not on an individual enterprise level, but at the level of the entire economy.

The imperialist state structure (Troika) dictates and arranges the terms of the payment on behalf of the banking and private investor interests outside Greece. The Greek state is the 'middleman' in the process, implementing the austerity and other measures from which wealth is extracted from Greece's economy and sent as interest and principal on debt repayments to the Troika. The Troika in turn redistributes the payments to the private bankers, investors and businesses from which it originally raised its bailout funds that it has loaned to Greece.

That is why, as the EMST study showed and concluded, 95% of the Greek government's debt payments ultimately end up in the private sector in the Eurozone outside Greece—i.e. in the hands of Eurozone bankers and investors. Of the 215.9 billion euros in credit extended by the Troika to Greece in the 2010 and 2012 agreements alone, 86.9 billion of principal was repaid *but 119.3 billion was repaid in interest*, to private investors or to recapitalize Greece's banks. Only 9.7 billion ended up in the Greek economy. What appears as a state-to-state structure transfer of wealth—from Greece to the Troika and its institutions— is really in essence a transfer of wealth from the Greek society and economy in general to private interests outside Greece in the Eurozone.

The recycling of the interest payments occurs through both Greece and the Troika—functioning together as interest aggregators from Greece to private banks and investors outside Greece. That interest aggregation and distribution process for each of the Troika institutions occurs in brief as follows:

The EC: The Greek government makes interest payments on loan debt incurred from the EC (EFSF, ESM, etc.). The EC raises the loans from its constituent country members, who raise it from their national banks and investors. Greek debt payments to the EC flow back to their respective member governments and in turn back to the private banks and investors.

The ECB: Greece's central bank repays ECB loans, which then are redeposited to its member central banks' accounts with the ECB. The funds ultimately contribute to ECB purchases of mostly German and core government bonds and now corporate bonds as well. The money ultimately is redistributed to the corporate sector via QE and other pre-QE liquidity injection measures by the ECB.

The IMF: Greek government payments to the IMF are then re-loaned by the IMF to other economies in crisis, which eventually redistribute it largely to western banks who participate as partners in all the IMF bailouts. Example: Ukraine IMF loans from 2005 to 2014 that went to repay loans from participating western banks and investors.

But the money used to repay the Greek government debt and interest must come from somewhere. Part appears to come from new debt incurred in order to be able to repay old. But the money to repay that new debt on old interest must also come from somewhere ultimately. Where it comes from is the aggregate Greek economy and society, from Greek production and commerce on a national (not private enterprise) scale, organized through the medium of Troika-Greece negotiated austerity policies and programs.

In Financial Imperialism, therefore, the extraction of wealth in the form of aggregate interest on debt is arranged through the medium of the state itself, as well as at the level of the individual enterprise. It is becoming one of financial imperialism's defining characteristics in the 21st century, emerging in the most vulnerable smaller economies, which are being consolidated into new free trade-single currency-banking union transnational capitalist economies like the Eurozone, European Union, TPP, NAFTA-CAFTA, and scores of others that exist or are in development worldwide.

Debt has become a major tool for extracting profit in the form of interest for globalized finance capital in the

21st century. The interest on ever-rising debt from loans and bonds and other securities paid to the Imperialist state are extracted from the entire Greek population—not just on an enterprise basis—though of course forms of interest as payment on credit extended to private enterprise continue. But superimposed on interest from the traditional production or trade exploitation, where goods are involved, is not just interest, but interest on interest due to rising levels of government debt and inability to make payments.

To pay principal and interest on its escalating debt, the Greek government is required to extract income and value from the Greek people by means of austerity: reducing wages, pensions, benefits and services while raising taxes. Greece must generate a sufficient increase in GDP to obtain tax payments with which to repay Troika and private debt. If GDP does not grow, which it cannot do in depression conditions, income taxes decline thus requiring raising of sales (VAT) and small property taxation. If sales taxes are insufficient to make debt payments, the Greek government must also cut spending. Spending cuts focus primarily on government employment and wages, pensions and health services, education and other social services. Labor market restructuring is often the means to reduce benefits and wages of government workers and thereby minimum wages and union-bargained wages and social security benefits for the rest of the private sector working class. When private sector jobs and wages in turn fall, the reduced income for working class Greeks becomes Greek government 'savings' that are available for redistribution to the Troika and private investors in the form of debt payments. Greeks must give up a greater share of their wages in the form of taxes to repay debt which they had not personally incurred. As austerity impacts the economy, they then become jobless due to the need to repay debt, or have their 'deferred wages' (pensions, health services, social security) reduced, the savings from which are redistributed to the Troika, and so on. The cumulative result is a reduction in economy-wide wage and other earned income that is extracted by the Greek government and paid to the Troika and private investors as debt principal and interest. Through this process of state intermediation, debt and the suffering and reduction in well-being it entails is spread to the entire population, irrespective of their role in incurring it.

Financial Imperialism from Privatization of Public Assets

If tax increases and Greek government spending reductions are insufficient to make debt payments, then the Greek government is forced by the Troika to raise additional funds by selling public goods and investment—i.e. privatization of Greek public assets—utilities, railroad and urban transport systems, airports and seaports, etc. Privatization results in a double form of financial exploitation: The Greek government sells the public assets to private investors, most of whom are German, British, Chinese and other investor groups, at a below market price, often at what are called 'fire sale' prices. By setting prices well below market value, the investors are thus subsidized by the Greek government. The investors make a financial profit in various ways. They may hold the public asset and then resell it in whole or part at a market price equal or above the asset's fire sale price. While awaiting the market price of the asset to recover, the investor reaps a stream of income that may be produced by the public asset as well. For example, purchased Greek railroad systems, electricity systems, or ports produce an income stream, which the private investor enjoys in the interim before resale. The asset may be still further exploited by investors' issuing new bonds on the asset. Or investors may reap a financial windfall through government provision of low cost, subsidized loans to purchase the public asset; or loan guarantees, which the government subsequently pays if the income stream from the privatization does not reach some contractually agreed upon level. Privatization thus creates multiple ways to exploit—i.e. to extract wealth—financially, once the government is on the hook for debt.

Foreign Investor Speculation on Greek Financial Asset Price Volatility

Financial imperialism includes generating interest and money flows from buying and selling government financial securities. This includes professional investors' speculation in Greek government bonds, notes, financial derivatives tied to bonds (credit default and interest rate swaps), and residential foreclosures and mortgage debt acquisition at below market prices, and even stock price speculation as Greece's stock market swings widely (contracts) in the run-up to the crisis and after a debt deal is signed (expands).

The periodic debt crises provide great opportunity for speculators and professional investors (mostly in the EU but globally and among Greek investors as well) to realize significant capital gains due to the volatility induced by the crisis. This is not interest on debt—private enterprise or state-to-state aggregated. There is no austerity required to pay for the financial gains.[30] But it is financial exploitation of the crisis based on the debt nonetheless, a kind of spin-off affording financial exploitation.

As the Greek debt rises, that precipitates an awareness of crisis, and as crisis negotiations begin between the Troika and Greek government, investors dump Greek bonds. Bond prices fall and Greek bond interest rates escalate just as the Greek government attempts to raise significant additional revenue from bonds in order to deal with the debt crisis (since the ECB and Troika insist the government raise funds

are enabled by the debt crisis indirectly and their capital gains that accrue to investors and bankers outside Greece are actual profits. But they do not accrue from interest based on debt paid for ultimately from production and trade, or even from austerity. But they are a consequence of the crises nonetheless.

The preceding represent the gamut of means whereby financial imperialism and financial exploitation of Greece, its people and economy takes place. What starts as private to private debt and interest is, in the wake of a crisis, transferred to government balance sheets to ensure the bailout of Greek banks and businesses in order in turn to ensure continued payments to private banks and businesses outside Greece. Economic crises and depression require still more borrowing and debt and renewed debt crises and negotiations. Austerity follows to enable Greece to make payments on its debt. Austerity includes privatization of pubic assets that permits financial exploitation in yet another form. The cycle of repeated debt crises and negotiations enable professional speculators to take advantage of the inevitable financial asset price volatility in Greek government bonds, stocks, derivatives, property values, and other financial assets as ways to realize still more financial exploitation. The process represents not only financial gains from the creation of ever-rising debt and endless austerity conditions, but financial gain from money made from money in a complex web of financial manipulation.

This edifice of financial exploitation based on debt, interest, privatization fire sales, speculation on sovereign bonds, and financial asset speculation and manipulation constitutes the essence of the new and emerging financial imperialism, as it has applied to Greece.

If one were to 'add up' the magnitude in the case of Greece alone, it would include interest on the $400-$500 billion in Greek government and central bank debt today, partly paid and to be paid; the tens of billions in privatization sales plus untold future income streams to foreign investors from the managing of the privatized public goods for years and decades to come; the countless magnitudes of private interest at above market rates paid by Greek banks and businesses to outside banks and investors over the last decade; the almost inestimable but at least hundreds of billions of dollars in speculative profits made on Greek bonds and derivatives transactions since 2010; and who knows how much from shorting Greek stocks by professional investors since 2010.

If Greece were not part of the Eurozone, its central bank could simply have issued its own Greek currency to bail out its banks itself, thus avoiding the need for ECB borrowing, ECB sabotaging of Greece's banking system during debt crises negotiations, and the massive bank withdrawals and capital flight that occurred with each debt crisis that required tens of billions of debt in order to recapitalize Greece's banking system in the wake of each debt crisis.[32]

If Greece had not been reduced to an economic protectorate of the Eurozone—i.e. of German financial interests and its Euro allies—Greece could also have devalued its own currency to stimulate export earnings in lieu of having to borrow from the Troika. But both avenues of issuing and devaluing its own currency were blocked by Eurozone structure and political realities.

There was no true Eurozone central fiscal authority willing to spend and invest in Greece to assist it to grow out of the contraction. Put simply, few in the Eurozone political or financial superstructure—i.e. the Troika pan-Eurozone state structure—cared much about the well-being of Greece and Greeks or felt much responsibility to the country mired in years of continuing economic depression. But imperialist policy makers seldom do care or feel much. Even with the structural limitations discussed above, steps could have been taken to ameliorate the harshness and share the pain. But German banker interests and allies among finance ministers and in governments insisted on the debt being paid, if necessary by still more debt imposed. Their economic ideology did not permit it. Nor, even more so, did their direct economic interests. German attitudes in that regard might be historically compared to US willingness in the 1930s to spend massively on infrastructure in its deeper depressed Southern states via creating the Tennessee Valley Authority and other fiscal injection of income measures at the time.

No currency independence. No central bank independence. No alternative fiscal assistance as its own fiscal action was rendered frozen by Troika imposed austerity. That was the outcome of membership in a perverted economic union called the Eurozone, or EMU 1999 that benefited the core economies of northern Europe at the expense of the periphery. The periphery served as a region of exploitation—first by rendering it an economic dumping ground for northern core exports and direct speculative investment in housing and construction, and thereafter as a source of interest from debt.

During the pre-2008 boom cycle years, credit flowed to Greece and the periphery to enable the purchase of core exports of goods. When the core stopped the flow of credit after 2008, what was left was debt. But interest on debt was as lucrative to the core banker interests as was purchase of export goods. Repayment of loans and other credit extended by the Troika to Greece's government and central bank were recycled back to Eurozone core private interests—95% of same, to be exact. Without true economic recovery after 2009 for the periphery, each time more debt had to be extended in order to repay old debt, and interest payments were added to interest payments and compounded. Financial imperialism increasingly assumed the form of state-to-state debt and interest flows, accruing eventually in the northern core banks and financial institutions. New means for financial exploitation were spun off and added in the process—financial gains from privatization and financial gains from government bonds and financial securities speculation. Greece was sucked into the debt machine where the fix itself became the cause of ongoing and ever worsening entanglement, with no release in sight. For Eurozone bankers, it was just too good a 'deal' to terminate: perpetual debt interest money flows back to them, guaranteed by credit extended by the Troika institutions. Overlay on top of that, cycles of opportunity for financial speculation on bonds, stocks, derivatives, and other financial securities. It was even better than Greeks buying German and northern core exports of real goods to Greece. Exports might decline with economic conditions and competition. But debt repayments were guaranteed to continue—for as long as Greece remained in the Euro system at least. Financial imperialism may just prove more profitable than older forms of imperialism based on production and commerce of goods.

The expansion of financial exploitation and new forms of financial imperialism is a harbinger of things to come for smaller economies and states that choose to integrate themselves into economic unions with larger, more economically dominant economies and states. It starts with a free trade zone or 'customs union', preferred by the dominant economies as sources for expanding their exports and direct investments. To further expand the dominant economy's production and trade within the customs union, a currency union is eventually added—as in the case of the 1999 EMU in Europe. Alternatively, a common currency may not arise from a treaty but may evolve over time. Smaller members' currencies are displaced by the single currency union. But a single currency in turn requires a regional central bank as issuer of the single currency. A banking union inevitably follows, which may occur in stages or by legal treaty arrangements. The region-wide central bank not only issues the single currency, but dictates the monetary policies for the member states, as well as the national banking systems of the members. By joining these various 'unions', the smaller economies and states thus lose control over their currency, their monetary policy, and their banking systems. The last and often most difficult phase is integration of fiscal policy. The smaller states are stripped of their fiscal independence in stages, which is absorbed by the supra-national economic institutions dominated by the larger, stronger economy and its allies.

This trajectory over time results in the smaller and weaker economies becoming 'economic protectorates' of the larger and stronger economies—as pan-region economic institutions, dominated and controlled by the larger economies, absorb the currencies, the banking systems, monetary policies and, eventually, the fiscal policy functions of the smaller and weaker economies. The outcome is intensified exploitation of the smaller and weaker economies by the stronger and larger, or by a coalition led by the stronger. This process is farthest along in the Eurozone in the case of Greece, but is occurring elsewhere in the Eurozone as well in various degrees. US economic dominance in Central America and the Caribbean is an example of a similar process in development, especially in the case of Puerto Rico. And as China develops its custom union, and as its currency, the Yuan, becomes dominant in the region in the next decade, Asia's smaller and weaker economies are likely to follow a similar path.

The thrust and trajectory of 21st century global capitalism is toward greater centralization and integration. The formation of free trade zones/customs unions, currency unions, banking unions, and eventually centralization of fiscal functions, are the institutional and policy framework prerequisites for expanding financial forms of exploitation. As the Eurozone has continued to evolve from a customs to currency union, and to develop a banking union in stages, and as Euro institutions like the EC drift toward dictating fiscal spending and tax policies to other Eurozone member states in parallel, a new form of financial imperialism is in the making. Greece is likely to be but the forerunner."

Endnotes

1   As well as other increasingly debt burdened economies in Europe's periphery and elsewhere beyond Europe.

2   Surplus grain production was a major source of state finance—i.e. taxes in kind—in ancient economies of the period.

3   J. A. Hobson, *Imperialism*, University of Michigan Press, 1967, p 22-23..

4   As British imperial power waned after World War I, both Canada and Australia clearly evolved from forms of economic protectorates to more independent economies. Economic integration per se does not represent an economic protectorate. Canada's economy is highly integrated with the US in the 21st century, but it is not an economic protectorate of the US. The latter depends significantly on who determines the essential policy directions of the economy—the indigenous elites or the imperialist elites. Puerto Rico today is more like an economic protectorate of the US—with vestiges of political protectorate as well still remaining.

5   The late 19th Imperialism focused on Africa as European powers carved it up after the 1885 Treaty of Berlin. According to Hobson, "this recent imperial expansion stands entirely distinct from the colonization of sparsely peopled lands in temperate zones, where white colonists carry with them the modes of government...of the mother country", p. 27.

6   They are both at the same time political and economic institutions

7   J.A. Hobson, *Imperialism*, University of Michigan Press, 1967, pp.

108-09.

8 An exception being the somewhat obscure banker-economist at the time, Henry Thornton, *An Enquiry Into the Nature and Effects of the paper Credit of Great Britain*, 1802, public domain reprint 2015.

9 See Jack Rasmus, *Systemic Fragility in the Global Economy*, ch. 16, pp. 320-324, on the errors of classical economics with regard to banking and finance, and Ch. 17, "Mechanical Marxism", pp 376-384, on how this bias has carried forward to contemporary Marxist economic analysis with its continuing bias against financial investment and its destabilizing impact on the modern global economy.

10 V. I. Lenin, *Imperialism: The Highest Stage of Capitalism*, International Publishers,

11 Rosa Luxemburg, *The Accumulation of Capital,* 1951, p. 421.

12 While Lenin clearly develops upon Hobson and Hilferding, he made no reference at all to Luxemburg's more or less contemporary work to his own.

13 For a summary of post-war perspectives, see Anthony Brewer, *Marxist Theories of Imperialism: A Critical Survey*, Routledge, London, 1980, pp. 131-294.

14 John Smith, *Imperialism in the Twenty-First Century*, Monthly Review Press, New York, 2016. As Smith himself notes, his primary focus is the connection between finance and the outsourcing (offshoring) of good production. Financialization is narrowly defined and is the consequence of changes in production, not vice-versa, nor even dialectically.

15 Except to claim, as did Lenin, that finance is synonymous with monopoly capitalism, which in turn is the driving force of Imperialism. In fact, Smith's analysis is in many ways an attempt to resurrect and adapt Lenin's basic theses to the 21st century. Monopoly capitalism in the Imperialist heartland leads to capital over-accumulation and/or class struggle there, which forces monopoly capital to seek overseas expansion to exploit cheaper labor and lower wages in order to raise global average rates of profit on capital. Whereas Lenin merely made this statement in his agitational 1916 pamphlet, Smith develops the details to show how trade, offshoring, and what he calls 'labor arbitrage' between the global north and super-exploited south produce that outcome.

16 Smith, *Imperialism in the 21st Century: Globalization, Super-Exploitation, and Capitalism's Final Crisis,* Monthly Review Press, New York, 2016, p. 282.

17 Smith, p. 298. Smith ascribes the origin of the financial crisis to August 9, 2007, located in the European banking system, with August 9, 2007

as "the day the debt bomb exploded". That of course is incorrect, as is his general understanding of the role of debt in the general crisis before and ever since.

18   David Harvey, *The New Imperialism*, Oxford University Press, London, 2001. Not surprisingly, Smith dedicates a good part of his chapter 7 to refuting Harvey. Other European Marxists, like Michael Heinrich, have also recently explored—based on previously unpublished notes of Marx—the role of finance capital as more independent.

19   David Harvey, p. 147.

20   Michael Heinrich, *An Introduction to the Three Volumes of Karl Marx's Capital,* Monthly Review Press, 2012, p. 168.

21   Heinrich, p. 216.

22   Joseph Schumpeter, *The Sociology of Imperialisms*, Meridian Books, 1966, pp. 1-96.

23   Piero Sraffa, *The Production of Commodities by Means of Commodities,* 1960.

24   As Pope Francis has raised in one of his recent world tours, there are 'new forms of colonialism' that have been developing. See Heidi Vogt and Francis Rocca, "Pope Decries 'New Forms of Colonialism'", *Wall St. Journal*, November 28, 2015.

25   Marxist 'reflexive' theories of imperialism acknowledge this and see financial exploitation as a secondary consequence of exploitation from production first. They disregard the other forms of financial exploitation and imperialism.

26   And behind the national central banks and governments stand the dominant national private banks, prominent investors, and national politicians they influence in terms of policy by various means.

27   Greek private banks and businesses thus 'make' their principal and interest payments to Euro bankers, but the Greek government and Greek central bank incurs at least an equivalent debt, which it must then 'make' or pay to the Troika that extended the credit to Greece's government and central bank. 'Debt' is reduced in Greece's private sector but an equivalent debt is added to the balance sheets of the Greek government and central bank.

28   For example, the French bank, Credit Agricole, was a major owner of at least one of the largest four Greek private banks, the Bank of Piraeus.

29   As was shown in early chapters, Greek government debt as a percent of GDP, hardly rose until the 2008 crash, and was quite stable from 2000 up to that point.

30   Although speculation on Greek government bonds that drives up the cost of bond issuance does add to the total Greek debt. So this

statement is qualified by that fact.

31   Quantitative Easing, QE, programs might be viewed as the central bank acting as the 'bad bank', buying up the bad assets, holding them on its balance sheet, and then as the price of the assets begin to recover again, selling them to private investors. The reselling always occurs well before the full price recovery, so the private investors reap the lion's share of the capital gains from the price recovery.

32   Capital flight from Greece to core northern Euro banks might actually be considered yet another form of financial imperialism, since the money flows to such banks are then re-invested by those banks to earn another return on investment for them. It is Greek depositors' money (mostly wealthy Greeks and businesses), but it is core bankers who earn the profits on that money.

INDEX